The Making of King Kong

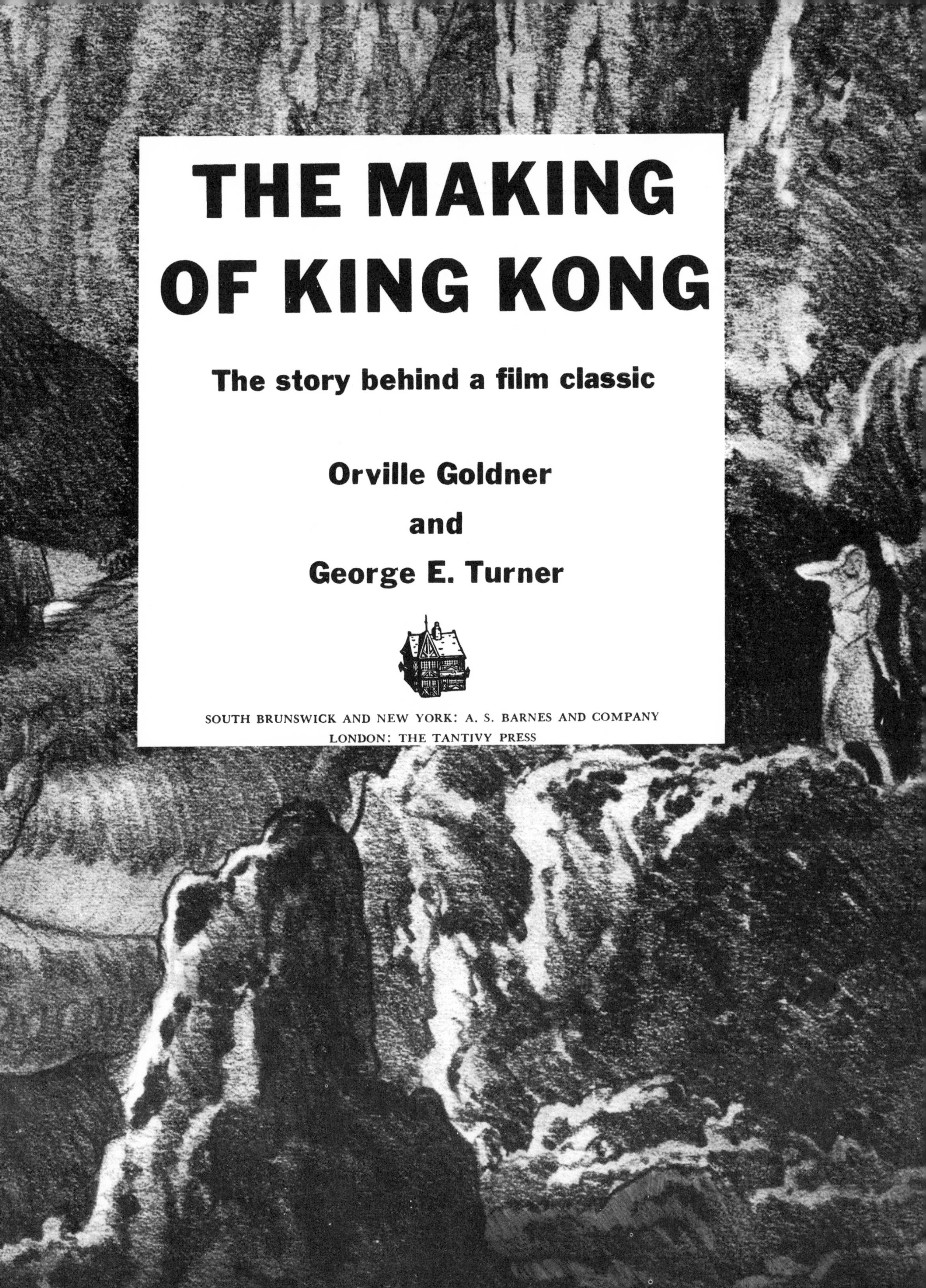

THE MAKING OF KING KONG

The story behind a film classic

Orville Goldner

and

George E. Turner

SOUTH BRUNSWICK AND NEW YORK: A. S. BARNES AND COMPANY

LONDON: THE TANTIVY PRESS

A. S. Barnes and Co., Inc.
Cranbury, New Jersey 08512

The Tantivy Press
108 New Bond Street
London W1Y OQX, England

Library of Congress Cataloging in Publication Data

Goldner, Orville.
The making of King Kong.

Includes index.
1. King Kong (Motion picture) I. Turner, George, 1925– joint author. II. Title.
PN1997.K437G6 791.43'7 74–18
ISBN 0–498–01510–6
SBN 0-904208-70-2 (U.K.)

PRINTED IN THE UNITED STATES OF AMERICA

The loving interest, encouragement and help of family and friends over many years made this book both inevitable and possible.

It is dedicated to three authentic motion picture pioneers, Merian C. Cooper, Ernest B. Schoedsack and Willis H. O'Brien. These men had uniquely different personalities and talents. Together and separately they made truly original and important contributions to the Motion Picture Arts and Sciences. Their influence on films and thus audiences around the world is still to be measured.

The Authors

Foreword

"It's weird, wild, wonderful—the stuff for which movies were made!"

So proclaimed a Hollywood ballyhoo man more than forty years ago. Need we add that the film he was publicising was *King Kong?*

Nobody ever has accused a publicity man of being married to the truth, but this anonymous "flack" would have given Diogenes cause for hope. *King Kong* truly *was* "the stuff for which movies were made," a logical extension of the works of Méliès, Porter, Griffith and every other film-maker who sought to record on film ideas beyond the scope of any other medium. Here, for once, was a movie that justified the most immodest claims put forth in its behalf. It *was* "a show sired by the spirit of P. T. Barnum," the "strangest adventure drama this thrill-mad world has ever seen," a "mastodonic miracle of the movies," an "adventure that leaps beyond the frontiers of the imagination," and "the picture that out-thrills your maddest dreams."

King Kong was released April 10, 1933, and has increased in popularity through the years. It is probable that as a folk hero the titular character today is known to more persons of all ages than is Paul Bunyan. Tourists visiting the Empire State Building buy postcards showing Kong perched atop the mooring mast. Youngsters wear lapel buttons declaring that *King Kong Died for Our Sins* or *King Kong Wears a Toupee* or *King Kong Has an Edifice Complex.* Comedians such as Bob Newhart, Jonathan Winters and Don Adams have Kong routines in their repertoires. Innumerable wrestlers, football players and weightlifters have adopted the film title as their sobriquets. There are *King Kong* model kits, comic books, mechanical toys and dolls.

Theatrical showings of this venerable film still break attendance records. "Time" named it "Movie of the Year" in 1952 when it was reissued and brought in two-and-a-half times the gross expected of a new "A" release. A New York City television station ran it seventeen times in one week and each time won higher audience ratings than were scored by any other station in the city.

There are valid reasons why none of the dozens of imitations has succeeded in duplicating its grasp upon the imagination of the public. One is that, however fantastic and implausible the film may be, it convinces because it is built upon solid, biographical fact. It is as personal a statement of its guiding geniuses—Merian C. Cooper, Ernest B. Schoedsack, Ruth Rose and Willis H. O'Brien—as is anything by Chaplin or Stroheim. This underlying reality is sensed by the viewer.

Carl Denham, the daredevil producer who seeks and finds Kong, is a personality composite of Cooper and Schoedsack. He possesses the same

courage and intentness of purpose that made possible the filming of *Grass, Chang* and *Rango* under incredibly difficult conditions. He accepts hardship and danger willingly as the price of the game. He knows he must avoid the monsoon because he ran afoul of it in Thailand, cranks his own camera because his cinematographer in Sumatra was rendered helpless by a fear of wild animals, seeks a girl to appear in his new film because exhibitors complained that if *Chang* only had "love interest" it would have made twice as much money. It is said that if Denham wants a picture of a lion he just walks up and tells it to look pleasant—an approach no more brazen than Schoedsack's method of provoking tigers into charging his camera.

It would probably never have occurred to Denham to visit the Bowery in search of a pretty girl desperate enough to accept a dangerous job had not Steve Clemente, the Yaqui Indian knife-thrower (who is in the cast of the film), done that same thing when he was unable to hire an actress for his vaudeville act. Denham's friend, the tough, reluctantly romantic Jack Driscoll, clearly resembles Schoedsack.

Ann Darrow, the film's heroine immortalised by Fay Wray's performance, springs as surely from the life of Ruth Rose, co-author of the shooting script. Like Ann, the writer was an unemployed actress who found adventure and romance in far away, primitive lands. Had she not met her future husband aboard the expedition ship "Arcturus" it is likely that the love scenes aboard the "Venture" would have been played in the Philip Barry style of dialogue that typified films of the period instead of a clumsily sincere tough-guy style that is touching because it seems real. The crusty Captain Englehorn and his roughneck crew seem lifelike because writer and producers knew well their living counterparts.

The technical virtuosity for which *King Kong* is celebrated is due in great measure to a career of experiment and innovation by the remarkable Willis O'Brien, who compensated for a life filled with tragedy and disappointment by pouring into his work unsurpassed imagination, dedication and exuberance. Those who knew him say that O'Brien *was* Kong, recognisable on the screen in every gesture and reaction.

Opposite:
Fay Wray, star of KING KONG (her hair was blonde in the film)

King Kong also bears the hallmarks of other creative individuals—the artists, craftsmen, technicians, actors and musicians who contributed the breath of life to the most intemperate imaginings of the film's principal creators.

Many writers have tried to justify the public's love affair with a gigantic, ugly ape by reading into the film a great deal more *significance* than was intended by its creators. European Communists insist that when Kong smashes the gates of the native village he symbolises Karl Marx. A French critic, apparently confusing Ruth Rose with Rose La Rose or Gypsy Rose Lee, attributed the picture's erotic aspects to the "fact" that it was partly written by "a former strip-teaser." Others insist Kong was black in order to represent the plight of the Negro in America, who also was brought to these shores in chains and exploited by the white man. Freudians point with glee to the irony of Kong retreating to the top of "the most elaborate phallic symbol in the world"—the Empire State Building. For Freudians, too, are the "mock crucifixion" of Kong, the "proxy gratification" of depression-angry audiences via Kong's destructive rampage in New York, a brontosaurus that reminds them of Leda's swan, and so on, *ad nauseam*. Such notions are firmly denied by the persons behind the film, who view them variously with disgust or amusement.

We earnestly suggest that simple explanations are best: Kong was not darker in hue than any other gorilla, he smashed the gates solely because he wanted to recapture Fay Wray, his atrocious behaviour in the city had nothing to do with politics or economic conditions and he climbed the Empire State Building because it was the highest point in the city, corresponding to his mountain-top lair in his homeland. *King Kong* is exactly what it was meant to be: a highly entertaining, shrewdly conceived work of pure cinema.

To understand the things that made *King Kong* the classic it has become, it is necessary to know some things about the persons involved in its making. It is essential as well to have a modicum of familiarity with several related films,

ranging from the early works of O'Brien, Cooper and the Schoedsacks to the DeMille Biblical epic, *The King of Kings;* the unfinished *Creation;* the tandem production *The Most Dangerous Game;* the sequel, *The Son of Kong,* and even the one film which possibly exceeds *King Kong* in popularity, *Gone with the Wind.*

All of these considerations are essential parts of this book that, at last, should dispel some of the controversy regarding the means used to bring to the screen a story many experts insisted could not be filmed. Little of this has been told until now despite the large body of material that has been published. The film was made on closed stages to protect the methods used in its production. Most of the published stories are based upon surmise and deliberately false information disseminated by press agents.

Although commercial success is anathema to many lovers of the arts (we all cherish lost causes and thwarted geniuses), it should be noted that one of the more important aspects of *King Kong* is that it made a great deal of money. It rescued RKO-Radio Pictures from bankruptcy, thus being directly responsible for the hundreds of films made by that lamented company during the last twenty-odd years of its existence. This is quite an important function when one considers the number of outstanding films that are, in a very real sense, the offspring of Kong. Among the many are the Fred Astaire-Ginger Rogers musicals, *The Lost Patrol, The Informer, Little Women, The Last Days of Pompeii, Gunga Din,* the Val Lewton thrillers, *All That Money Can Buy, Citizen Kane . . .*

Casts, credits and synopses of *King Kong* and nine other films that are discussed in this book may be found in the appendices.

Opposite: "Coop" studies the teeth of a prehistoric monster for a publicity shot

Acknowledgements

The authors wish to acknowledge with gratitude those who provided information vital to this book:

Mr. Robert Armstrong
Mr. Bruce Cabot
Mr. Wah Ming Chang
Brigadier-General Merian C. Cooper
Mrs. Merian C. Cooper (Dorothy Jordan)
Mr. Marcel Delgado
Mr. Linwood G. Dunn, A. S. C.
Mr. Mario Larrinaga
Miss Bessie Love
Mr. Archie S. Marshek
Mrs. Willis H. O'Brien
Mr. Sam Peeples
Mrs. Zoe Porter
Mr. Ernest B. Schoedsack
Mrs. Ernest B. Schoedsack (Ruth Rose)
Mrs. Jo Ann Schov
Mr. Carroll Shepphird
Mr. Murray Spivack
Mr. Max Steiner
Mr. Clifford Stine, A. S. C.
Miss Fay Wray

The American Society of Composers, Authors, and Publishers, and the American Society of Cinematographers, gave inestimable help.

Contents

Foreword 7
Acknowledgements 13
List of Illustrations 16

PART I
GENESIS OF KONG 21
1 Cooper-Schoedsack Productions 23
2 Adventure for Three 31
3 The Ultimate in Adventure 37
4 OBie 41

PART II
THE MAKING OF KONG 51
5 Production 601 53
6 The Perils of Pathe 65
7 A Happy Company 77
8 Inventions Become Necessary 87
9 The Skull Island Expedition 101
10 People, Primroses and Other Problems 115
11 It Wasn't Easy 133
12 The King in New York 159
13 The Finishing Touches 187

PART III
POSTLUDE 195
14 The Inevitable Sequel 197
15 Remember Cavalcade? 207

APPENDICES IV 215
Appendix 1: Grass 217
Appendix 2: Chang 219
Appendix 3: The Four Feathers 221
Appendix 4: Rango 225
Appendix 5: The Ghost of Slumber Mountain 227
Appendix 6: The Lost World 229
Appendix 7: Creation 233
Appendix 8: The Most Dangerous Game 237
Appendix 9: King Kong 241
Appendix 10: Son of Kong 263

Index 269

List of Illustrations

Fay Wray, star of KING KONG 9
"Coop" studies the teeth of a prehistoric monster 11
Self-portrait photograph of Schoedsack 24
Ancestor of the Kong Tyrannosaurus 29
Self portrait of O'Brien in the style of Rembrandt 43
OBie with model figure and Monoclonius 43
The "Missing Link" 44
THE LOST WORLD. The Allosaurus menaces the explorers 47
THE LOST WORLD. Actors hide from the Brontosaurus 48
CREATION. Tyrannosaurus in the temple 54
CREATION. Master drawing of dramatic action before the temple 55
CREATION. Drawing of the mother Triceratops and her young 56
CREATION. Lush jungle with wooden Triceratops 56
CREATION. Sketch by Larrinaga 57
CREATION. A happy family group 57
The important telegram 57
CREATION. A miniature set with river and birds 58
CREATION. Ernest Smythe pictures the action for the chase by the Triceratops 59
CREATION. A miniature set after Larrinaga drawing 60
CREATION. The Triceratops chases Ralf Halolde 60
CREATION. Side angle process shot of the chase 60
CREATION. The Arsinoitherium traps the Chilean sailors 61
CREATION. The angered mother Triceratops 61
The lemur (Kinkajou) in CREATION 61
A stand-in for testing scenes in CREATION and KONG 62
CREATION. The jaguar 66
THE MOST DANGEROUS GAME. Zaroff's castle 67
THE MOST DANGEROUS GAME. San Pedro with buoy lights in the distance 68
Bruce Cabot. Studio portrait 69
Robert Armstrong. A portrait 70
Lay-out from "The International Photographer" 71
Kong had many faces 78
Fay Wray in jungle 79
Merian C. Cooper admires his brain-child 81
Another portrait of Robert Armstrong 82
Fay Wray and Bruce Cabot 83
Vernon L. Walker and Linwood G. Dunn 85
The deepest set of all 88
A sketch by Larrinaga 89
Larrinaga's sketch realised 89

Fay Wray reacts to the "reel" thing 89
A complicated test for the dramatic ledge sequence 90
Mario Larrinaga in a moment of relaxation 90
Model of Fay Wray 91
Miniature trees, foliage and log 91
Side angle of miniature and glass surrounding the Arsinoitherium 92
Styracosaurus 92
A typical reaction 92
Cabot and the cave projected into the miniature 93
Cabot in the small cave surrounded by glass painting 93
Matte without the miniature 93
Cabot in matte watches the miniature Kong 94
Armature for the full-scale hand 95
The clay model that guided construction 96
Scale of the head becomes apparent 96
Intricate construction 96
Fred Reese watches progress on the colossal head 97
"What big eyes you have!" 98
The "big one" nearly finished 98
The wall, the gate, and the altar 102
The Great Wall set unfinished 103
Before the shooting starts 105
Night scene at the wall with Kong matted in 105
Sacrificed to Kong! 106
The Great Wall and native torchlight parade 106
Milling natives prepare for the sacrifice 106
First appearance of Kong 107
An early sacrificial altar test 108
Another test for the early appearance of Kong 108
Details of the model carved altar 108
A test with dowels where the altar will be 109
Another view of the "Venture" 110
Cardboard plates and brass escutcheon pins! 110
The non-floatable model of the "Venture" 110
On the way to the gate 111
Another Larrinaga master drawing that sets the scene 111
From the "Hollywood Reporter" 116
Another montage from the same issue 117
More personalities from the "Hollywood Reporter" 119
Another montage from the same issue 121
Kong fighting the reptile outside his cave 121
Articulated wooden figure 122
OBie animates the fight scene in the great cave 123
Drawing of the great fight 126
Fay Wray and Bruce Cabot 127
The Arsinoitherium deep in lush jungle 128
Wooden Kong stand-in 129
Fay Wray and miniature Kong 129
At the entrance to the cave 129
Miss Wray swoons for the composite test 130
The miniature reptile snaps at Fay Wray 131
Kong and the reptile struggle 131
Kong fights the Pteranodon 136
Miniature foreground with cardboard cut-out 137
Kong at his lair 138
Kong slays the Pteranodon 140
The lovers escape the beast momentarily 141
Stegosaurus in the middle distance 142
The Brontosaurus splashes through the foggy swamp 143
The Brontosaurus pursues a sailor 144
Just before the big fight 145
Just after the big fight 146
The Stegosaurus enters the scene 147
Skull Island 148
Foreground glass with artist's marks 150
Foreground glass 151
Almost completed glass painting 152
Full-scale tree and foliage textures 153
Miss Wray in a full-scale test 154
Walter Daniels sits for a test 155
Reverse angle in the finished composite 156
Fay Wray in the big hand 157
Press photographers and flashbulbs anger Kong 160
Madness in the street 161
The break away 161
The wrecked car 161
As Byron Crabbe saw the bedroom scene 164
Another original concept by Crabbe 164
Kong at the bedroom window 165
Another Crabbe concept 166
Ready to smash the marquee 167
Buz Gibson starts Kong up the Empire State Building 168
Schoedsack with his flight commander 169
Full-scale top of the Building 170

An incomplete process shot using a studio mock-up 171
A miniature plane is crashed in flames 172
The plane lands on a pad 172
At the top, with Fay Wray projected in 173
The animation as it appeared in the composite 174
Machine guns weaken Kong 175
A passing shot for the final sequence 175
Kong falls to the street 178
"It was *beauty* killed the beast" 179
Miniature details 180
More miniature details 181
As Kong sees the elevated 182
How the elevated was photographed 183
Kong waits for the train 184
Rampaging through the native village 189
A commanding view of the city 193
SON OF KONG. The ape expresses concern over his wounded finger 198
SON OF KONG. Denham bandages Kong's finger 199
SON OF KONG. The fight with the cave bear 200
SON OF KONG. The sea monster 201
SON OF KONG. Players in lifeboat during storm sequence 202
SON OF KONG. Little Kong in quicksand 203
SON OF KONG. Helen Mack, Robert Armstrong, and Little Kong in the lost temple 203
Robert Armstrong with Little Kong 203
SON OF KONG. A monster enters the temple 205
The Pathe jungle 208
THE LOST ISLAND. The puppet of Mae West 209
Leroy Prinz and Sid Grauman 211
THE LOST ISLAND. Puppets in the great cave 212
THE FOUR FEATHERS. Clive Brook and Richard Arlen 222
THE FOUR FEATHERS. Richard Arlen 223
Drawing for the bottom of the canyon 242
Kong shakes the log 244
The "real" stuntmen 244
Six-inch models on the log 244
Mostly glass, with Bob Armstrong matted in 246
Incomplete composite of a canyon scene 246
Unfinished canyon composite 246
The waterfall 248
A beautiful composite 250
The waterfall with miniature Kong 252
Natives 254
Native huts 254
Kong-trampled mannequin 254
Kong arrives at the beach 256
Kong after being shelled with gas bombs 258
A roof-top interval 260
Kong defies the airmen 261
The wounded Kong in his last moments 262
The big head at its frightening best 268

The Making of King Kong

I.
Genesis of Kong

The Three D's:
Keep it Distant,
Difficult and
Dangerous.

—*Motto of Cooper-Schoedsack Productions*

1. Cooper-Schoedsack Productions

"The biggest money picture of the year will be *King Kong*," David O. Selznick told his fellow executives at RKO-Radio Pictures, Inc., at the beginning of 1933. Selznick had great faith in this picture which had been in production for more than a year and consisted, at this point, of 238,000 feet of unedited negative from which a 10,000 foot feature had to be extracted.

Selznick's faith was not universally shared. B. B. Kahane, president of the company, felt certain the picture was strictly a novelty item that would flop with the public. Selznick had been heavily criticised for allowing more than $1,000,000 to be spent on King Vidor's *Bird of Paradise,* a sum the studio could not hope to recoup at the box-office. *King Kong* had not cost nearly so much, but it had been responsible for the abortion of one major production and it was common knowledge that some of its costs had been cribbed "under the table" from the budgets of other films.

And there were the producers, Cooper and Schoedsack—a colourful pair of vagabonds more noted for their willingness to take risks than for any understanding of the intricacies of big studio production. Kahane also felt that the story was utterly implausible.

King Kong, admittedly, is a fantastic fable, but it is only slightly more fanciful than the genuine story behind it, an epic adventure that had its origins many years before and was dependent upon those whims of fate that brought together the curious assortment of individuals necessary to its realisation. The initial links were forged at the close of the First World War, when Captain Ernest Beaumont Schoedsack, a six-foot-six movie cameraman from Iowa, was mustered out of the U.S. Army Signal Corps in France.

Schoedsack had become interested in the plight of war-torn Poland, which declared its independence on the day of the Armistice—November 11, 1918. A huge German force had to be evacuated from what had been the western part of the old Russian Empire, the several provinces lying between Poland and the new Russia. As each strip of land was vacated by the Germans it was quickly re-occupied by the Red Army. The resulting tense situation was welcomed by Germany, which stood to benefit from a Russian-Polish conflict, and by Lenin, who was determined to break down the only physical barrier that separated the Soviet Union from revolutionary Germany.

Schoedsack decided to cast his lot with the heroic Poles. He joined a Red Cross relief mission and from the outset was active in helping Polish refugees escape from Russian occupied territories. The country was in a pitiable condition, divided by ethnic and political differences and plagued by famine, epidemic diseases, unemploy-

Self-portrait photograph of Schoedsack while making GRASS

ment, unstable currency and an almost total loss of industrial and agricultural capabilities. Both the Czechs and Germans were making trouble. By the end of January the Red Army had advanced to the line of Brodno-Brest-Kovel and on February 9 the Polish counter-offensive began. Schoedsack, finding his charges endangered by Czech combatants while on his first mission, arranged for a Swiss military guard to escort his group out of the hostile areas.

In mid-February he arrived in Vienna, which was occupied by the Italian Army. It was a bitter winter and most of the city's trees were being chopped down for firewood. Occupation troops roamed the streets, smashing and looting. At the railroad station Schoedsack encountered a short, emaciated and battle-scarred young American who carried a Naval Academy sword. He was clad in a filthy, rag-tag uniform and wore mismatched French and German boots. The Americans struck up an acquaintance and Schoedsack, for once in his life, was in the company of a man as remarkable as himself.

Captain Merian Coldwell Cooper, of Jacksonville, Florida, had just been repatriated from a German prison. He sold his sword when he left Annapolis in 1914 after one high-spirited escapade too many; now he had found it and bought it back. After Annapolis he was a sailor, a newspaperman in Minneapolis, Des Moines, San Antonio and St. Louis, and served in the Georgia National Guard in the Pancho Villa campaign. Later, he joined the infantry and then transferred to the Aviation Corps, receiving his "wings" at Mineola in September, 1917. He served on the Western Front as a special tactical observer with the 20th Aero Squadron of the First Day Bombardment, flying low over German lines to mark enemy placements for the benefit of the Allied gun crews. General Billy Mitchell took note of Cooper's heroism and put him in charge of tactical missions in the Battle of Saint Mihiel. It was a veritable suicide mission in which many of his comrades were killed. After Cooper's plane was shot down, crashing inside the Allied lines, he was officially awarded the Distinguished Service Cross. He refused to accept the honour because he felt that he should not be singled out from the other pilots of his squadron. "We all took the same risks," he said.

Later, in the Argonne, Cooper was brought down in flames and captured. A German surgeon restored his badly burned face and he remained in a prison hospital until a month after the Armistice. Like Schoedsack, he saw in the Bolsheviks a potential enemy, and when he arrived in Vienna he was on his way to Warsaw to join the American Relief Association, which had been organised by Herbert Hoover to aid the famine-stricken portions of Europe.

Schoedsack remained in the thick of the war until its end, convoying supplies across a still hostile Germany, driving ambulances, shooting movies for the Red Cross and even making a long and dangerous journey to the Black Sea to bring back Polish refugees from the Russian oil fields.

Cooper went to Paris in August to join with Major Cedric E. Fauntleroy, late of the Lafayette

Escadrille and the American Air Service, in forming a group of American war pilots to be incorporated into the Polish Army. Their ten-man Kosciusco Aerial Squadron, named for the Polish national hero who aided Washington during the American Revolution, reported for duty on October 1 as a fighting unit of the Polish Air Force, with Fauntleroy in command. The Americans soon were flying patrols over the Bolshevist lines. The mission was hardly glamourous; pay ranged from $8 to $10 per month, disease was rampant, death was everywhere. Three American pilots were killed, another was crippled for life and two others were wounded.

When Fauntleroy was made Aviation Chief of the Second Army on July 3, Cooper succeeded him as Squadron Commander. He flew more than seventy strafing missions against General Budenny's advancing force until, on July 13, his aircraft was disabled by ground fire in Galicia. He made a forced landing twenty miles from Rovno and, pursued by Cossack horsemen from Budenny's cavalry, he fled into a clump of woods. He was soon surrounded and was beaten severely in the fight which followed. The Cossacks were about to kill him when one soldier who spoke English interceded for him.

Cooper represented himself as Corporal Frank R. Mosher—the name was stenciled on the second-hand underwear the Red Cross had given him. He was taken to Bolshevik headquarters where he was questioned by Budenny, who asked him to join the Red Army as a flight instructor. When Cooper refused, he was held prisoner for five days before escaping. Two days later he was recaptured and taken under heavy guard to Moscow.

Heavy fighting continued as the Poles retreated slowly before the massive onslaught. Captain Arthur D. Kelly of the Kosciusko Squadron was killed on the day following Cooper's capture. Fauntleroy was wounded by machine-gun fire a short time later.

Schoedsack was in the Ukraine when the Polish lines broke southwest of Kiev and the great retreat began. Kiev was occupied by Polish troops under General Edward Smigly-Rydz, who resisted courageously until ordered to evacuate the city and retreat westward. On July 12 the withdrawal from Kiev began. Much of the action was captured on film by Schoedsack, whose movies of this war are unparalleled. He was the last man to cross the great Dnieper River Bridge, which the nervous Poles detonated just as he raced to the shore. He was unable to photograph the explosion itself, but he turned in time to "shoot" the bridge as it went down. Somehow, Schoedsack got back through the Russian lines to Warsaw.

Cooper, in the months following his capture, was moved from jail to jail, finally being transferred to Wladykino Prison, a work camp near Moscow. He spent much of the winter shoveling snow from the railways.

The tide of war turned in August when President Pilsudski led a counter-offensive that resulted in an amazing series of Polish victories. As tens of thousands of Russian soldiers fled across Lithuania and East Prussia the Poles advanced rapidly and by October had regained most of the territory occupied during 1919. An armistice was signed at Riga on October 12.

Cooper remained in prison because the Russians considered him an American criminal rather than a Polish war prisoner. No word had been received of him outside other than reports from peasants who witnessed his capture, and the Russians were unaware of his identity. Cooper felt certain that he would be executed should it become known that he was the commander of the American flying squadron. As efforts to secure his release were intensified it became evident to him that his masquerade soon would be over.

With two Polish officers, Lieutenants Zalewski and Sokolowski, he escaped on the night of April 12, 1921. The fugitives ran and walked until morning, then hid in the woods and slept during the day. At nightfall they resumed their flight, following the railroad tracks because they had no compass. When they met peasants, Cooper represented himself as a German prisoner on his way home. Sometimes they "hopped" freight trains and on the third day they found themselves in a boxcar full of Russians. Because he could not speak the language, Cooper put his fingers in his mouth and made choking sounds to indicate that he was mute.

After five days they were forced to travel on foot through forests and swamps. All of the bridges were heavily guarded and one of the Poles could not swim, so long detours were necessary.

They had only enough money to buy two pounds of bread and when this was exhausted they traded articles of clothing to the peasants for enough black bread to keep them alive. Once, to elude guards, they hid for thirty-six hours above a brick stove in a peasant hut.

By the time they reached the Latvian frontier they barely had sufficient clothing to cover their bodies. A professional smuggler agreed to guide them across the border in exchange for a pair of shoes and an overcoat. Cooper relinquished his shoes and as a substitute cut off his shirt tail and wrapped the cloth about his feet; Sokolowski gave up his coat. As they neared the border the smuggler threatened to turn them over to the Bolsheviks unless he received more money and clothing. He was told that he would be killed if he attempted to betray them. After studying their grim faces he gave them no more trouble.

The group reached Latvia on the morning of April 23 after a journey of fourteen days and five hundred miles. A few days later Cooper was in Warsaw at Belvedere Palace, where President Pilsudski decorated him with the "Virtuti Militari" (Cross of the Brave), the highest honour Poland can bestow, and General Haller awarded him the Polish Service Medal. A statue was erected in his honour.

On his way to the United States Cooper again met Schoedsack—this time in London, where the latter was working as a freelance newsreel cameraman. These men, opposites in many respects, shared the same keen appreciation of danger, adventure and natural beauty. They discussed the idea of creating together an epic film of some little-known part of the world, but both men were in financial straits and such a venture was hardly feasible. Cooper went on to New York City to settle down, temporarily, as a feature writer for the "Times."

Schoedsack soon afterward joined the Near East Relief and became involved in the Greco-Turkish War of 1921–22. He was present when the Greeks were driven out of the seaport of Smyrna (now Izmir) on the Aegean Sea. In this savage engagement more than three-fifths of a city of some 400,000 inhabitants was destroyed and a large portion of the Greek population was massacred. Schoedsack's films of the embattled countries were shown widely, but he did more than crank a camera. Years later, a delegation captured him as he was leaving New York on the "Arcturus" expedition—*captured* is the proper word, inasmuch as Schoedsack tends to flee in the face of any sort of publicity or accolade. He had been the object of a long search and now, cornered, he was presented the Distinguished Service Medal "for humanitarian work in Smyrna and the refugee camps of the Near East." It was stated that "he risked his life in the performance of duty and was instrumental in the saving of many lives."

Cooper, meantime, encountered Captain Edward A. Salisbury, owner of the eighty-three-ton "Wisdom II," a two-masted schooner used for ethnological expeditions. Salisbury had been touring the world for two years under the auspices of the Southwestern Museum of California and now had returned to seek further financial support. His object was to produce motion pictures, a book and some magazine stories about little-known places.

Salisbury was a skilful promoter but as a writer and cameraman he was quite limited. In September, 1922, he hired Cooper as "first officer"—actually as his writer—for $25 per month. When the cameraman quit, Cooper cabled Schoedsack, who travelled from Turkey to Africa to join the cruise. The balance of the ship's company included four other Americans, a Danish youth, two Samoan deck hands and a comical Ceylonese cook known as Shamrock. Most of the original crew had jumped ship in the Pacific. The eighty-eight foot ketch-rigged yacht was a rusty old tub but she was solidly constructed.

The crew of the "Wisdom II" saw strange sights indeed, including the Pigmies of Murderer's Island, but the high-point of the cruise was a week in Addis-Abbaba. There Ras Tafari, Prince Regent of the Abyssinian Empire (later Haile Selassie, Emperor of Ethiopia) assembled his mounted knights for review before the camera. The future "Lion of Judah" did not "take" to the gold-braided skipper, but he entertained Cooper and Schoedsack in barbaric splendor and decked them out in full military regalia. Salisbury was anxious to move on, but Cooper and Schoedsack managed to get the photos which appeared with their celebrated three-part series in "Asia Magazine" and shot a great deal of movie footage from which they planned to edit a feature film.

The "Wisdom II" left the port of Djibouti, French Somaliland, in February, 1923, sailing up the Red Sea into a strong monsoon wind. The water was extremely turbulent and most of the crew were seasick. Following an erratic, zig-zag course, the ship often was carried dangerously close to the coast of Yemen. During the night, while the ship was moving at full sail on a landward tack, the navigator anxiously watched for the Mocha lighthouse, which was supposed to be visible for eighteen miles. Suddenly, the ship struck a submerged reef. Stuck fast, broadside to the wind, the "Wisdom II" was buffeted by heavy waves which swept over the deck. All hands were required to haul down the sails and save the craft from destruction. A huge comber swept the ship off the reef, ripping away the heavy leaden keel. She was anchored before she could be driven ashore. Now trapped in the lagoon beyond the banks, the ship wallowed helplessly, striking bottom with terrific force with each swell. Water poured into the bilge through the holes left by the torn-out keel bolts.

Morning revealed a terrifying sight: the Arab wreckers, who had destroyed the Mocha light, were waiting on the beach. Fortunately, the morning tide made it possible to get the ship under way. The anchor line was cut and the auxiliary motor started. The ship scraped over the reef and then was free. The bilge was hand-pumped sufficiently to allow partial repair of the leaks and the top-heavy craft headed northward into the monsoon.

After making port at Jedda, Schoedsack shot the first movies of pilgrims journeying to Mecca. A few weeks later the "Wisdom II" was in drydock at Savona, Italy. Workmen accidentally cut into a gas pipe in the bilge and when an Italian watchman entered the hold that night his lantern precipitated an explosion. The ship was burned, and with her the films that would have become the first Cooper-Schoedsack production.

Even before their Abyssinian footage was lost, Cooper and Schoedsack were planning another production. By the time they made their way to Paris they determined to make a film dealing with man's struggle against nature using as protagonists members of some nomadic tribe which must migrate to survive. They had no intention of making a travelogue; their plan was to tell a story of dramatic conflict as Robert Flaherty had done in *Nanook of the North.* At this early stage of their long and happy partnership they already had established the working methods that would characterise their future work together: full collaboration on all important aspects of production with their duties divided according to the abilities and preferences of each.

Among Cooper's assets was a knack for selling ideas to persons who were in a position to finance them. Accordingly, he returned to the United States to seek backing for their project. In New York he encountered unexpectedly a dear friend, Mrs. Marguerite Harrison, author of books and articles about her experiences in Russia and the Orient. Cooper first met the courageous Baltimore widow at a ball in Warsaw during the early days of the Russo-Polish conflict. Later, she smuggled food, money and tobacco to him during his imprisonment in Moscow before she, too, was jailed as a spy. The grateful Cooper, after his escape, organised a daring attempt to rescue her. Fortunately, she was "deported" to America before the foolhardy plan could be launched.

Cooper returned to Paris with $10,000—which was supposed to finance the entire expedition including the purchase of 40,000 feet of 35mm film. To Schoedsack's dismay Cooper also brought along a partner—Mrs. Harrison, who had been instrumental in raising the money. Schoedsack was opposed to taking a woman on a dangerous journey, but the die was cast.

The adventurous trio went to Turkey, planning to cross Anatolia to Kurdistan and there film the migration of one of the mountain tribes. Their youthful enthusiasm was not shared by the new Turkish government of Mustafa Kemal Ataturk. Having just fought a bloody war with the Greeks and the British-French alliance, the Turks viewed all westerners with suspicion. Secret agents spied on the Americans continually while officials stalled for many weeks without granting permission for them to continue east beyond the capital Angora (Ankara). During weeks of waiting, Schoedsack shot newsreel and travelogue footage in order to bring in some money.

The Americans managed to avoid surveillance long enough to flee to the Taurus Mountains, hiding in a small village where they became snowbound. They were treated royally by the peasants, who took them hunting for mountain goats and hid them from the police. When the snow broke, the party crossed over to French-occupied Syria and thence across the desert (in an ancient

Model T Ford) to Bagdad. Schoedsack went on to Mosul in search of a Kurdish tribe for their film, but the Kurds were fighting the British and Turks there and it was impossible to photograph their usual customs.

Cooper, meantime, learned from Sir Arnold Wilson, High Commissioner of Iraq, about the Bakhtiari tribes of Southern Persia (Iran), who lived under a medieval feudal system with little interference from the central government. They were nomads whose existence depended on the search for grass to keep their sheep and cattle alive, living in winter near the Persian Gulf where there was pasturage until late spring. In summer every blade of grass was seared by the sun and the tribes were forced to migrate to the mountains of Western Persia, across the awesome Zardeh Kuh range.

Making haste to the gathering place of the tribes, the film company arrived just as the migrations were about to begin. Most of the money and half of the film supply had been exhausted. There was no turning back because there wasn't enough money to pay for the return trip. With no supplies of their own they joined the Baba Ahmedi tribe and lived as the tribesmen did, Cooper and Schoedsack sleeping on the ground (or snow) with only one blanket each while Mrs. Harrison carried a small tent. Their diet consisted of sheep's buttermilk and stone-hard bread—the latter being so hard that Mrs. Harrison cracked a tooth with her first Bakhtiari meal. Schoedsack damaged his revolver-butt while trying to break up a chunk of bread. The only concession to luxury was the wearing of shoes; the Bakhtiari travelled barefoot. The Americans won the respect of their 30,000 hosts by being just as tough as the most hard-boiled of the lot.

During the early days of the march, because of the intense heat of the day, camp was broken after midnight and new camp-sites established before sunrise. As the trek proceeded into higher altitudes the weather became progressively colder until, at last, the caravan reached the snow-buried Zardeh Kuh mountain, a 12,000-foot barrier. The crossing of this wall of snow was an awesome sight which, captured on film, became one of the most spectacular motion picture sequences of all time.

Mrs. Harrison, Cooper and Schoedsack were the first foreigners ever to cross Zardeh Kuh, a journey of forty-six days. Schoedsack reached the other side of the mountain with eighty feet of film, which he used to shoot an ending for the picture. From Isfahan Cooper cabled several editors in New York and received enough advance money on articles to take the partners home. It was planned that Schoedsack would get more film and spend several months in Persia shooting human interest footage with a specific Bakhtiari family and Cooper would return in the fall for the return migration. Their plans did not materialise, however, and they were forced to use their film as it was. They were far from satisfied with the result and always considered their film, *Grass,* to be "a lost opportunity." After *Grass* was edited, Mrs. Harrison, no longer interested in film-making, withdrew from the partnership—to the relief of her co-producers. While Cooper searched for a distributor for *Grass,* Schoedsack, in order to bring some money into the destitute company, took a six months' job as cinematographer for the New York Zoological Society's oceanographic expedition to the Sargasso Sea and the Galapagos Islands, sailing February 10, 1925 aboard the "S. S. Arcturus."

Grass, whatever its imperfections, remains the cornerstone of an important school of picture-making and the foundation of the firm of Cooper-Schoedsack Productions. It led to many good things, the one of most immediate importance being the friendship of a pioneer film-maker who was quick to recognise the genius and dedication behind the making of *Grass,* Jesse L. Lasky.

Ancestor of the Kong Tyrannosaurus from the American Museum of Natural History

2. Adventure for Three

Jesse L. Lasky, vice-president of the Paramount-Famous Players-Lasky Corporation, premiered *Grass* at a charity benefit on February 19 at the New York Plaza Hotel. The critics were impressed. When the film opened on March 30 at the Criterion with symphonic accompaniment by Dr. Hugo Riesenfeld and Dr. Edward Kilenyi, it proved a sensation. A long New York run re-paid the $10,000 investment and brought in a modest profit, but without stars or "love interest" it was not a box-office success in its national release. Lasky was sufficiently pleased that he offered to subsidise another Cooper-Schoedsack expedition.

The "Arcturus" venture also proved to be important to the future of Cooper-Schoedsack Productions, for it served to bring a new member into the company.

Ruth Rose, historian and research technician of the expedition, was raised in the theatre by her father, Edward Rose, a leading theatrical producer and dramatist. Ruth, who lost her mother while still a youngster, grew up in the company of the great theatrical personalities of the day. Her idol and mentor was William Gillette, author and actor who still is remembered as the stage's definitive Sherlock Holmes. As a petite and beautiful young woman she appeared in numerous plays and acted in films at Fort Lee. She had been leading lady to Otis Skinner for three seasons when the Actors' Equity strike of 1919 caused the shutdown of Broadway's show houses.

The direction of Ruth Rose's career changed abruptly when she heard about the New York Zoological Society's Tropical Research Station at Kartabo, British Guiana. Although she had no scientific training, she applied to the director, Dr. William Beebe, volunteering to do whatever unskilled task should be required if permitted to join the expedition. Impressed with her zeal, Beebe hired her as "supercargo." Soon she was hard at work with six trained technicians, capturing, looking after and studying an astonishing variety of creatures found in a vast and largely unexplored jungle in which the only other human inhabitants were Akawi Indians and the inmates of a penal colony.

Displaying remarkable adaptability, she became in a short time a valued member of the research team, working in a bat-infested laboratory at an abandoned mining camp. She overcame a fear of serpents by making a pet of a small whipsnake; a short time later she helped to capture alive a gigantic boa constrictor. During her several years with Beebe she survived earthquakes, army ants, tropical storms, eye-to-eye encounters with jaguars and meetings with innumerable exotic snakes. Her writing ability was recognised early and she was made official historian of the Beebe expeditions. Magazines published her reports and she wrote portions of some of Beebe's popular books. A love of all living beings, even those that generate fear in man, is evident in her writing.

The "Arcturus" sailed 12,000 miles and crossed the equator eighteen times. Schoedsack, while not at all stimulated by his chores as a photographer of marine fauna, was charmed by the lovely Ruth Rose. By the time Schoedsack returned to New York, Cooper was straining at the leash. Paramount had okayed the idea for their second "natural drama" (a term coined by the producers).

Man's conflict with the jungle was the theme of the new Cooper-Schoedsack film. In their search for the most untouched of jungles the producers went to Bangkok, the capital of Siam (now Thailand). For some weeks they searched for a fitting locale for their film, Schoedsack exploring Indo-China while Cooper investigated lower Siam. Both men encountered too many big game hunters and automobiles for their liking. Then they heard tales of the Nan district of Northeast Siam, said to be the most remote jungle in the world. While Cooper remained in Bangkok to make the necessary arrangements with the king, Schoedsack journeyed as far north as the country's one single-line railroad would carry him, then continued by horseback, on foot and by log canoe to the Laotian Province of Nan.

Here, separated from the rest of the country by mountains, jungles and sixty-seven river crossings, he found a tropical forest that no white hunter ever had penetrated. From the only white inhabitants, a Presbyterian missionary and his assistants, he learned that nearly four hundred area villagers had been killed by tigers and leopards during the preceding five years. In some settlements the mortality rate attributable to predacious cats was as high as twenty percent. Lao houses were set upon high posts as a precaution against prowling beasts. Although native hunters occasionally killed troublesome leopards with their primitive flintlock rifles, little effort was made to control marauding tigers. This was because of a religious belief that whoever kills a tiger will be changed into a "god horse" (tiger) for the slain animal's demon spirit to ride upon. It was considered dangerous even to utter the word *suar* (tiger), for should the spirit overhear and take offence, a terrible vengeance would ensue.

Here, indeed, was an ideal setting for "natural drama": a jungle regarded not merely as a gigantic concentration of undergrowth but rather an actual, living personification of evil dominating the lives and thoughts of its human occupants.

Cooper arrived shortly and production began on the film known eventually as *Chang*, the title being a Lao word meaning elephant. The producers selected an attractive family as their principals, concocted a story sufficiently flexible to allow for the utilisation of actual situations that might develop, and began filming sequences with regard for natural dramatic development. The other players were beasts of the jungle—cats, pythons, bears, monitor lizards, buffalo, elephants and monkeys. Comedy relief was provided by Bimbo, an affectionate white gibbon ape whose antics on film have the appearance of real acting ability. It proved fairly simple to capture most of the animal actors but not the tigers, which eluded them through cunning and were made more elusive because of the superstitious awe with which they were regarded by the native crew. Cooper and Schoedsack were careful not to kill any animals except when it became necessary to do so for the protection of human life.

The most notorious man-killer in the region was a legendary tiger known as "Mister Crooked," whose tracks had been found at many a scene of tragedy. After a great deal of difficulty, the producers managed to capture this beast and several other known man-eaters. A significant drop in the mortality rate of the province became apparent. It was later reported by the governor that the work of Cooper and Schoedsack reduced by two-thirds the number of deaths caused by tigers in Nan.

Although some writers have suggested otherwise, there is no trick or studio photography in *Chang*, nor were any tame animals used. Schoedsack's equipment consisted of two tripod-mounted French Debrie cameras—four hundred-foot capacity hand-cranked models with no provisions for special effects. Cooper sometimes cranked the second camera when he wasn't needed to man a rifle. Photography in the dense jungles was extremely difficult and was done for the most part with the f 4.5 lens wide-open. The slow-speed orthochromatic film was overexposed purposely so that a "soft" developer could be used to produce a negative of fine definition. Climatic conditions made it mandatory to keep the film in sealed, dehumidified containers until it was ready to be used.

No telephoto lenses were used in photographing *Chang*, Schoedsack having decided that the obvious safety advantage was less important than the greater field of vision, definition and steadiness afforded by the normal two-inch lens. All the photography, therefore, was done at close range, primarily from camouflaged shelters and pits placed near animal trails and waterholes.

During one sequence, a tiger chased two natives up a tree. Sensing a chance to get an unusual shot for intercutting, Schoedsack later built a light platform in the tree thirteen feet above the ground while Cooper, armed with a rifle, was stationed in another tree nearby. Native beaters then chased a tiger to the vicinity and Schoedsack, lying on his perch alongside his camera, attracted the tiger's attention (and wrath) by proffering a "Bronx cheer." After angrily circling the tree, the beast leaped suddenly and fastened his claws in the trunk, trying desperately to climb to the platform. Cooper aimed his rifle at the cat's head, but Schoedsack called to him to hold his fire. Although tigers are not supposed to be able to climb trees, this one left claw marks on the trunk eleven feet above the ground and was so close to his goal that his face completely fills the frame in the resulting shot. After he had dropped to the ground, the tiger had to be killed to halt his rampage.

Even more harrowing was Schoedsack's method of filming an elephant stampede. A pit was dug, measuring about five feet square by seven feet in depth, and roofed over with heavy logs. A low turret of logs was built in the centre, projecting several inches above the roof and cut away underneath to permit the camera to project above ground-level and give Schoedsack head-room to view the action. The turret was necessarily weaker than the rest of the roof. Natives then drove a nearby herd of wild elephants toward—and over—the covered pit. For several anxious moments, as the pachyderms thundered overhead and fragments of the roof sifted into the pit, Schoedsack wondered if the logs would hold. After the herd had passed over the weakened structure, several of the elephants turned around and started back. One of the returning animals stepped directly on the turret and it gave way, showering the cameraman with splintered fragments of broken logs. Luckily, the elephant pulled his foot free and continued on his way.

Three of the native crew members were attacked by pythons, and one night a twenty-foot python invaded Schoedsack's room, which was thirty feet above the ground. Cooper's expert marksmanship more than once saved Schoedsack or others of the company from death.

There were other perils more difficult to combat. The coming of the monsoon forced the producers to move to a different jungle area to complete their work. A cholera epidemic was responsible for the deaths of seven of the native assistants. Schoedsack fell victim to malarial fever and during eleven of the fourteen months he was in Siam often worked while on the verge of delirium. Both men returned to New York so emaciated as to be almost unrecognisable, but they brought back the picture they consider to be their best.

"Coop and I made *Chang* with the raw materials we found there and no help whatever," Schoedsack says. "There was hard work, sweat and malaria—but in dollars it only cost what it takes to operate a 'B' unit for two days."

While Cooper and Schoedsack were editing *Chang* in New York, Schoedsack broke the news that he was going to marry Ruth Rose. Cooper was horrified at the thought of having another woman on the team after having herded Mrs. Harrison across Zardeh Kuh. Nevertheless, the wedding took place. Cooper's fears were not lessened by Mrs. Schoedsack's declaration that her husband would no longer be called "Shorty" and thereafter would be called "Monte" instead. Nor was his morale improved when Lasky agreed to pay Mrs. Schoedsack's expenses on the next Cooper-Schoedsack expedition for Paramount.

Chang opened in New York City at the Rivoli on April 28, 1927, with titles by Achmed Abdullah, a popular novelist. Hugo Riesenfeld's score was performed by an augmented symphony orchestra with two six-foot thunder-drums concealed behind the screen to emphasise the tumult of the elephant stampede. The sequence was further dramatised by the use of Paramount's "Magnascope," a device which opened the screen from its normal size to full proscenium width as the first elephant started to run over the camera. After three-hundred pachyderms had trampled the village, the "Magnascope" closed down on a scene of a little monkey playing with a broken pot.

Chang was enormously successful, justifying fully Lasky's faith in his *protégés*. The reviews almost without exception were enthusiastic and the Academy of Motion Picture Arts and Sciences nominated it in the category of "Most Artistic" production (it lost to F. W. Murnau's *Sunrise*.) Paramount's chiefs were delighted; a genuine epic costing only $60,000 would be profitable.

Lasky consequently invited the producers to make their own story in their own way. They wanted to try something new: to combine a "natural drama" with studio production to yield a film version of A. E. W. Mason's African warfare novel, "The Four Feathers."

In the late spring of 1927, only a few days after the *première* of *Chang*, they set out for Africa. From Dar es Salaam they went south to the mouth of the Rovuma River and thence upstream to film jungle scenes. One of these shows two white men being chased by Sudanese slavers into a parched jungle. The natives set the woods on fire, the flames driving out a horde of terrified baboons. After crossing a river, the fugitives weaken a bamboo bridge, which collapses when the apes swarm over it. Then a herd of hippopotami stampede over a bank and submerge. When the pursuers try to ford the stream, the hippos rise to the surface and drive them back.

Neither hippos nor baboons are co-operative as actors, hence several months were required to film these scenes. The District Commissioner, in order to stress the danger of working with hippos, showed the Americans a photo of a woman who had been bitten in half by one. Schoedsack once took a nocturnal stroll down a narrow trail and met a hippo weirdly limned by the moon. "It's a strange feeling," Schoedsack says with typical understatement.

A large number of the ponderous beasts were rounded up and herded into a corral made of massive, five-foot walls. By morning all had climbed out and another round-up was necessary. They were made to stampede over the cliff by crowding them against a log barricade that could be cut free on signal, permitting the animals to slide down into the river. Cooper was standing under the logs when Schoedsack called to him. The man who was assigned to release the logs mistook "Coop!" for "cut!"—and severed the trigger rope. Logs and hippos plunged down the bank and Cooper leaped to safety.

Later, the Schoedsacks were filming from a platform in the river when Ruth moved suddenly, jarring the camera. Schoedsack began bawling her out, then realised she had nearly been seized by a hippo. The hippopotamus stampede had to be staged thirteen times before the desired result was obtained.

Baboons are ferocious, cunning and possessed of incredible strength. They also are among the most intelligent of animals and the producers were fascinated by their near-human actions.

Working in the jungle, Cooper soon changed his mind about Ruth Schoedsack. She proved an invaluable member of the team, managing the commissary, keeping the payroll, acting as doctor for about two hundred native employees and manning gun or camera when necessary. She only fired one shot in Africa, but it saved someone from becoming a crocodile's dinner. She never forgave herself for killing the saurian.

In December they sailed north along the coast on the Indian Ocean, through the Gulf of Aden and the Straits of Bab el Mandeb, then up the Red Sea to Port Sudan. Christmas was spent aboard a Mohammedan ship crowded with pilgrims bound for Mecca. Overland they trekked seven hundred miles southwest to the Nuba Mountains, thence north and east to the Atbara River and at last into the Red Sea Hills, home of the famed "Fuzzy Wuzzy" fighting tribes.

They found that the old slave port of Suakin, which had been deserted during the dervish uprisings, was unaltered, preserved perfectly by the desert. The costumes of the Sudanese likewise had not changed in more than a century.

It was in the Red Sea Desert that the battle scenes were staged, with hundreds of descendants of the fanatical dervish warriors recreating the warfare of Kipling's time in the actual locale of the battles. The running charge of the "Fuzzy Wuzzy" army, photographed from many angles, is a terrifying spectacle rivalling in excitement the elephant stampede of *Chang*.

Several of the natives were selected to fall as though shot during the charge, which was across a flat plain studded with chunks of lava. To the chagrin of the directors, these men merely stopped running and lay down on the ground, carefully avoiding any contact with the rocks. Cooper called a halt and told the actors he would demonstrate how they must fall. Running a short distance, he spun as though hit and fell heavily to the earth. The jagged lava cut his leg so badly that Cooper might have bled to death but for an incredible bit of luck: a visitor who had just arrived to watch the battle happened to be the only doctor within many miles. Cooper was rushed away to a distant hospital, leaving Schoedsack to work alone for several weeks.

The war scenes were a long time in the making because most of them had to be shot during the early morning hours. Soon after sun-up the temperature soared daily to around 110 degrees, making it impossible to work natives, camels and horses.

In August 1928, Cooper and Schoedsack arrived in California and set to work directing dramatic scenes at Paramount and in the desert between Indio and Palm Springs, where the company built a replica of the British fort seen in the African footage. They drew strong performances from a cast that included Richard Arlen, Clive Brook, William Powell, Theodore von Eltz, Noah Beery and Noble Johnson. The feminine lead was played by a charming "WAMPAS Baby Star" from Canada, Fay Wray. The producers were highly impressed with the actress, both as an individual and as a performer, and she has remained their close friend. Johnson likewise formed a long association with Cooper-Schoedsack pictures.

Adolph Zukor rejected plans to make *The Four Feathers* a talking picture and appointed as supervisor the young David O. Selznick, for whom Schoedsack had shot some documentary films. Through careful planning, Cooper and Schoedsack were able to cut together their African, California desert and studio scenes without resorting to any kind of composite photography. The intricate and continual intercutting is matched so expertly that many critics have incorrectly assumed that only a few brief shots were made in Africa.

After the producers had edited the film and left Hollywood, Selznick decided additional scenes were needed and assigned the chore to Lothar Mendes. These are unimaginative and damaging to the show. By the time the picture was ready to screen, non-dialogue films were "dead" except in the small town theatres which had not yet installed sound equipment. An excellent musical score by William Frederick Peters and an effects track by the multi-talented Roy Pomeroy were added before the film was given a gala launching at the Criterion Theatre in New York on June 12, 1929. Paramount again used the "Magnascope" to enhance the spectacle.

"I thought David Selznick made a great mistake in putting in all that titling and those phoney scenes directed by Mendes," Cooper said. "It was a much better picture when Monte and I left it, when I went to New York to go into aviation and Monte went off to make a picture in Sumatra. However, I was confident that the stuff Monte and I had shot would be sufficient to make it a success, and it was despite the fact it was the only 'silent' picture playing in New York when everything else was a 'talkie.' "

Cooper's venture into civil aviation was the outgrowth of investments he began making in 1927, using most of his profits from *Grass* and *Chang*, in a mutual fund restricted to aviation stocks. Even the depression failed to halt the growth of the airlines and Cooper in a short time found himself deeply involved in the future of American airpower. These interests made it essential that he remain in New York even though Lasky was anxious to get another Cooper-Schoedsack jungle film under way.

Schoedsack, unable to reconcile himself to the confines of civilisation, accepted Paramount's offer. After conducting voluminous research at museums and geographical societies in New York he wrote his own script and, in May, 1929, set out with Ruth to the Dutch East Indies, where he would film *Rango*.

Cooper, despite his success, was painfully aware that life as a business executive was a pallid anticlimax to a decade of high adventure. It would not be the end. There would be other movies, other expeditions to unexplored worlds. In his spare time he studied maps at the Explorer's Club and the National Geographic Society.

It was during this time that Cooper's imagination caught fire with what was to become the most celebrated of his creations. It was then that Cooper conceived *King Kong*.

3. The Ultimate in Adventure

"To thrill myself," Cooper replied when he was asked why he dreamed up *King Kong*. "To please the public, too, of course, but I also wanted to please myself. I wanted to produce something that I could view with pride and say, 'There is the ultimate in adventure.' "

So it was that while Schoedsack was shooting his latest "natural drama" in the wilds of Sumatra, Cooper turned his thoughts to a wholly imaginary adventure in which he set out to magnify the spirit of the Cooper-Schoedsack expeditions. His first concept was of a gigantic ape, forty or fifty feet tall, perched atop the tallest building, fighting a fleet of warplanes.

One of Cooper's friends in New York was W. Douglas Burden, the noted explorer and naturalist whose experiences in Brazil, Nicaragua and the Far East were the stuff of high adventure. Cooper was particularly intrigued by Burden's account of his American Museum of Natural History expedition to the Lesser Sunda Islands of Malaysia, which was undertaken at the same time *Chang* was being filmed. The highlight of the expedition was a collecting trip to the island of Komodo, home of the fabled Komodo dragons, the world's largest lizards.

Komodo itself was something of a story-book "lost world," a weird, volcanic jungle-land inhabited only by a handful of Malay convicts exiled there by the Rajah of Sumbawa. The Komodo lizards were first reported in 1912 by P. A. Ouwens, a Dutch scientist from Java, who followed native legends of living dragons to their source. Burden was the first to bring the great reptiles to the New World, the beautiful habitat group at the American Museum being composed of specimens bagged during the 1926 expedition. Two dragons were brought back alive and exhibited at the Bronx Zoo but they languished and died in a short time.

"Komodo was relatively unexplored, only a few white men having landed there," Burden wrote in the "National Geographic Magazine." "With its fantastic sky line, its sentinel palms, its volcanic chimneys bared to the stars, it was a fitting abode for the great saurians we had come to seek. Deer, wild boar, water buffalo, and game birds were abundant on the island . . .

"The lizards, which attain a length of ten feet and a weight of 250 pounds, are known to scientists as *Varanus komodoensis*. They are vicious, carnivorous reptiles, which attack their food much as the great flesh-eating dinosaurs must have done, ripping off great chunks of meat with their sharp, recurved saw-edged teeth and swallowing them whole, bones and all.

"The Varanus lizards first appear as a genus in the early Eocene, some sixty million years ago;

so that we have here not only the largest, but also the oldest, of living lizards."

Burden's description of the nearby island of Wetar also suggests an ideal setting for mystery and the possible discovery of prehistoric survivals:

"As it arose out of the sea, the island appeared a vast mass of torn and splintered mountains. The central portion is unexplored, and small wonder, for the tumble of jagged peaks presents insurmountable barriers opposing the traveler's way." Burden noted that Bali and other islands of the region were inhabited by Malays, but that "Wetar, on the other hand, is inhabited by Papuans, who belong to a large group of peoples classified by anthropologists as Oceanic Negroids. The Malays, being a mixture of Mongoloid-Polynesian, have no negroid blood."*

It is not difficult to imagine how great a lure these islands exerted upon the adventurous spirit of Cooper while he was beached in New York, often wishing he could be with his friends in Sumatra giving the "Bronx cheer" to raging tigers. His own jungle experiences, his agonising need to explore the unknown places of the world and finally his talks with Burden combined to form the genesis of *King Kong*. To his original idea of a gigantic gorilla pitted against modern man he added, after his talks with Burden, other elements basic to the final story: the discovery of gigantic prehistoric reptiles still existing on a remote island "'way west of Sumatra," an isolated race of savage Blacks who worship strange gods, an expedition from New York capturing and bringing home an awesome monster to amaze the public, the inability of such a creature to survive as a captive of man. Even the name, Komodo, possessed an exotic quality that influenced him in creating the name of the central figure of his story. In a 1933 press release Cooper said:

"I got to thinking about the possibility of there having been one beast, more powerful than all the others and more intelligent—one beast giving a hint, a suggestion, a prefiguration of the dawn of man.

"Then the thought struck me—what would happen to this highest representative of prehistoric animal life in our materialistic, mechanistic civilisation? Why not place him at the pinnacle of the tallest building, symbol in steel, stone and glass of modern man's achievement and aspiration, and pit him against modern man?

"As I mulled the story over in my mind, I saw that I had conceived the climax rather than the beginning. How would *King Kong* get there? I saw that man would have to go to *King Kong's* world first: I conceived him as impregnable to gun-fire and too huge and swift to be killed by sword at close quarters.

"How, then, to capture him? I had it! Schoedsack and I had gone to remote places to make wild animal pictures. *King Kong* would be found in such a remote place—a survival of the early world —and he would be captured through a fragile and beautiful girl. There is only one thing that may undo a brute, provided the brute approximates man, and that is beauty!

"It is beauty that kindles the spark of something the brute never has sensed before. He is amazed, he is subdued by this strange thing of beauty. So I decided it would be Beauty, personified by a girl, that would lead to *King Kong's* capture and, ultimately, to his death."

If this touch of the sensual appears foreign to the thinking of one whose earlier films had pointedly avoided such complications, it must be remembered that exhibitors had tempered their enthusiasm for *Chang* with the criticism that the film would have drawn bigger audiences had it contained a love story. There had been a leading lady in *The Four Feathers,* but the stiff-upper-lip tone of that he-man picture permitted no hint of brute passion. In some post-war articles in the New York "Times," written under the by-line of "A Fortunate Soldier," and in his book, "Things Men Die For" (Putnam, 1927), Cooper had much to say about women he had known regarding their fierce loyalty to their men in times of danger or deprivation.

Schoedsack had taken a cameraman to Sumatra, so he could concentrate on story and direction. He began to feel uneasy at sailing time when the photographer failed to appear. His anxiety increased when the man finally came aboard unconscious, borne aloft by several inebriated friends and accompanied by a large sack of bottled goods.

* "Stalking the Dragon Lizard on the Island of Komodo," by W. Douglas Burden: "National Geographic Magazine," August, 1927.

Rango was made in the high mountain jungles at the northwestern end of Sumatra, among the fierce Atjehnese natives and an abundant concentration of wildlife. The Dutch government, which had been having trouble with the tribes, reluctantly granted the film party permission to enter the region but refused to accept responsibility for their safety. The Schoedsacks quickly befriended the natives and for nine months worked at a location 3,000 feet above sea level, living in a bamboo hut alongside a mountain torrent. The area was free of the excessive heat, malaria and mosquitos that plagued the *Chang* expedition, the only climatic problem being an over-abundance of rain peculiar to the monsoon belt.

Schoedsack's misgivings about his cameraman soon were confirmed: the first encounter with a tiger so terrified the man as to intensify his drinking problem until he was virtually useless. In the evenings the man usually drank a little Dutch beer with the Schoedsacks, but afterwards he would slip out to the native huts and quaff the local brew. He nailed his windows shut and kept a huge sword by his bed. Often he was heard to mutter that "those tigers aren't gonna get *me!*" and once he locked himself in the darkroom and refused to come out. Schoedsack eventually put him aboard a ship to Europe and photographed most of *Rango* himself.

Schoedsack returned in June, 1930, and began cutting the negative of his picture at the Paramount Eastern Studio, Astoria, Long Island. He opened *Rango* with a talking prologue in which a little American boy hunts cardboard tigers with his pop-gun. An uncle, who has lived in the jungle, then tells him a real story about a boy, a gun and a tiger. The body of the story is told visually, with the accompaniment of sound effects and a symphonic score. The talking prologue was innovative at the time and became a standard part of most expeditionary films thereafter.

Schoedsack tried to remain in seclusion while occupied with these time-consuming chores, but his employers, who had sent out numerous press releases as to the dangers he had encountered with wild beasts and hostile savages, were insistent that he allow himself to be interviewed by the press. Until then he had managed to relinquish this distasteful part of the business to the more flamboyant Cooper. When at last a press conference was arranged, Schoedsack, to the despair of the publicity department, went to great lengths to minimise any suggestion of personal adventure in the making of *Rango*. When the "Times" reporter asked about the studio's hair-raising press releases, Schoedsack "looked perplexed," then replied:

" 'Dangers?

" 'As dangerous as your poison liquor and your automobiles here in New York, I suppose. Wild animals? Why, yes, there are the tigers. Naturally, the big cats come down into the village now and then and kill a few goats or oxen. But your taxi drivers kill a few people from time to time, don't they? New Yorkers don't go around in perpetual fear because of that.' " When asked if he had narrow escapes while photographing tigers, he said, " 'Certainly not. I went to Sumatra to make a picture, not to risk my neck. No natives were killed. Three tigers were shot—for the picture. Aside from that I only killed tigers when necessary . . .

" 'Seriously, there were no thrills. The finished film may seem packed with excitement, but making it is a long, slow, tedious business stretched over eight or nine months. Remember, only eight percent of the stuff I shot appears in the picture shown to the public. And, honestly, there weren't many difficulties . . . The weather was wonderful . . .

" 'The point is that I have my own ideas about making motion pictures. Everyone seems to think that stories, to be vital, must have a love interest. A picture can't be good unless it's built around a throbbing scene between a male and a female. That's a mistake, as Cooper and I tried to show with *Grass* and *Chang*. We focus our lenses, not on silly close-ups of love-sick females, but on the elemental clashes between nations and their fundamental problems, between man and nature.

" 'Another thing to remember is that when I go off like that, I don't have to take orders from producers. I work out my picture in my own way.' "

Five days after the *première* of *Rango,** Cooper received news that shattered one of his fondest hopes. For five years he had been planning an expedition into the largest unexplored land area in the world, the so-called "Empty Quarter" or

* *Rango:* "The New York Times," January 4, 1931.

"Abode of Loneliness" of Arabia. No expedition had ever penetrated this region containing more than 500,000 square miles of desert—nearly half the area of all Arabia—because there was no water to be had at any of the known entrances and the surrounding areas were peopled by tribes hostile to any intrusion by outsiders. Now it was reported that Bertram Thomas, Wazir to the Sultan of Muscat, had just made the first crossing of the "Empty Quarter." Hiding his personal disappointment, Cooper issued a statement to the press saying that Thomas's feat "required a courage that modern explorers have not been called upon to show . . . I cannot imagine any expedition on earth more surrounded with danger . . . I consider it the greatest individual accomplishment, and the bravest one, in our day." Exploration proved, as Cooper had believed it would, that tribes heretofore unknown existed deep within the region Cooper called "truly the No Man's Land of the world."

In less than a month Cooper was off on a dangerous adventure of his own, but this time there was no joy in the undertaking. His young friend, Varick Frissell, who had been making sound movies of a sealing expedition in the North Atlantic, was reported missing after the sealing ship "Viking" exploded and burned off the coast of Newfoundland. After talking to Frissell's father, Cooper arranged a flying mission to search for survivors. With the famed Bernt Balchen, the first pilot to fly over Antarctica, Cooper left Boston in a large twin-engine Sikorsky amphibian plane. Storms hampered rescue efforts as ships became ice-locked and the heavy airplane was buffeted by Arctic winds. The steamer "Sir William," crushed by ice, was lost (all hands escaped). Eventually, all but twenty of the 155 men who sailed on the "Viking" were brought back, but Balchen and Cooper, after a week of scanning the ice floes, returned with the report that Frissell and his cameraman, Arthur Penrod, were among the lost. The tragic quest reached its climax when the searchers returned to Boston—and were fined $500 for failing to conform to customs regulations!

When Paramount acquired filming rights to "The Lives of a Bengal Lancer," Francis Yeats-Brown's popular book about British and native troops in strife-torn India, Lasky envisioned a production done in the manner of *The Four Feathers*. He proposed to send Cooper and Schoedsack to India to make location footage, then have them complete the film with Hollywood players and sets. The assignment held great appeal, but Cooper, whose airline interests were paying off in a big way, was forced to decline his participation.

Schoedsack, therefore, undertook the Indian expedition on his own, beginning preparations in May. He set out early in July 1930, accompanied by his wife, his cameraman brother, Felix, cameraman Rex Wimpy and several assistants. After seven weeks at sea the party arrived at Calcutta on August 27 and travelled by train into the interior. During the next fifteen weeks they shot scenes in the northern mountain country, at Delhi and Simla, in the Khyber Pass, at Peshawar, Kohat, Risalpur, in the jungles around Jhansi and Jaipur, in the southern states of Madras and Mysore, and finally in Bombay. Much of their work was done among the warlike Afridis, Mahduhs and Wasiris.

David Selznick had terminated his job at Paramount on June 8 and, with his brother, Myron, attempted to find backing to start his own movie company. During this time he again came into contact with Cooper, who showed him the latest of several treatments he had prepared on his prehistoric gorilla story. Although David found the idea interesting and believed that Cooper had the ability to see it through, he was in no position to do anything about it.

During the summer of 1931, Cooper tried to interest executives at Metro-Goldwyn-Mayer and Paramount in sponsoring his project, including expeditions to Africa and Komodo, but none of them was willing to risk such an expensive and possibly impractical scheme.

Cooper's aviation interests had snowballed to the extent that he was elected to the board of directors of Pan American Airways, of Western Air Express (the first chartered domestic airline, now called Western Airlines), of General Aviation and National Aviation. His financial future was secure, but his creative instincts were thwarted. Often his thoughts returned to his half-formed adventure film idea which, it seemed, would never be born.

4. OBie

There was, in fact, a man who possessed the know-how to make practical the filming of Cooper's mad daydream. He was Willis Harold O'Brien, a two-fisted, hard-drinking Irishman from Oakland. O'Brien was the outstanding practitioner of something he called "animation in depth," a method by which inanimate objects are given an illusion of life and movement on film.

The basic idea, known as stop-motion, is a simple one that was exploited before 1900 by a pioneer French producer, Georges Méliès. A subject is placed in position and a single frame is shot of that placement. The subject then is moved slightly and another frame is exposed. Further related positions are photographed in this manner, describing the increments of movement of whatever action is to be simulated on the film. The strip of "still" frames, when projected in the usual way, are blended by the "persistence of vision" into a semblance of motion. The speed at which the subject appears to move is determined by the distance between the positions photographed: fast-moving objects require less footage and therefore the placements are farther apart than would be necessary for slow-moving effects. It was by this method that a bed was made to dance and leap all over the room in Edwin S. Porter's wonderful trick film of 1906, *The Dream of a Rarebit Fiend.*

Although O'Brien was far from being the first film-maker to utilise dimensional animation, his efforts were more ambitious than those of his predecessors or contemporaries and it was he who refined and developed the technique until he attained near-perfection.

O'Brien had been a cowboy, a prize-fighter, a cartoonist for the "San Francisco Daily World" and a sculptor for the San Francisco World Fair of 1915 before he entered the film industry. While he was making some clay models of boxers for an exhibit, his brother began manipulating the arms of one of the figures, saying, "My fighter can beat yours." This led O'Brien to experiment with stop-motion photography of pliable clay models. Manipulating the mannikins by hand in gradual steps and photographing them with a borrowed newsreel camera, O'Brien produced a film in which they appeared to be moving about on their own, albeit jerkily and too rapidly.

Late in 1914, O'Brien made a picture seventy-five feet in length featuring a caveman and a comical brontosaurus. An interested spectator at the screening of some of O'Brien's experiments was Watterson R. Rothacker, president of the Rothacker Film Company of Chicago.

O'Brien later filmed *The Dinosaur and the Missing Link,* a comedy involving cavemen, an ape-man and prehistoric beasts. The protagonists were constructed in miniatures of clay over joint-

ed wooden skeletons and photographed among settings made from rocks and tree limbs, which were set up in the basement of the Imperial Theatre in San Francisco. Two months were required to produce the film, which was completed late in 1915. The Thomas A. Edison Company of the Bronx, New York, bought the reel for $525—one dollar per foot—for theatrical distribution. O'Brien quickly set to work in another "studio" on the roof of the Bank of Italy Building at Powell and Market Streets, where he made two trick pictures, *Morpheus Mike* and *Birth of a Flivver.*

In 1916 O'Brien went to New York to make more dinosaur comedies for Edison's Conquest Film Programs. For this purpose Mannikin Films, Inc., was formed with O'Brien as president. Mannikin then produced *R.F.D. 10,000 B.C., Prehistoric Poultry* (two versions), *In the Villain's Power, Curious Pets of Our Ancestors, Mickey and His Goat, Sam Loyd's Famous Puzzles—the Puzzling Billboard* and *Nippy's Nightmare.* The last-named has the distinction of being the first film to combine living actors with the mannikins, the live action being intercut with the animated scenes. At this point O'Brien suddenly was dissatisfied with his earlier efforts, convinced now that a good movie must have human elements.

The models in the Mannikin films were designed after the popular conception of the appearance of prehistoric animals with no particular attempt at authenticity. When the Conquest Program was discontinued by Edison, O'Brien was asked to edit a weekly series in which a continuing educational feature would be a brief depiction of various extinct animals. In order to make his reconstructions scientifically correct, he consulted with Dr. Barnum Brown, the distinguished vertebrate paleontologist at the American Museum of Natural History.

Edison sold out to Lincoln & Parker before the weekly series got under way and the new owners decided to abandon the educational portions of the series. At this time O'Brien met Major Herbert M. Dawley, a pioneer film technician and cameraman, who had been experimenting with a plastic dinosaur and had pasted a great number of exposures of the animal in a small book so that when the pages were flipped the subject appeared to move. O'Brien and Dawley entered into an agreement to film *The Ghost of Slumber Mountain.*

Opposite: this self-portrait in the make-up of Rembrandt is the last known picture of O'Brien. It was made as a gift to Don Weed of Film Effects Studio, Hollywood, during the trick work and animation for IT'S A MAD, MAD, MAD, MAD WORLD. (Loaned by Don Weed)

OBie in 1930 with a model figure and a Monoclonius (from a badly damaged print in the collection of Marcel Delgado)

O'Brien set to work without a scenario, using only a sheet of titles as a guide. He constructed five prehistoric monsters under Dr. Brown's guidance, making them as realistic as possible. Brown also suggested much of the animal action used in the film. There is no slapstick and the dinosaurs are not caricatured. The entire film was made by O'Brien using methods he pioneered and all of the animals in it were his. The original was approximately 3,000 feet in length but it was cut to 520 feet before release. It is thought that Dawley used some of the excised footage in *Along the Moonbeam Trail* (1920), which is, at this writing, among the lost films.

When *The Ghost* opened at the New York Strand, full credit was given O'Brien for its production. O'Brien's name was absent from the release prints, which bore the single credit line, "Produced by Herbert M. Dawley." The producer

The "Missing Link" from Willis O'Brien's 1916 comedy. O'Brien called him "Kong's ancestor." (Library of Congress photo)

also accepted sole credit when he was interviewed for a popular magazine. The publication told its readers that:

"Major Dawley began his unusual work with a camera, some film, and several tons of prehistoric bones in the American Museum of Natural History. The bones were of value only so far as they gave scientists the basis on which to furnish him accurate data. Thus he would proceed to build his own monsters.

He laid in a supply of lumber, cloth, paint, clay and other materials with which to construct his million-year-old animals. He first prepared a rugged wooden skeleton, finished it off with a covering of clay to express the muscles, tendons and bones of the living animal, and over this placed a skin-like covering of cloth painted a dark brown color. After building several animals—one of them was seventeen feet high—he was ready to make them act for the camera . . . By utilizing what is technically known as the motion-stop process—a process so laborious and time-consuming that it is practically abandoned in these days of quick production—he made thousands of exposures of his animals in thousands of different attitudes, with the result that when the film was run through the projecting machine it gave the impression that these wood, clay and cloth figures were actual animals, alive and moving . . . In addition to placing the legs in the proper posture each time an exposure was made, he had to change the position of the neck, the trunk, and the tail each time a new step was taken. This is comparatively easy to do when the model is small, but when it is seventeen feet high, it requires an effort and patience that few men would care to exercise.

*In one of Major Dawley's films two animals are shown fighting. The photographing of this film required, of course, twice as much effort as a film showing but one monster in action. Yet this sculptor did not stop with two in the same picture; he put in three and even four, and the difficulty in making the animals move in a life-like way was quadrupled . . ."**

A viewing of the film reveals that the monster "seventeen feet high" is one of O'Brien's clever miniatures photographed in a miniature setting designed to match full scale scenes of the human actors photographed on location in the mountains. The one exception is a close-up of an Allosaurus which appears to have been made using a large head. Evident are a number of trademarks familiar to anyone who has studied O'Brien's work. Despite an amusing "framing story," the body of the work is calculated to amaze and shock the spectator and the dinosaurs are strikingly realistic. The story, which is sufficiently uncomplicated to be unfolded in about fifteen minutes, carries a fair measure of suspense.

The most conspicuous weakness of the film is its scarcity of close-ups, there being only two in the entire reel. The animals, however, are excellent. They seem properly heavy and ponderous, their actions are surprisingly smooth and there are many bits of business peculiar to O'Brien's work (i.e., the great Diatryma pauses to scratch itself a moment after it enters the scene). The camera itself is animated twice, panning across the landscape to reveal an approaching Triceratops and moving slowly up the towering body of the Allosaurus to a shot of the grinning head.

This film was released in 1919 by Paul M. Cromelin's World Cinema Distributing Company of Fort Lee, New Jersey. It cost only $3,000 to produce and grossed more than $100,000. Dr. G. Clyde Fisher, of The American Museum of Natural History, commented, "I was greatly pleased. It is astonishing how lifelike those old dinosaurs and the giant bird, diatryma, were. The whole thing was extremely well done."

Another who was impressed was Watterson Rothacker, who was horrified at the blatant attempt to discredit O'Brien. Placing O'Brien under contract, he set him to making novelty reels. Both men lost interest in short films, however, when Rothacker secured photoplay rights to Sir Arthur Conan Doyle's "The Lost World," a fantastic novel about prehistoric monsters discovered on a Brazilian plateau.

It quickly became evident that the spectacular action envisioned for this project would necessitate technical work well beyond the scope of O'Brien's usual one-man *modus operandi.* To this end Rothacker arranged to co-produce the feature with First National Pictures, Inc., at their Burbank lot. Here O'Brien would have the collaboration of the head of the studio's special effects department, Fred W. Jackman, whose genius embraced every facet of motion picture technology. O'Brien realised, too, that dinosaurs made of wood, clay and cloth were inadequate for the needs of so ambitious an undertaking. He needed assistance of a highly specialised kind.

O'Brien was attending night classes at the Otis Art Institute. There he met twenty-year-old Marcel Delgado, a grocery clerk who was working as a student assistant in order to finance his studies. Some sixth sense told O'Brien that the wiry and pugnacious young sculptor possessed the determination and unique talents needed to help bring "The Lost World" to the screen. How right he was!

In his native village of La Parrita, below the border near Laredo, Texas, Delgado watched the labours of a bearded old man called "The Patron Saint" who earned his bread by carving statues of the saints. By the time he was six Delgado was making sculptures of his own as well as developing mechanical skills by creating his own toys. During the Mexican Revolution his large and impoverished family moved to California, where they worked in the bean fields and walnut orchards around Saticoy. He had little opportunity to go to school and did not speak English until he was seventeen. Delgado well remembers his meeting with O'Brien:

"Mr. O'Brien took an interest in my work and one night he asked me, 'would you like to work

* Charles W. Person: "Making Actors of Prehistoric Animals." "Illustrated World," November, 1919, p. 380.

in motion pictures?' I told him I would not because I wanted to be an artist and didn't want to lose any time. Every time he saw me he asked again and offered me $75 a week to come to work for him. I always said no, and I don't really know why; I was only making $18 a week but I guess I felt secure. One Friday he asked me to lay off work and visit the motion picture studio. OBie left a pass at the gate and when I went in OBie met me and took me to his little shop. There was a 'phone, some cameras and pictures all around. 'How do you like your studio?' he asked. 'It's yours if you want it.' It was a twenty-year-old boy's dream! So I signed up and worked for the next couple of years building dinosaurs for *The Lost World*. I made forty-nine or fifty of them and it was all done under cover with no visitors allowed —although some of the studio big shots came in anyhow."

Delgado used the paintings of Charles R. Knight to guide him in the appearance of the prehistoric animals. Knight's celebrated reconstructions at the Field Museum of Natural History and the American Museum of Natural History are the finest art of this highly specialised kind in that they are not only as accurate as scientific knowledge can make them but they are amazingly lifelike. The same lifelike quality is evident in Delgado's creations. They have personality.

Delgado's dinosaurs averaged eighteen inches in length, with the stegosaurs and ceratopsians being somewhat smaller and the brontosaurus being considerably larger. The skeletons were made of tempered dural with articulated backbones and ball-and-socket joints for all movable digits and appendages. Sponge-rubber muscles were applied and made to flex and stretch as real muscles do. The armature then was padded and shaped out into the basic form of the animal. The skins were made of latex and rubber sheeting. All spines, plates, warty growths and other protuberances were made separately and applied to the realistically textured skins. Some of the reptiles were equipped with a breathing apparatus consisting of a bladder placed between the skin and the armature. By use of an air compressor device, the amount of air in the bladder could be controlled and animated along with the other bodily movements so that the animal appeared to breathe.

By mid-1922, O'Brien had produced a reel of test footage in which the dinosaurs cavorted about very much as they must have done in life. A print was given to Conan Doyle, who had come to America to give a series of lectures on spiritualism. While Sir Arthur was in New York, he was invited by his doubting-thomas friend, Harry Houdini, to attend the annual meeting of the Society of American Magicians held at the Hotel McAlpin on June 2. Doyle at first refused, having become wary of magicians because of their tendency to ridicule his spiritualistic beliefs. At the last minute, however, he did attend in the company of Adolph S. Ochs, publisher of the New York "Times," and other special guests. After all of the greatest magicians in America had displayed their latest tricks, Doyle topped them easily with a stunt of his own which was emblazoned next morning on the front page of the "Times."

A movie projector was brought in, a screen erected and the lights extinguished. In a brief speech, Doyle said that he would answer no questions about the film he was about to present. "These pictures are not occult, but they are psychic because everything that emanates from the human spirit or human brain is psychic," he said. "It is not supernatural; nothing is. It is preternatural in the sense that it is not known to our ordinary senses. It is the effect of the joining on the one hand of imagination, and on the other hand of some power of materialisation. The imagination, I may say, comes from me—the materialising power from elsewhere."

O'Brien's test reel was then screened without titles or comment. The audience was astonished. The "Times" reported that "Dinosaurs of one tribe appeared on the screen and rubbed jowls in an affectionate manner. Then entered the tyrannosaurs or dinosaurs of the killing type which preyed on the browsing members of their family. The tyrannosaurs fought among themselves, interlocked their great jaws and wrestled. Finally one broke the back of the other and was about to devour it, when up dashed a triceratops, the three-horned ancestor of the modern rhinoceros, who drove the tyrannosaur away. Then appeared the stegosaurus, an armour-plated monster, whose defensive equipment saved him from repeated attacks of the dinosaurs." The newspaper, undecided as to whether Doyle was "making merry . . . or was lifting the

THE LOST WORLD. The Allosaurus menaces the explorers

veil . . ." concluded that Doyle's "monsters of the ancient world or of the new world which he has discovered in the ether, were extraordinarily lifelike. If fakes, they were masterpieces."

Not only had Doyle paid back the magicians in their own coin by eclipsing their best performances; he also had given O'Brien's film monsters an acid test that could only be considered a triumph. After seeing page one of the "Times," Doyle realised that things were getting out of hand and he immediately issued a statement explaining the origin of his films.

Within days O'Brien's former producer, Major Dawley, brought suit against Rothacker and Doyle, issuing a public statement that Doyle's dinosaurs had been filmed by a process invented by Dawley and pirated from him by one of his former employees. He threatened to sue Rothacker for $100,000 for patent infringement and to file an injunction halting filming of *The Lost World* and preventing sale or use of any of the existing footage. Nothing came of the case, however, and O'Brien continued his work.

In July 1924, First National announced that the full-scale work of *The Lost World* had been started after "six and a half years' preparation and research," and that more than $1,000,000 would be spent on the production. Nor was this figure a press-agent's boast. A set representing two streets in the heart of London was one-eighth of a mile long. The maximum lighting capacity of the studio was required to light the set, on which were deployed two thousand players, two hundred automobiles, six omnibuses, twenty-five assistant directors and eighteen cameramen. Equally impressive were exterior and interior views of the Royal Museum which were reproduced at the studio. Jungles, a trading post, caverns and a precipice were constructed on the lot along the Los Angeles River.

Direction of the live action was begun by Harry O. Hoyt, a graduate of Columbia and Yale who had been a lawyer before becoming a scriptwriter (initially for D. W. Griffith), editor and director. Such was the scope of the production that supervisor Earl Hudson established a second unit when it became evident that a year would be needed to complete the film as it was progressing. William Dowling directed the second company, which eventually was merged with Hoyt's main unit during the final weeks of production. The leading players were Wallace Beery, Lewis Stone, Bessie Love, Lloyd Hughes and Bull Montana. Arthur Edeson was in charge of the corps of cameramen filming the live action.

The dinosaur scenes were staged on a set measuring about two hundred by three hundred feet wherein was depicted a vast jungle properly scaled to make Delgado's monsters appear at home. Miniature trees were constructed solidly to avoid unwanted jiggling, with leaves and fronds in some instances being cut from sheet metal for greater stability. For scenes in which the animals seem to leap at one another, special backgrounds were devised to permit the combatants to leave the ground. Animation was shot with seven cameras mounted on dollies which could be locked securely into position. The shutters were operated simultaneously from a single control.

The Lost World's greatest innovation was the showing of live actors and animated monsters in the same frames. D. W. Griffith moved a life-size Ceratosaurus through scenes with the players in *In Prehistoric Days* (1913) but the mock-up lacked the agility of O'Brien's animated beasts. Lubin's *On Moonshine Mountain* (1914) used living reptiles, which were lively enough but never were shown with the players, being intercut with shots of the human performers. For *The Lost World,* O'Brien placed actors in the miniature settings by masking off portions of the negatives and printing into the masked areas scenes of players photographed against matching backdrops. Bessie Love, in her recently completed autobiography, "Love From Hollywood", remembers acting under these circumstances. She says, "In place of yelling 'Run!' when the prehistoric animals started chasing us, Mr. Hoyt explained in detail why we should run, namely, the tyrannosaurus was a carnivorous dinosaur. The animals were not actually on stage . . . it was double exposure. It didn't really matter if you called them Joe, Gus and Heimie as long as

THE LOST WORLD. Wallace Beery, Arthur Hoyt, Lewis Stone and Bessie Love hide from the Brontosaurus as he destroys their log bridge

you looked terrified and scampered."* When one sees husky Wallace Beery dwarfed by a monster convincingly one hundred feet long, the effect is startling even today. The effect on the spectator in 1925, when nothing of the like had been seen before, can be imagined.

Even more striking are the shots of the Brontosaurus running wild through the streets of London as hordes of extras scatter in terror. These scenes were accomplished through an early travelling matte process. The dinosaur was animated against a stark white background and the resulting film was made up two ways: as a negative with the animal appearing against a black background, and as a high-contrast positive with the figure in silhouette against clear film. The high-contrast positive was used as a mask through which to print the street scene, producing a copy in which the contours of the animal were left unexposed. The negative then was employed to print the Brontosaurus into the masked areas. This process was made obsolete by the more dependable ones invented by C. Dodge Dunning and Frank Williams and by the development of optical printing. It was effective, however, and marred only by occasional matte-bleeds caused by variable shrinkage of the different emulsions. The matching of miniature and full-scale perspectives was superbly managed. Several scenes used full-scale props: a life-size Brontosaurus head crashing through a wall to invade a chess tournament and a gigantic tail sweeping through a crowd of extras to tumble them like tenpins.

The real *tour de force* of the show is a stampede of monsters during a volcanic eruption, which remains the most spectacular animation sequence in any film. Dozens of dinosaurs are seen fleeing through the forest, sometimes in the same frame with the live actors, an exploding volcano, flame and smoke. Even in this situation the allosaurs prey upon the other animais, which fight them off as they race along. One grim tableau has an entire family of allosaurs feeding upon a fallen herbivore. The volcano sequence was printed on red stock in the release prints.

The Lost World was released early in 1925 (by all odds *the* vintage year of the silent cinema) and was given a deluxe roadshow treatment. The original version was in ten reels with a running time of about two hours. Audiences and critics were so wild about the dinosaurs they were willing to tolerate the long and unexciting portions dealing with a standard romantic situation.* The players were well liked, however, particularly Wallace Beery in his robust performance as Professor Challenger, the most uncharacteristic role of his long career, and the vivacious Bessie Love.

Production manager Earl Hudson soon announced that O'Brien and Hoyt were planning a sequel to *The Lost World* and that it would be "entirely different" from the original. Despite changes of ownership and policy, the studio continued plans for the sequel as late as February, 1928, when negotiations were made with Rothacker to begin production. With more management changes, however, O'Brien's film was abandoned. His disappointment was compounded as other proposed subjects—including a version of *Frankenstein* in which the Monster would be portrayed by an O'Brien "mannikin," and an adaptation of H. G. Wells' *Food of the Gods*—were never born. O'Brien soon fell into obscurity while Delgado found employment in the First National property department.

"While *The Lost World* was in work I got to be well known at the studio," Delgado recalls. "Big stars like Milton Sills, Colleen Moore and Wally Beery were my friends. But after I was demoted to the prop shop they treated me like I had the mange. A couple of years later Warner Brothers bought out First National and I was laid off, but I was quickly hired to build miniatures and special props at the old William Fox Studio. I stayed there until OBie called again."

O'Brien continued to submit his ideas but nobody was willing to back them. The sensational emergence of "talkies" created a frantic atmosphere in which potential investors regarded O'Brien's wholly visual ideas as being hopelessly outmoded.

By 1930, fortunately, the novelty appeal of talking pictures had waned sufficiently to set the studios searching for other means of enticing audiences. Most of the studios launched wide-film productions, but these failed because depression-stricken theatre owners, already forced to acquire

* Used with permission of the author.

* Existing prints are in five reels.

sound equipment, were unwilling or unable to install the equipment necessary to their presentation. Technicolor and other two-colour processes enjoyed a sudden boom that proved transitory because added expense and unresolved technical problems made colour production a formidable undertaking. What the movies needed was virility, not gimmickry.

Outdoor adventure thrillers returned to studio schedules as audiences became increasingly apathetic to the visual dullness and excessive talkiness of the majority of new films. Films like W. S. Van Dyke's *Trader Horn* and Howard Hughes' *Hell's Angels,* both of which were conceived as silent epics; Wesley Ruggles' *Cimarron,* Roland West's *The Bat Whispers,* Schoedsack's *Rango* and numerous others appeared in answer to the cry that movies must move as well as talk.

Here, at last, was an era in which O'Brien could function.

II.
The Making of Kong

"Kong was the product of many contributions."
Ernest B. Schoedsack

5. Production 601

While Cooper was working on his giant gorilla story, O'Brien was planning a rather similar project which he called *Creation*. This collaboration with Harry Hoyt was envisioned as an epic production combining elements of *The Lost World* and *The Admirable Crichton*.

Early in 1930 Marcel Delgado received a call from an elated O'Brien: *Creation* had been bought for production by RKO-Radio Pictures. Leaving his job at Fox, Delgado reported to the Gower Street studio to begin construction of a new menagerie of prehistoric monsters. O'Brien was permitted to create his own production unit within the studio to develop the property.

Creation was one of the most intricately planned film projects ever launched. Every aspect of lighting and action necessary to produce the ultimate dramatic value of each shot was decided before consideration was given to the mechanical means of producing the desired effect. O'Brien made numerous sketches depicting highlights of the scenario. These were developed into large, comprehensive illustrations. Continuity sketches were then made in shot by shot sequence, linking the larger drawings so that each scene in the script was pictured. Lighting, camera angles, sets and props, planned action and the relative scale of all elements were illustrated. Precise diagrams showed camera positions, lenses, and perspectives.

The illustrations were the work of three gifted artists, Mario Larrinaga, Byron L. Crabbe and Ernest Smythe. Larrinaga, born in Baja California of Basque parents, started his professional art career without formal training at the age of sixteen. As an apprentice to his older brother, Juan, at a scenic studio in Los Angeles, he painted sets and curtains for opera, drama and vaudeville. In 1916 he became a technical artist at the new Universal Studio, where he painted everything from miniatures to huge cycloramas. Eventually he headed the art effects department at Warner Bros. He retired to Taos, New Mexico, in 1951 and has gained a notable reputation in fine arts and architectural design. Crabbe had an outstanding reputation as a set designer and effects artist and died at the peak of his career in the middle 1930s. Smythe was an illustrator who had produced hundreds of posters and advertisements for Universal.

Animation now was more difficult than in the days of *The Lost World* because it had to be prepared for projection at twenty-four frames per second, the standard speed for sound films, whereas the earlier film was shot at sixteen f.p.s. O'Brien, therefore, had to provide animation with eight additional steps per second of screen time. This reduced by one-third the amount of footage that could be completed in a specific time. Twenty-five feet of finished film (running less than twenty

CREATION. Tyrannosaurus in the temple

seconds) was considered a good day's work.

Scenes of a shipwreck and an island rising from the sea were staged in a heavily braced glass tank with plates four feet square. The tank was filled with water one night so shooting could begin next morning, but the glass broke during the night. It was not sufficiently heavy to withstand the pressure of the water. New and heavier glass failed to sustain the weight of the water. A third and much stronger tank held the water but the thicker glass caused the cameramen to complain. Lighting and distortion problems had to be faced. The first takes of the headland rising lacked the desired ponderousness. This problem was finally solved by thickening the water with clear gelatin.

Composite effects in which Delgado's monsters, live animals and actors were combined were achieved with stunning realism undreamed of in the days of *The Lost World*. Except for the cameramen, Delgado and the glass artists, the men who assisted O'Brien in achieving these superb effects were borrowed from the art, property and miniature departments. These grips, artisans and technicians were trained in the intricacies of O'Brien's complicated and time-consuming methods amid a great deal of trial and error.

The studio chiefs despaired with each passing day. RKO, hard-hit by the depression, was on the verge of bankruptcy and in a state of organisational upheaval. William Le Baron, vice-president in charge of production, was under intolerable pressure from the New York office. By the late summer of 1931, Le Baron had escaped to a job at Paramount, and *Creation* had run up costs in excess of $100,000. Miniscule as this sum may appear by today's inflated standards, it represented a considerable outlay at a time when five profitable "quickies" could be made for that amount and a respectable "A" feature could be brought in for $200,000. *Creation* could cost millions.

Le Baron's successor, who arrived in September, 1931, was the former "boy wonder" of Paramount, David O. Selznick. The new boss was instructed to make whatever changes were necessary to put the company back on a solid footing and it was clear that drastic surgery was mandatory. Salaries were slashed. All productions were halted for re-evaluation, some to be aborted (a notable casualty was Luther Reed's ambitious *Babes in Toyland*), some to be revised with new sequences and others to be re-made entirely. Several directors were replaced in mid-film and others were given New York stage directors as collaborators to bring up the quality of dialogue. "Script doctors" arrived to rescue troublesome scenarios. Budgets, which had been flexible, were set in advance of all future production with $200,000 established as a standard for "A" features.

Selznick soon realised that he needed a hard-nosed assistant to help in appraising the welter of unfinished films, scripts and properties. He made a wise choice.

CREATION. Master drawing of dramatic action before the temple, credited to O'Brien and Larrinaga

CREATION. Byron Crabbe made this key drawing of the appealing mother Triceratops and her young

Merian Cooper arrived from New York in response to Selznick's summons and accepted the job. Among the unfinished films screened by Cooper was O'Brien's *Creation* footage. Cooper was fascinated by the technical aspects of the work but felt that the project, after nearly a year, was getting nowhere. Selznick agreed, and *Creation* was struck from the schedule.*

Although Cooper could see no commercial possibilities in *Creation,* which he described as "just a lot of animals walking around," he perceived in O'Brien a means of producing his giant gorilla epic in a practical manner without leaving the lot. From Selznick he received permission to shoot a test reel to be submitted to the board of directors. He was permitted to retain O'Brien and his unit until it could be ascertained whether or not the picture could be made successfully. The film went on the schedule as Production 601.

* See Appendix 7 for more about *Creation.*

CREATION. Here the lush jungle is created largely out of carefully selected small plants. The fallen tree is yet to be textured. A wooden Triceratops stands in for the test

Now Cooper was faced with the problem of how to shoot, on an almost non-existent budget, a reel of film spectacular enough to impress a group of executives who were unable to agree on anything other than the need for careful budgeting of each dollar. The manner in which he achieved the desired result illustrates the genius for organisation for which Cooper was well known.

After consulting with O'Brien, Cooper asked Delgado whether it would be possible to build a gorilla which, on the screen, could be made to appear as large as a dinosaur. Delgado replied that he could and was told to get to work on it. After Cooper had left, O'Brien told Delgado to "make that ape almost human." Accordingly, Delgado designed a monstrosity in which were combined the features of man and ape.

"That's the funniest looking thing I've ever seen!" Cooper declared when he saw the completed job. "It looks like a cross between a monkey and a man with long hair. Damn it, I want to put a pure gorilla on that screen!" After a great deal more work, Delgado produced a second Kong that was more lifelike but yet retained certain man-like characteristics. Cooper was again dissatisfied.

"I want Kong to be the fiercest, most brutal, monstrous damned thing that has ever been seen," Cooper demanded. O'Brien argued that it would be impossible to win audience sympathy for a monster ape lacking any human qualities, but Cooper was adamant. "I'll have women crying over him before I'm through, and the more brutal he is the more they'll cry at the end." Cooper returned to his office and called the American Museum of Natural History in New York City, requesting the exact dimensions of a large bull gorilla. On the afternoon of December 22, 1931, he placed in O'Brien's hands a telegram from the Curator of Zoology:

DIMENSIONS LARGE MALE GORILLAS HEIGHT HEEL TO CROWN SIXTY

CREATION. This sensitive drawing by Larrinaga manifests his great skill and feeling for light and shade

SEVEN INCHES SPAN OUTSTRETCHED ARMS HUNDRED TWO INCHES CHEST OVER NIPPLES SIXTY CIRCUMFERENCE AROUND BELLY SEVENTY TWO STOP PHOTOGRAPHY OF ADULT HUMAN AND GORILLA SKELETONS COMPARED SEE HAECKEL E NINETEEN THREE ANTHROPOGENIE VOLUME TWO PAGE SEVEN NINETY EIGHT FOR OTHER DATA YERKES NINETEEN TWENTY NINE THE GREAT APES AND DUCHAILLU EIGHTEEN SIXTY TWO ADVENTURES IN EQUATORIAL AFRICA = HARRY C RAVEN

"Now that's what I want," Cooper declared, whereupon O'Brien announced his resignation and stalked out of the studio. After a few drinks at a neighbourhood speakeasy, O'Brien returned to work. The scene would be repeated several times during the year to come.

Edgar Wallace, the popular English author, had arrived from London on December 5, having accepted a lucrative contract to write originals for RKO. Within days Cooper arranged for Wallace to be assigned to script *The Beast,* the studio's work title for Cooper's gorilla story, as soon as he should complete "Death Watch," a mystery story later retitled "Before Dawn."

On December 12 Cooper took Wallace to meet O'Brien and watch the filming of a test shot of men fighting a dinosaur. An entry in Wallace's diary tells of his visit to a converted projection room that had become O'Brien's workshop. There he examined the frame of "the giant monkey which appears in this play.

CREATION. A happy family group

The important telegram that established the proportions, though not the size, of Kong

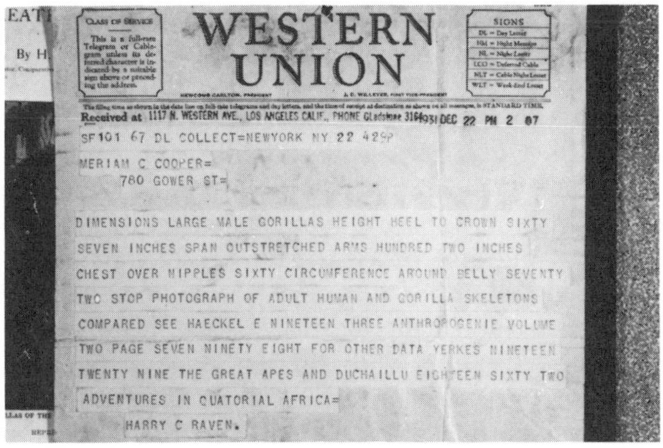

WESTERN UNION

Received at 1117 N. WESTERN AVE., LOS ANGELES CALIF., PHONE GLadstone 3164 1931 DEC 22 PM 2 07

SF101 67 DL COLLECT=NEWYORK NY 22 429P

MERIAM C COOPER=
780 GOWER ST=

DIMENSIONS LARGE MALE GORILLAS HEIGHT HEEL TO CROWN SIXTY SEVEN INCHES SPAN OUTSTRETCHED ARMS HUNDRED TWO INCHES CHEST OVER NIPPLES SIXTY CIRCUMFERENCE AROUND BELLY SEVENTY TWO STOP PHOTOGRAPH OF ADULT HUMAN AND GORILLA SKELETONS COMPARED SEE HAECKEL E NINETEEN THREE ANTHROPOGENIE VOLUME TWO PAGE SEVEN NINETY EIGHT FOR OTHER DATA YERKES NINETEEN TWENTY NINE THE GREAT APES AND DUCHAILLU EIGHTEEN SIXTY TWO ADVENTURES IN QUATORIAL AFRICA=

HARRY C RAVEN.

CREATION. A miniature set built after the original Larrinaga concept. The Los Angeles river is matted in and the birds were animated by Orville Goldner

"I saw a woodcarver fashioning the skull on which the actual figure will be built. In another place was a great scale model of an actual gorilla. One of the gorilla figures will be nearly thirty feet high. All round the walls are wooden models of prehistoric beasts. There are two miniature sets with real miniature trees, on which the prehistoric animals are made to gambol."

On Christmas Day Wallace wrote:

"Merian Cooper called and we talked over the big animal play we are going to write, or rather, I am writing and he is directing." The next entry, dated December 29, adds: "An announcement has been made in the local press that I am doing a super-horror story with Merian Cooper, but the truth is it is much more his story than mine. I am rather enthusiastic about it, but the story has got to be more or less written to provide certain spectacular effects. I shall get much more credit out of the picture than I deserve if it is a success, but as I shall be blamed by the public if it's a failure, that seems fair."

Delgado this time made the gorilla to Cooper's specifications, cheating only to the extent of paunch and rump.

"Kong was eighteen inches high," Delgado says. "The skeleton was made of high-tempered dural and I gave him muscles that react, which is why Kong looks alive instead of stiff. I was given pruned rabbit fur to cover him with and I never was satisfied with that because I knew it would show the fingerprints of the animators."

Early in February, both Cooper and Wallace were stricken with pneumonia. Cooper checked into a hospital and tried to persuade Wallace to do the same. The author elected to remain in his apartment, which he maintained at a high temperature, and drink large quantities of heavily-sweetened hot tea. On February 10, 1932, Wallace died of pneumonia complicated by diabetes.

"Actually, Edgar Wallace didn't write any of *Kong,* not one bloody word," Cooper says. "I'd promised him credit and so I gave it to him."

About two weeks later, Cooper and O'Brien began shooting technical scenes for the test on Stage 3 at the Radio lot. The working title now was *The Eighth Wonder.* Visitors were barred as technicians and cameramen set to work in units separated by high, black drapes designed to keep light from spilling into neighbouring sets. The only actors employed at this point were the eighteen-inch ape and several of the dural-and-rubber dinosaurs originally built for *Creation.* James Ashmore Creelman, a veteran writer with a knack for concocting imaginative adventure tales, was recruited to collaborate with Cooper on the story while Larrinaga and Crabbe were kept busy putting the resulting ideas into illustration form.

Along with photo-copies of the story drawings, O'Brien issued to his artisans a collection of woodcut illustrations by the Nineteenth century French artist Gustave Doré. These were taken from "The Bible," "Paradise Lost," "The Divine Comedy" and other classic editions. "This is what I want," he explained, indicating the play of light over the tortured trees and menacing rock formations of Doré's demonic landscapes. A comparison of Doré's art with finished scenes of the film reveals that the chiaroscuro and mood of the jungle scenes is that of Doré. The settings were intricate com-

CREATION. Ernest Smythe pictures the action for the chase by the Triceratops

CREATION. A miniature given depth with glass painting, and the Los Angeles river matted in. It follows Larrinaga's key drawing.

CREATION. In a process shot the Triceratops chases Ralf Harolde

CREATION. Side angle process shot of the chase. Miniature tree and foliage foreground

The lemur (Kinkajou) in CREATION

CREATION. The angered mother Triceratops charges after the killer of one of her offspring

CREATION. The Arsinoitherium traps the Chilean sailors (six-inch models) on the log

binations of miniature construction and paintings on flats and glass.

Glass painting had been used since the early days of film-making to add the upper portions of sets only partially built (i.e., the towers of a castle or the ceiling of a cathedral), to create desired backgrounds which otherwise were unavailable and to add clouds to bleak skies. By the mid-Thirties the method was displaced by improved matte and optical processes.

Glass paintings were rendered on sheets of plate glass that was flawless and iridescence-free, in tones of opaque grey (and, later, in colour). A high degree of precision was necessary in the matching of proportions, perspective, lighting and textures. Detail was critical inasmuch as the product would be greatly enlarged on the screen. Painted areas were backed with opaque black paint while the remaining portions were left clear. The glass was placed between the camera and the set in such a position that, as seen through the camera lens, the lines of the set and the artwork were matched perfectly.

O'Brien's adaptation of glass art was unique. As many as three planes of painted art were prepared for many of the jungle scenes, with constructed miniature set elements positioned between glasses. The art flats and the solid forms were carefully aligned and blended to produce scenes possessing a realistic atmosphere and a convincing illusion of depth. The settings were lighted by the cameramen to match the light patterns of the original designs. Sometimes the sought-for effect could not be achieved through actual lighting, whereupon paint technicians spray-painted the offending areas to conform to the original conception.

The dramatic jungle trees were modelled in plasticine clay over wood-and-wire forms. These were covered with toilet tissue, then shellacked and painted. The tree foliage in some instances consisted of sprays from small shrubs, such as genista, which were wired onto the constructed branches. Palm fronds, ferns and certain other leaf forms were cut from copper sheeting thinner than writing paper. Mingled with man-made plants were small succulents, desert shrubs and other living plants. A "green man" obtained grape roots from vineyards where old orchards were being replaced or destroyed and these were used in making gnarled miniature trees and vines.

Animation is comparatively simple when applied to objects that operate from a fixed axis, but walking or running animals are much more difficult because their body weight shifts with each step. For this reason the sets were built on tabletops made of two-inch pine through which numerous holes were drilled. The holes were designed to accommodate specially designed clamps that could be inserted from underneath into the metal feet of the beasts as they "walked." By this means the animals' feet were held securely in position each time they touched down. The perforated tabletop was hidden from camera view by glass art, foliage, and a low camera angle. O'Brien's first assistant spent a great deal of time crawling about under the tables to set and tighten clamps. Rods were sometimes concealed in the sides of the animals and anchored into the sets to hold the figures firmly in position.

The animators studied slow-motion films of elephants to aid them in developing the body movements of the dinosaurs. Eadweard Muybridge's sequential photos of animals and humans were consulted as well. The human figures used in some scenes with the animals were six inches tall. The detailed characters were carved in wood and were firmly jointed so they would remain in any given position.

Tiny archaeopteryxes and other birds were made to flit among the trees on invisible wires. The birds were about one-and-a-half inches in length, with bodies carved in wood and wings made of pliable copper. They were advanced on the hair-thin piano wires in steps of one-fourth of an inch per exposure and the wings were made to "flap" with minute cycles of animation. It was quickly learned that white birds are harder to animate than dark ones because they cannot be "lost" among the foliage and branches of trees.

Stand-ins for the dinosaurs were necessary because the latex skins of the working models suffered under the heat of the studio lights. The wood-carved versions were identical in size and colour to the movable animals seen on the screen.

Each scene was tested until its various elements were properly aligned and lighted. For this pur-

Opposite: a stand-in for testing scenes in CREATION and KONG

pose a portable darkroom, measuring six by nine feet, was kept on the stage. After a short length of movie film was exposed, the camera magazine was taken into the darkroom without disturbing the position of the camera and the exposed strip of negative was developed. Frame enlargements printed from these negatives guided the technicians in adjusting artwork, properties and lights until the desired effects and necessary alignments of all components were achieved. Such precautions, although time-consuming, made it possible to avoid the errors in matching that compromise so many trick scenes. It is fortunate that some of the crew members kept a few of these tests as souvenirs, because these faded prints (they weren't *fixed* for permanency) are all that remain of many scenes of the film.

While designing, constructing, and testing were proceeding at RKO Schoedsack was experiencing difficult times at Paramount. Returning from India early in January, he found the studio chiefs wrangling over the script and casting of *The Lives of a Bengal Lancer* and unable to decide whether it should be completed at the studio or on location in the Sierra. A parade of noted writers tried re-writing the script and each version was rejected. Clive Brook, Phillips Holmes, Fredric March, Cary Grant and Richard Arlen were among the players whose names appeared on and then vanished from the casting lists. Schoedsack, a devotee of direct action, became increasingly exasperated by the postponements of his film and was not enthusiastic about time-marking assignments to shoot re-takes for other directors. In March, John Cromwell was assigned to co-direct *Lives* with Schoedsack, but when there were further delays Schoedsack secured his release from Paramount and joined Cooper at RKO, where he signed a contract as producer and director. Cromwell soon followed suit. Stephen Roberts next was named to direct *Lives,* which eventually was completed by Henry Hathaway—in 1935.

In May 1932, Cooper and Schoedsack initiated pre-production work on *The Most Dangerous Game,* for which James Creelman prepared an ingenious adaptation of Richard Connell's award-winning short-story of 1924. A large chunk of the film's $200,000 budget was allotted for the construction of an elaborate set on Stage 11 at the RKO-Pathe lot in Culver City. An eerie swamp, man-made cliffs, a waterfall and a ravine bridged by a fallen tree were dressed with authentic tropical trees and undergrowth. These elements were so designed by Carroll Clark, the art director, that they could be rearranged to create a variety of different settings. With the addition of glass art by Larrinaga and Crabbe and atmospheric effects by Harry Redmond Jr., the total set became, as far as the camera could discern, a vast jungle.

This accorded perfectly with Cooper's plans for *The Eighth Wonder.* Here was Kong's native heath, made to order and paid for.

6. The Perils of Pathe

Production 602, *The Most Dangerous Game,* was started early in June under Schoedsack's direction with Irving Pichel assisting as dialogue director. The cast included Joel McCrea, Fay Wray and Robert Armstrong.

Leslie Banks, a London and Broadway stage star who had never appeared in films, was imported for the pivotal role of Count Zaroff. He was witty and charming, a specialist in the sophisticated type of comedy. His features had been marred seriously in the First World War with the result that his face presented two dramatically different profiles, the right side being handsome while the other appeared rather brutish. This Jekyll-Hyde quality was useful in depicting the changing moods and warped longings of a man who displays Chesterfieldian manners and composes waltzes but is possessed by bestial desires.

Connell's story depicts a battle of skills between two celebrated hunters when Rainsford falls overboard in the Caribbean and is cast ashore on General Zaroff's private island. A Cossack aristocrat in exile, Zaroff lives only for the hunt. After stalking every big game animal he decides that only one creature has the intelligence and will-to-live that make a challenging quarry. He arranges fake channel lights so ships will be wrecked on nearby reefs. Survivors are treated as guests until he is ready to hunt them down. Rainsford survives the hunt, kills the madman in a duel and inherits the game preserve.

While Connell concentrated on the predatory concept of man against man in a struggle for survival, Creelman twisted Zaroff's aberration a turn farther by making it explicit that for him the joy of the hunt was a prerequisite to sexual indulgence. "He talks of wine and women as a *prelude* to the hunt," Zaroff says of a guest. "We barbarians know that it is after the chase, and then only, that man revels. You know the saying of the Ogandi chieftains: 'Hunt first the enemy, then the woman.' It is the natural instinct. The blood is quickened by the kill. One passion builds upon another. Kill, *then* love! When you have known that, you have known ecstasy!"

This refinement was made possible by the presence of a woman, the radiant Fay Wray. The addition of romantic interest made it necessary to dispense with Connell's sardonic ending, but Creelman compensated by providing for Zaroff an exit considerably more dramatic than the fencing bout of the original.

Creelman spun wonderful adventure yarns, but he had an impractical side that occasionally created production problems. He insisted, for example, that it would be more frightening if Zaroff used leopards rather than hounds to track his prey. Schoedsack, who knew the ways of the big cats, reluctantly borrowed a jaguar from the Selig Zoo. The animal was in the charge of a famous woman animal trainer, Olga Celeste, and her male helper.

O'Brien had earlier used a jaguar in *Creation*. The beast, when released from its cage, was supposed to run out into a clearing, pounce on a live chicken which was concealed in some foliage, then run out of camera range into another cage. A man was stationed on top of the cage to close the gate once the cat was safely inside. Jaguars are unpredictable and this one refused to do as the script demanded. Finally, the cat ran out and seized the bird, but instead of devouring it on the spot he carried it to the other side of the set, intent on jumping on top of the cage to finish his meal. Terribly vulnerable as he crouched on the cage, the technician held his ground while the beast stared and snarled. At last the jaguar, brushing past the technician, jumped over the top of the cage with the one objective of finding a quiet place to eat the chicken. He then jumped the low wire barrier which separated the set from the camera and crew. Although Olga Celeste told everybody to stand still, some members of the crew scurried to places where they felt more secure. However, at least one electrician who had manifested great fear from the beginning of the shooting scrambled up the ladder to the rafters of the sound stage. The big cat, still wanting only his kind of habitat for devouring his feathered catch, finally crouched beside the barrier. Miss Celeste grabbed the beast by the wonderfully loose skin over the shoulders and rump and heaved him into the cage.

Schoedsack's jaguar was equally unco-operative. Escaping onto the fog-shrouded set, the cat created a general panic before being recaptured. Understandably, Schoedsack returned the cat and hired

CREATION: The jaguar that only Olga Celeste could handle

THE MOST DANGEROUS GAME. Zaroff's castle as visualised by Byron Crabbe

Harold Lloyd's pack of great danes and their trainer, also a woman. The dogs' hair was darkened to make them appear more vicious and they were sent in pursuit of Fay Wray and Joel McCrea through the fog-shrouded swamp, Banks following with his precision rifle.

In the course of the chase, Banks came bounding out of the fog, clutching his backside with his free hand.

"I say! One of those animals *bit* me!" the actor declared. The trainer protested that her pets absolutely would not bite. "Perhaps it was a cameraman, then," Banks replied, turning around to reveal a badly lacerated *gluteus maximus,* "But *something* bit me on the ass!" Both the actor and his costume required patching before shooting could be resumed.

Another annoyance at Stage 11 was the nervous omnipresence of the company filming Production 601, now re-titled *Kong.* Cooper hovered in the wings with his cast and crew, ready to pounce onto the set between takes on Schoedsack's film. To make matters worse, he insisted on borrowing Armstrong and Miss Wray for hours at a time while Schoedsack fidgeted. A daily spectacle in the Kong-Zaroff jungle was a Mutt-and-Jeff confrontation with the two producers gnawing their pipestems and growling at each other.

The situation came to a head while Cooper was shooting some difficult process scenes in which Miss Wray lay pinned beneath a log while Kong and a dinosaur fought over her. These shots required a great deal of intricate preparation because they combined full-scale properties, the actress, foreground glass art and some previously filmed animation. Setting up and matching these various elements was a tedious business. Cooper

THE MOST DANGEROUS GAME. San Pedro in the foreground matted with a glass having two unpainted spots through which the "buoy lights" shine

was adjusting the actress's wig for the ump-teenth time (she was a brunette in *Game* and a blonde in *Kong*) when Schoedsack rebelled.

"The camera is so far away you could have a prop boy under that wig and nobody would know the difference," Schoedsack insisted. Cooper felt otherwise but compromised by using Linden, Gibson and a cut-out figure as stand-ins for the actress between takes. In order that Schoedsack could meet the production schedule imposed by Selznick, Cooper was obliged to do much of his filming at night.

Cooper had approached Fay Wray with the news that he had chosen her to be the leading lady in a film about "a discovery of gigantic proportions" and that she would play opposite "the tallest, darkest leading man in Hollywood." Her initial enthusiasm changed to panic as he showed her Larrinaga's official portrait of her film suitor stalking through the jungle with Miss Wray clutched in one hairy paw. The role called for a blonde (for contrast) and Cooper had considered several blonde actresses, including Jean Harlow and Ginger Rogers, but his high regard for Miss Wray made him want her for the part. He decided, then, to cover Miss Wray's brown hair with a blonde wig and cast her as Kong's "golden woman."

Her *other* romantic lead, Bruce Cabot, was a young contract player who hadn't yet been in a film. He came to Cooper's attention when he submitted some photos of himself made up as Zaroff, according to the description in the Connell story, with military moustache and white hair. Although he didn't get the Zaroff role, Cabot was upset at seeing his photo in an ad for *The Most Dangerous Game*! Cabot was given the role in *Kong* after a rather unusual screen test: Cooper

Bruce Cabot. A studio portrait

Robert Armstrong. A portrait

made him climb down a rope that was suspended from the log bridge on Stage 11.

Armstrong, between scenes of *The Most Dangerous Game,* was instructed to exchange his dress suit for a soiled and tattered safari get-up for his first day's work with Cooper. There was no script as yet, but Cooper and Creelman had decided that there would be a chase through the jungle.

"I hadn't been able to read a script, but I did know that I was playing an adventurous motion picture director who took a company to a mysterious island and this was about all I knew," Armstrong recalled. "Mr. Cooper explained to me that this shot would be of myself and my crew in single file coming through the woods, and when I got to the log I was to hold up my hand and stop my followers. As I looked across the log I was to see, across the chasm at the other end, a fifty-foot ape.

"At this point I said, 'Excuse me, Mr. Cooper, but if I understood you correctly you said that I saw a fifty-foot ape.' He said, 'Yes, that's right, Bob. Why?' I said, 'Well, am I supposed to take it big?' He said, 'Yes, Bob.' I said, 'Well, I've been in this business a great many years, but *you* tell *me* how to take a fifty-foot ape *big*!'"

Script troubles continued. Creelman's fertile imagination produced good ideas but he had difficulty keeping inside the bounds of financial and technical practicality. Here, for example, is his description of Skull Island:

FADE IN on a general view of Skull Island, at dawn, with the bridge of the ship in the foreground. Captain Englehorn is leaning over the rail looking out at the grandeur of the spectacle. Sea and jungle are still in purple shadow. But high above, the east has drenched the mountains in the glory of its burning. One by one the columnar peaks of snow are kindling downward, chasm by chasm, each in itself a new morning;

Willis O'Brien and the full-scale Kong in a lay-out from "The International Photographer"

white glaciers blaze their winding paths like fiery serpents; long avalanches cast down keen streams, brighter than lightning, each sending its tribute of driven snow, like altar smoke, to the heavens. The rose light of the silent domes flushes that heaven about them until the whole sky, one scarlet canopy, is interwoven with a roof of waving flame and tossing, vault beyond vault, as with the drifted wings of many companies of angels.

Another knotty problem was the need to bridge the action highlights so there would be no dull lapses to impede the action. How to get the romantic leads from Kong's clutches and back to the native village, how to bring Kong to civilisation without a plethora of explanations, how to tell the purpose of Denham's expedition in as few words as possible—these were stumbling blocks that plagued Cooper and Creelman. A young performer named Horace McCoy, who had joined the writing staff at RKO after his acting career failed to get off the ground, received his first assignment as a writer when he was told to help Creelman with *Kong*. McCoy became a well-known scenarist and author of novels including ' They Shoot Horses, Don't They?"

One usable bit of story material came from an unexpected source. Esteban Clemente (Steve Clemento), a Yaqui Indian who was known in vaudeville as the world's greatest knife-thrower, was playing in *The Most Dangerous Game* as Zaroff's Mongolian servant. Although he possessed an incredibly malevolent face, Clemente was a likeable and mild-mannered little man who became a friend of Cooper and the Schoedsacks. One day he told them of the difficulty he encountered in obtaining a pretty girl to be the "target" for his stage act. After all the talent agencies had refused to help him, he began walking the streets searching for somebody sufficiently comely and courageous to handle the job. Finally, he saw a shabbily dressed but very attractive girl standing at a lunchroom window, gazing in like a child outside a toy store. Clemente suggested that she have dinner with him. Frightened, but too hungry to refuse, she accepted. After Clemente managed with considerable difficulty to explain why he was interested in her, she accepted the job. This incident, combined with episodes from Ruth Rose's early career, may be seen to resemble closely the opening sequence of *Kong*.

Bruce Cabot's role required him to slide down a vine from the log bridge and swing into a cliff-side cave. The ravine was built high above the floor of the stage and the stunt extras had to fall from the log into a net. Bruised and fatigued after several days of this, the inexperienced actor became increasingly perplexed as to his role. He was relaxing one day with the stuntmen when one of them asked him, "What part are you supposed to be playing in this crazy picture?"

"They tell me I'm the leading man," Cabot said.

"Then they lied to you," the stuntman told him. "You're just doing the rough stuff for Joel McCrea while he finishes that other picture." The other men agreed.

Cabot tried to convince himself that the story was just a studio rumour, but when he learned that the stuntmen were being paid more than his modest contract salary brought him, he decided the rumour was true. Cabot stormed up to Cooper and announced that he was quitting.

"But what about *Kong*?" Cooper demanded, unconsciously supplying a line for his film.

"You can shove *Kong*!" the actor shouted as he stamped off the set.

Cooper found Cabot before he could leave town and assured him that he definitely had the lead in *Kong*. It was true that McCrea, then the studio's "fair-haired boy," had been announced for the role, but the studio's insistence that he be doubled in some strenuous scenes led Cooper to seek out a less demanding actor.

"Don't go," Cooper urged. "You'll ruin us if you walk out now." Cabot agreed to return and it only occurred to him later that he should have asked for more money. As things turned out, his salary was reduced a short time later during a Selznick economy move.

Archie Marshek, film editor assigned to *The Most Dangerous Game*, was one of the few men at the studio who believed that the moderately budgeted picture was potentially a classic. Even Schoedsack had his doubts, saying later that he "didn't think it would be very good so I just decided to keep it moving so fast that nobody would notice. If a scene lasted thirty seconds I'd say, 'I think it would play just as well in twenty seconds.' We didn't know what a good picture we had until it was finished." Marshek says that Schoedsack sometimes hid in the editing room when Cooper was on the set because each producer had his own ideas of how the chase should be filmed. By avoiding the issue he was able to do it his own way. *The Most Dangerous Game* was brought in on schedule and within the budget.

The screening revealed that the Cooper-Schoedsack team had exceeded all expectations. Their first "all-talkie" provided ample proof that Schoedsack could no longer be typed as an "outdoor" director, that his abilities embraced a far wider range of film-making than the documentary and the "natural drama." His first studio film had atmosphere comparable to anything achieved by the German directors. Schoedsack insists that he had no intention of making a "horror" film, that he wanted only to tell an adventure yarn. Nevertheless, as a spine-chiller *The Most Dangerous Game* can hold its own with the best of Whale or Browning.

Especially notable is the characterisation of Zaroff, wherein a fantastic character is made to seem disconcertingly real via subtle touches seldom applied to melodrama. Early in the film he is shown in evening clothes being the perfect host and playing on the piano a lovely waltz of his own composition. Standing among the exaggerated shadows of his big-game trophies as he chats with his guests, he absently runs his fingers over the scar that symbolises his madness. His eyes glisten with tears when he realises that the only man in the world he dared to hope would share his mania considers him insane, and he seems genuinely hurt when the woman he admires upbraids him for murdering her brother. In the jungle, garbed in black hunting togs, he becomes an unfettered savage as he races through the fog, gleefully sounding the horn to summon the hounds to the kill.

The mood is captured perfectly by cameraman Henry Gerrard and heightened by Max Steiner's music. Steiner wrote Zaroff's piano music, which was performed for the soundtrack by Norma Boleslawski, and founded much of his score upon its theme. The score is one of the most elaborate of the Thirties, containing eighty-three musical cues involving fourteen compositions. The prolonged chase contains some of the most exciting film music extant.

Realism is evident even within the framework of fantasy. Schoedsack visited a medical morgue to learn how human heads are preserved. He already knew how to construct jungle traps because he had seen it done in Siam and Sumatra. The Malay deadfall was real and the heavy log shook the stage when it landed.

"I think of a film as though it were music," Schoedsack says. "It must have a beginning, a middle and an end, and should build up to climaxes, then allow some rest, then build again. I believe in pace. If necessary I use a stopwatch on the actors." This credo is evident in *Chang*, which both Cooper and Schoedsack consider their best work, and in *Rango*. It is fully crystallised in the thrilling pace of *The Most Dangerous Game*, which in this respect has yet to be surpassed.

The producers were convinced that most films of the period were too stagebound in execution, with static photography and plodding scenes played more for the benefit of microphone than camera. They were upset when Paramount added such sequences to their otherwise cinematic *The Four Feathers*, and were determined that none of their future productions would be similarly crippled. To this end they utilised in their initial "talkie" the best features of silent film technique —fluid camerawork, creative cutting and strong musical scoring—with dialogue calculated to complement the action rather than dominate it. The shipwreck sequence, for example, begins with an interruption of dialogue as the players are tumbled by the impact of the ship hitting the reef. A series of twenty "flash" shots show in only a few seconds the horror of the situation: the lurching ship, water rushing through the bulkheads, consternation on the bridge, pressure gauges with indicators swinging to the danger point, the engine room crew floundering in scalding water and steam, a superb miniature of the exploding ship, men and debris falling into the sea. Montage of this sort was not unusual in later films, but in 1932 it was a daring experiment.

Zaroff's aberrations are exposed early in the show so that no further explanations need intrude once the chase has begun. Suspense builds slowly at first, gathering momentum almost without interruption right to the end title, the few brief pauses in action being artfully placed to allow the spectator a chance to catch his breath. Each shot is of the exact duration needed to sustain the unrelenting tempo. The camera angles are superbly varied, with the hounds and hunters sometimes shown from below ground-level, rushing over the camera like the elephants of *Chang* and taking on the aspect of gigantic beasts. Shots wherein the camera is static while observing the action and those in which it races along with the players are skilfully intercut.

The opening titles are superimposed over a door-knocker depicting a wounded centaur holding in its arms the body of a woman. This motif symbolises the story as adapted for the screen. Marcel Delgado made some of the special properties, such as the dessicated human heads in Zaroff's trophy room.

By the time *The Most Dangerous Game* was in the can, *Kong,* despite the secrecy surrounding it, was the talk of the studios. The test reel, consisting of approximately ten minutes of outrageous but enthralling action, was calculated to make the viewer want more. A dozen large, detailed drawings served to illustrate dramatically the highlights planned for the feature. Larrinaga and Crabbe rendered these scenes in carbon pencil after O'Brien's action sketches.

Cooper unveiled the drawings to the studio's board of directors at the time the test reel was screened. Although they were drawn when only a hazy idea of the screen story existed, most of the action depicted in them appears in the final production. The scenes:

(1) A Brontosaurus rises from the water, capsizing a lifeboat containing a girl and the male players; (2) Kong, carrying the girl, approaches the log bridge; (3) Kong shakes the log, tumbling men into the chasm; (4) gigantic insects and a huge spider attack the sailors in the bottom of the gorge; (5) Kong fights the flesh-eating dinosaur, Tyrannosaurus; (6) Kong, seated on a ledge near the summit of Skull Mountain, tears Ann's clothing; (7) Kong seizes a pterodactyl which tries to carry Ann away; (8) Kong fights native warriors in the island village; (9) Kong, chained in the center-field of Yankee Stadium, breaks free; (10) a scene of panic on a New York City street as Kong holds an automobile above his head as though to dash it to the ground; (11) a girl in a hotel room awakens to see Kong reaching in through a window; (12) Kong, atop the Empire State Building, holds Ann in one paw and roars defiance at approaching navy pursuit 'planes.

The test reel contained about 147 scenes, the first being the shot from *Creation* in which a Triceratops pursues and kills a man. Then:

> The remaining nine men, including Denham and Driscoll, race madly through the jungle until they approach a gorge which is bridged by a fallen tree. They halt when they see Kong, who carries Ann, crossing the log bridge. An Arsinoitherium spies the men and charges them. The men, led by Driscoll. run to the log. Kong stops in a clearing and listens, then deposits Ann in the top of a dead tree and hastens back to the gorge. The men are across the log when they see Kong approaching. Driscoll climbs down a vine hanging from the bank and swings into a cave about ten feet below. Denham, at the other end of the log, ducks out of sight into some underbrush. The men on the bridge are trapped between Kong and the Arsinoitherium. Kong lifts the end of the log and shakes two men off into the chasm. They land in deep mud at the bottom. A third man falls, then two more and then another, until only one remains clinging to the log. Angrily, Kong lifts the end of the tree and lets it drop into the gorge. Monstrous lizards and insects, a gigantic spider and an octopus-like creature swarm out to devour the struggling men. The spider then climbs up a liana toward Driscoll's cave. Driscoll cuts the vine with his sea-knife and sends the spider tumbling just as Kong reaches into the cave. Eluding the huge paw, Driscoll slashes out. Kong withdraws his hand and licks it, then reaches down again. Meantime, Ann awakes from her faint and looks down to see a monster snake at the foot of the tree. Then a tyrannosaurus enters the glade. Ann screams, whereupon the dinosaur stops and scratches its ear. Kong almost has Driscoll in his grasp when he hears the scream. Hurrying back, Kong arrives just as the meat-eater is about to seize the girl. The two monsters engage in a titanic battle in which Kong's semi-human tactics compensate for the greater size of the dinosaur. Kong is flung against the tree, which falls, pinning Ann to the ground. Kong finally kills the tyrannosaurus by tearing its jaws apart. Carefully, he lifts the log from Ann, picks her up and carries her farther into the jungle. Driscoll climbs

to the bank and is hailed by Denham from the other side. Unable to cross the gorge, Denham heads back to get help while Driscoll continues to trail after Kong. The sequence ends as Driscoll steals past the bleeding, still breathing body of the tyrannosaurus, frightening away a huge vulture.

The methods devised by O'Brien and his crew to film this remarkable phantasmagoria, while deriving from O'Brien's earlier work, were more sophisticated by far. Cooper's imagination was even more vivid than O'Brien's and the greatest ingenuity was required to put his ideas on film. Several of Cooper's colleagues assured him that many of the scenes he envisioned could not possibly be produced.

"However, I knew that there was nothing a man could mentally conceive that the cameraman could not re-create or excel by any number of processes available," Cooper said later. 'Frankly, I didn't know the details of how we were going to produce these strange prehistoric animals and mingle them with real persons in modern settings, but I was able to secure the services of two men eminently fitted for the work to be done. One was Mr. Schoedsack, who had made pictures with me before. The other was Willis O'Brien."

The reception of the test film was predominantly enthusiastic, although several highly placed executives were not sympathetic to the project and did their utmost to block it. Selznick offered it his highest endorsement and Cooper, with admonishments to keep the budget within realistic bounds, was given the green light to produce his feature in association with Schoedsack.

The producers did not dare to wait until a script could be prepared. Creelman was assigned to write the screenplay while Schoedsack began working with the actors. Cooper continued his collaboration with O'Brien in planning and developing the animated sequences. The technicians continued to build settings and went to work constructing some large props the like of which never had been seen in any studio. Delgado built five more Kongs identical to the first one, so that repairs could be made to the "star" during the wear-and-tear of production.

Many months of work lay ahead before the cameras would cease turning on Production 601.

7. A Happy Company

On an NBC radio interview Cooper reconstructed the circumstances that led to his creation of *King Kong*:

"The world is getting smaller every year. I mean it's becoming too civilised. I can remember when the world was a grand old place—a place full of unexplored lands, choked with adventure. In those days Schoedsack and I used to run away to the ends of the world, confident of finding real motion picture material. But now, what's a fellow to do? Where is he to go?

"Persia, where Schoedsack and I made *Grass;* Siam, where we made *Chang,* and all the other colourful spots where we have made films: Borneo, Sumatra and the Archipelago—no longer is there any mystery or hidden adventure in those places. Although there are few spots left to explore, I can't give up the idea of making adventure films. And this very obstacle . . . has made me dream again. And that dream is: if I had it in my power to plot the greatest adventure of a lifetime, one I could actually participate in, what would it be?

"It would be this. Halfway around the world, somewhere in the Malay waters, there would be an unexplored land known as Skull Island. On this island would dwell a tribe of strange savages but not half so queer as their god whom they worship, a frightful god known to them as King Kong, a towering beast, fifty feet in height, who would have the power to crush a human being in the palm of his hand. To capture that animal and bring him back to Broadway, New York, to my way of thinking, would be a swell adventure. I don't know what the details of the story would be, I only know that in the story I would have a crazy motion picture producer go in search of this monster. He would take with him a motion picture company which would include only one girl. This powerful beast, King Kong, who never in all his life had gazed on a beautiful thing, would be strangely attracted to this pretty white girl—attracted to her, perhaps as he might be to some frail but beautiful flower. In some manner I could bring this beast back to New York; and then the monster, thinking of this beautiful human toy . . ."

Although the foregoing was stated "after the fact," it and the previously described drawings used to "sell" the test film combine to provide a pretty accurate reconstruction of the concept of *King Kong* before an actual shooting script had been prepared. Creelman contributed many good ideas to the further development of the story but was unable to produce a screenplay that satisfied Cooper or Schoedsack. They found too many stumbling blocks to the pace they envisioned, too

Kong had many faces

much dialogue that seemed unsuited to the characters.

As Selznick's assistant, Cooper was in a position to take his pick from the aggregation of writers under contract to the studio—a group that included Beulah Marie Dix, Robert Benchley, J. Walter Ruben, Ralph Spence, Bernard Schubert, Garrett Fort, Ralph Block and other dependable craftsmen. Instead, to the surprise of everybody at the studio, he handed the script to Ruth Rose.

Mrs. Schoedsack had never written a screenplay. Her literary experience consisted of some articles about the Beebe expeditions and one romantic short-story, "Trade Winds," which was published in the "Ladies' Home Journal." Cooper felt that, more important than studio experience, she knew what it was to be a member of a dangerous expedition in a tropical jungle infested with wild beasts, knew the rough-hewn sailors who man tramp steamers and the sort of men who make pilgrimages to unexplored lands—how they talk and how they react to danger. She was equally familiar with Broadway jargon.

"Put *us* in it," Cooper told her. "Give it the almost Victorian kind of dialogue that it needs to make the fantasy stand up. Establish everything before Kong makes his appearance so that we won't have to explain anything after that. Give it the spirit of a real Cooper-Schoedsack expedition."

The studio executives were opposed to the idea of introducing Kong so late in the story, all of them insisting that he should appear at the beginning. Cooper and Schoedsack, however, were adamant in their insistence upon using their own formula in constructing the script. It was highly successful when applied to *Chang,* for which it was invented, *Rango* and *The Most Dangerous Game.*

Mrs. Schoedsack concentrated at first on some

"live sequences" which her husband staged before the official script was completed and mimeographed. This script retained intact Cooper's test reel, including the *Creation* scene with the triceratops. Although it was sufficient to satisfy the home office as to what to expect, the official shooting script differs considerably from the finished product. The writer stayed on the set with the producers during the months of shooting that followed, editing and rewriting day by day, throwing out anything that proved superfluous or impeded the flow of action, changing dialogue and situations to conform to the exigencies of production and to maintain the celebrated Cooper-Schoedsack pace.

The producers knew they had the writer they needed when they read the opening line of dialogue: "Hey! Is this the moving picture ship?" She had thrown out several pages of explanation and in only seven words succeeded in getting the story under way! A few more lines inform us that the leader of the expedition, Carl Denham, is "crazy," that the "S. S. Venture" carries a crew three times larger than the normal complement, that there is "enough ammunition to blow up the harbour" on board, that Denham has had some pineapple-size grenades made up that contain a gas "strong enough to knock out an elephant" and that Denham has been unsuccessful in his attempts to find an actress willing to join the expedition. By the time Denham has told an out-of-work actress that she is headed toward "money and adventure and fame and a long sea voyage" and she has met the handsome first mate, the story is established. More dark hints about the destination of the voyage and the nature of the mysterious god-spirit, Kong, and introduction of the Beauty and the Beast theme follow. After that, nothing had to be spelled out.

The originally cold-blooded Denham emerges

Graphic evidence that monster-infested jungles are not recommended for actresses who insist on being ever-glamorous

as a flesh-and-blood man in whom are combined the personalities of Cooper and Schoedsack. Traits of the latter also are evident in Driscoll, the hard-surfaced, gentle-hearted woman-hater. Captain Englehorn somewhat resembles the intrepid William Beebe. The lovely Ann Darrow, the beauty who kills the beast, became an extension of Ruth Rose, although the writer insists that such an idea never occurred to her. Schoedsack said that his wife's script was easy to shoot because:

"The characters are believable—I didn't have to ask them to do anything impossible or ridiculous—and she never bothered me with descriptions of sets, only mentioned the locations where the scenes took place. She probably knew it wouldn't do any good because I always had to figure something out with the location or with the art department—something practical and something I could use. Nothing annoys me more in a script than long-winded descriptions of settings by writers whose only experience is behind the typewriter and who have no idea of the technical and expense problems involved. Of course studio techniques are entirely different from the ones we used out in the jungle, making things of what already was there. The secret of our success with animals in these pictures was that we first found out what the animal would do and then incorporated this into the action of the story. This is quite different from trying to force something to happen as dreamed up by some dope behind a typewriter in Hollywood who has had no experience with the actual things he's writing about. That's why Ruth's scripts were so good: she knew all her characters."

King Kong is essentially a fantastic version of the realistic *Chang,* an expansion of genuine adventures encountered by the producers and writers into the realm of the impossible. The slow, deliberate build-up was necessary so that the viewer's suspension of disbelief could be maintained to the end. It would have been ruinous to permit the viewer to stop and think during the extravagant scenes following the introduction of Kong and the other monsters; he must be swept along with the action. The success of this formula has been demonstrated often by default by the majority of fantasy films which attempted to duplicate the success of *King Kong,* however well-made they may be.

The writer created a language for the natives of Skull Island, identified in the film as being similar to "the language the Nias Islanders speak." The censors, fearful that the mumbo-jumbo might contain some indelicate phrases, demanded that an English translation of all native dialogue must be submitted for approval. The author complied, although she felt it unlikely that the picture would be seen by the isolated inhabitants of Palau Nias, which lies in the Indian Ocean west of Sumatra. Herewith is an example of the Australasian-based language, as spoken in the film by Noble Johnson (the native chief), with the translation:

"Malem ma pakeno! (The woman of gold!) Kong wa bisa! (Kong's gift!) Kow bisa para Kong! (A gift for Kong!) Dana, tebo malem na hi? (Strangers sell woman to us?) Sani sita malem ati—kow dia malem ma pakeno. (I will give six women like this for your woman of gold.)"

The Hays office invoked the same rule in later years when Mrs. Schoedsack created the Arabic-based language of the mythical kingdom of Kor for *She* (1935) and the speech of a fictitious African tribe for *Mighty Joe Young* (1949).

"Ruth used just the kind of romantic dialogue I wanted; it was perfect!" Cooper said. "Monte and Creelman and I wrote some, but Ruth did ninety percent of it." One of Cooper's contributions was the "old Arabian proverb" that opens the film: "And the Prophet said: And lo! the Beast looked upon the face of Beauty. And it stayed its hand from killing. And from that day it was as one dead." Schoedsack's distinctive touch is evident in some of the salty dialogue aboard ship and in the jungle.

One of Ruth Rose's greatest improvements in the story line was the avoidance of an involved sequence showing how Kong was brought to New York. The writer moved the action directly from Skull Island to Broadway with a few lines spoken by Denham as he surveys the unconscious Kong:

"Send to the ship for anchor chains and tools. Build a raft and float him to the ship. We'll give him more than chains. He's always been king of his world, but we'll teach him fear. Why, the whole world will pay to see this! We're millionaires, boys—I'll share it with all of you! In a few months it'll be up in lights: 'Kong, the Eighth Wonder of the World!'" Dissolve to a shot of a

Merian C. Cooper admires his brain-child

Broadway theatre displaying Denham's very words "up in lights."

Slickly dialogued love scenes were the order of the day in 1932, when writers and directors from the stage were a strong influence. Even Johnny Weissmuller's pidgin-English romancing in *Tarzan, the Ape Man* had a certain *élan,* having been specially written by the European *matinée* idol, Ivor Novello. Ruth Rose eschewed this approach for Bruce Cabot's wooing of Fay Wray on board the "Venture," striving instead for the sort of talk one might expect from a tough seafaring man who has fallen in love for the first time.

JACK: "Don't laugh! I'm scared for you! I'm . . . I'm sort of scared *of* you, too. Ann, I . . . Say, I guess I love you!"

ANN: "But Jack, you hate women!"

JACK: "Yeah, but you aren't women. Ann, I don't suppose . . . You don't feel anything like that about me, do you?"

The lovers embrace. The scene is both amusing and touching. Cabot, who was anything but shy around women, had a great deal of difficulty with this scene, one of the few in the picture for which Schoedsack asked for numerous takes.

Cabot, scion of an aristocratic French-Indian family of Carlsbad, New Mexico, was handicapped by a lack of acting experience when he made *Kong.* Prior to that he had played a few bit parts under his real name, Jacques de Bujac. After attending New Mexico Military Academy, Swanee Military Academy and New Mexico University, he worked his way over much of the world at a variety of unusual occupations (bone gatherer on the Plains, seaman on a freighter, sparring partner for a boxer, oil field roughneck, road surveyor, civil engineer, Wall Street broker and night-club manager). David Selznick met him at a Hollywood party and placed him under contract.

"I didn't know enough about pictures at that time to know what *Kong* was all about," Cabot said. "I just did what I was told and collected my weekly paycheck." Three years later the New York "Times" would hail his highly professional performance in *Show Them No Mercy* as one of the year's finest. "Bruce Cabot gives a terrifying performance as a surly killer who is transformed by liquor and nerve into an irresponsible madman," reported critic André Sennwald, citing the "cold brutality and macabre humour" Cabot brought to the role of a kidnapper. He was equally memorable as Magua in *The Last of the Mohicans* and as gangster Tom Keefer in *Let 'Em Have It.* For forty years the six-foot-two actor alternated playing heroic and villainous roles, taking time out for Second World War duty as an Army intelligence officer in Africa, Sicily and Italy. His off-screen life was as colourful and exciting as the roles he played.

When he died of throat cancer on May 3, 1972, at the age of sixty-eight, Cabot's obituaries invariably were headlined with the words, *"King Kong" Hero,* despite the fact that he followed this first featured role with scores of others.

Robert Armstrong had a notable career in the theatre and motion pictures before he portrayed the fast-talking Carl Denham, the role for which he is best remembered. He dropped out of law school at the University of Washington in Seattle in order to tour with a vaudeville company, later becoming leading man in New York with Jimmy Gleason's stock company. A hit play, Gleason's "Is Zat So," brought him a movie contract with Pathe in 1926. His first film was *The Main Event,* in which he played a prizefighter.

"I had been in Hollywood just long enough to establish myself as a silent actor when sound came

Another portrait of Robert Armstrong

Fay Wray and Bruce Cabot caught in a moment that shows the strain and hard work endured in an adventure film like KING KONG

in," Armstrong said. "Then the producers started looking for stage actors and paying them big salaries to come out here. I kept shouting, 'Hey! How about me? I was raised on the stage! Listen to me! Me! ME!' But they wouldn't notice, and I soon found myself playing support to the guys who had supported me on the stage a couple of years earlier!" By the early Thirties he was getting better roles, such as that of the dynamic fight promoter of Universal's *The Iron Man*. "I was fortunate to get the Denham role," Armstrong said.

A thoroughgoing professional, Armstrong made more than a hundred pictures as well as stage and TV appearances before a coronary attack forced his retirement in 1952. He played heroes, villains and character roles (such as Tojo in *Blood on the Sun*) with equal success. One of his last TV performances was as a guest star on the Red Skelton Show. In the middle of a sketch, Skelton suddenly ad-libbed, "Say, did you ever get that monkey down from the building?" The line "stopped the show."

Armstrong died on April 21, 1973, at the age of eighty-two. Although in his later years he was white-haired, Bob Armstrong had the look and manner of a sportsman and his voice remained that of Carl Denham. His closest friends to the last were the Schoedsacks and Fay Wray.

Several years ago, Armstrong was reminiscing about some of his experiences in silent pictures. "Phyllis Haver was a sweet, lovely girl," he said. "She was almost as nice as Fay—but, of course, *nobody* is *that* nice." Anybody who has ever known Fay Wray probably concurs in this opinion. There have been better actresses and there have been a few with greater physical beauty, but never have the often contradictory qualities of sex appeal and virtue been blended more perfectly in one woman. The girl every red-blooded man would like to rescue and protect, she was the perfect choice to play Beauty.

The daughter of a rancher, Fay Wray came to California from Alberta. While a student at Hollywood High School she appeared in an area pageant, the annual Pilgrimage Play. By 1923, at the age of sixteen, she was doing "bits" at various studios, moving on to leads in Hal Roach comedies and Universal Westerns. In 1926, Erich von Stroheim selected her to play the lead in his monumental Paramount picture, *The Wedding March,* which led to a long line of roles opposite the reigning actors at the studio. Cooper-Schoedsack Productions brought her to RKO for *The Most Dangerous Game.* She was at that time married to the brilliant but erratic author, John Monk Saunders (*Wings, The Dawn Patrol*), whose career was blighted by drugs and alcohol and ended in suicide. A second marriage, to writer Robert Riskin, ended in tragedy when Riskin was paralysed by a stroke, dying several years later. Mrs. Riskin gave up her career to look after her husband, resuming it again after his death.

Her blue eyes and fair skin made her seem a natural blonde in *Kong,* and that is the way the public still regards her. In her scores of other pictures she appeared with her natural brown hair. For years she was typed as an ingenue in "horror" pictures, legacy of her effectiveness playing opposite Kong. She fled to England in the mid-Thirties in an attempt to break the mould—and was cast in similar roles. For reasons difficult to understand, this very popular actress was denied stardom although she usually was featured opposite the top male stars of all the major studios.

A gifted writer and musician, the intelligent Miss Wray disliked most of the horror films and adventure melodramas in which she appeared, hoping always to be able to return to the kind of roles she played for von Stroheim and von Sternberg. Curiously enough, she and her "thrillers" have retained their popularity, some of them attaining the status of classics, while the titles and stars of many "serious" pictures of the Thirties have been forgotten.

The doughty Captain Englehorn was superbly realised in the person of Frank Reicher, Munich-born writer, director and actor. A wiry little man who kept himself fit by swimming, Reicher was a leading figure in the theatres of Berlin, London and New York. He made a few films as long ago as 1915, went back to the stage until the late Twenties, then returned to the film industry and remained there. He was eighty-nine when he died on January 19, 1965.

Reicher's acting required little direction. Occasionally Schoedsack would say, "That was a little strong, Frank," or "Let's give it a little more," and Reicher would be perfect in the next take. "He was the best actor we had and he helped the other actors along," Schoedsack said. "He knew exactly what tempo was right for any scene."

Noble Johnson was blackened and covered with tattoos and ceremonial scars for his role as the native chief of Skull Island. The veteran actor was a mulatto but was so light-skinned that he could play a wide variety of racial types including the Cossack of *The Most Dangerous Game,* a Chinese in *The Mysterious Dr. Fu Manchu,* a Nubian in *The Mummy,* a Polynesian in *Moby Dick,* a Persian prince in *The Thief of Bagdad* and a Cuban zombie in *The Ghost Breakers.* His most oft-played role was as an Indian chief, which led many viewers to assume him to be an Indian. He came from Colorado Springs.

"He was like his name, noble," a fellow actor said of him. An impressive figure, six-foot-two and heavily muscled, he could appear primitively cruel in one film and highly sympathetic in another. He was soft-spoken and gentle off-screen.

Johnson left the film industry in the early Fifties and invested in Nevada real estate. What became of him after that is a mystery several film historians have tried to solve without success.

Sam Hardy, cast appropriately as a Broadway character, was a stage actor for twenty-three years, dividing his time between stage comedies and dramas and leading roles in silent movies. A big, sociable man, he was a close friend of W. C. Fields and other bigger-than-life show business characters. Most of his film roles were more prominent than his brief appearance in *Kong.*

Steve Clemente is virtually unrecognisable under the witch doctor make-up in *Kong.* The Indian actor, who most often portrayed the villainous half-breed once considered indispensable to Western films (his only rivals being Apache Charles Stevens and Turkish Frank Lackteen) died in 1950 at the age of sixty-five.

The plug-ugly crew of the "Venture" was made

up of Western heavies and stunt men, most of whom have died since then. Among the more conspicuous are Dick Curtis, who earned the title of "the meanest man in Hollywood" while menacing innumerable Western heroes from 1918 until his death in 1953, and the husky ex-fighter John P. "Blackie" Whiteford (1889-1962). The one clean-cut crew member was James Flavin, a young New York actor who also co-starred that year with his future wife, Lucile Browne, in the Universal serial *Phantom of the Air*. Flavin has since specialised in playing tough police detectives in films and TV. Chinese actor Victor Wong, scheduled for a bit part, proved so effective as a laugh-getter that his role was enlarged during production.

King Kong was not an easy picture to work in because of the many technical problems to be surmounted, but a pleasant camaraderie developed among the players and staff. "We really had a happy company there," Schoedsack recalled.

The late Vernon L. Walker, ASC, left, and Linwood G. Dunn, ASC, in 1932 with the new optical printer used in filming much of the effects work in KING KONG

8. Inventions Become Necessary

"*King Kong* . . . was not made entirely by enlarging miniatures," a credulous "Time" writer told the world on March 13, 1933. "Kong is actually 50 ft. tall, 36 ft. around the chest. His face is 6½ ft. wide with 10-in. teeth and ears 1 ft. long. He has a rubber nose, glass eyes as big as tennis balls. His furry outside is made of 30 bearskins. During his tantrums, there were six men in his interior running his 85 motors."

"Modern Mechanix and Inventions" for April, 1933, informed its readers that Kong was a "normal size actor in ape costume." Two pages of drawings show the actor climbing a building model built horizontally along the studio floor, emoting in front of a process screen on which flying warplanes are projected and being filmed in composite against a red screen on a "negative insensitive to red light, recording only the ape's actions, taken in blue light, to add to scenes already on the negative." The girl, we are told, having been photographed separately, "is cut and placed in the ape's hands, each frame individually photographed to show progress of action, as moving arms, etc. This is known as 'animating.' "

A French publication reported that the actor in the ape-skin was reduced by trick photography and superimposed into drawings of the jungle. Many writers have repeated this claim.

Another oft-repeated story is that Charles Gemora, the Filipino actor who portrayed gorillas in innumerable film dramas such as *Ingagi* and *Murders in the Rue Morgue,* also was Kong. One writer, after allowing that Kong was a stop-action model in most scenes, declared that it was Gemora who climbed the Empire State Building in the long-shots of that sequence. To add to the confusion the newspaper obituaries of Gemora stated that his "most famous role was that of King Kong."

In the "Chicago Sun-Times" for December 21, 1969, however, we learn that one Ken Roady "really is King Kong. During his time Ken Roady made 133 films, but his biggest was as the fifty-foot gorilla in the 1933 classic." Roady was quoted as saying he "worked on that picture for more than a year. Got paid $150 a week and never could get along with either Fay Wray or Robert Armstrong, who were the stars of the picture. They never realised how important I was to them, I guess."

Reams of such misinformation have been printed —the result, presumably, of the traditional journalistic reluctance to let the facts stand in the way of a good story. The fact is that *no gigantic motorised robots or men in ape-suits were used at any time in the making of the film.*

Kong was, as Ernest Schoedsack has said, "the product of many contributions." One contribution

The deepest set of all. Three animation tables, a foreground glass, two "in-between" glasses and a painted backing

of inestimable value was that of Sidney Saunders, supervisor of the studio paint department, who unveiled an important new technical development just as the *Kong* test reel was getting under way. This was a refinement of the rear projection process, the cellulose-acetate screen, which was destined to become a basic necessity in studio production technique. Rear projection permits actors to perform in front of a translucent screen, on the back of which is projected a previously filmed scene. The camera records both the new action and the projected background in a single take.

Cameramen for years had been experimenting with the principle of rear projection but were seldom successful because of the many difficulties inherent in the process. The celebrated German cameramen, Karl Freund and Günther Rittau, had managed some successful projection effects in *Metropolis* (1926) and O'Brien is said to have used a projected background in one scene of *The Lost World*. One knotty problem was that of synchronising the shutters of camera and projector. In projection an image is flashed on the screen for one forty-eighth of a second, then the shutter closes and blots out the light until the succeeding frame moves into the aperture and is projected. The eye, through the phenomenon known as "the persistence of vision," holds one image long enough for it to blend into the next so that the intervals between frames are not perceived. The camera's eye is not deluded, however, and the camera and projector must therefore be operated in perfect unison, otherwise the variability of exposure will cause the re-photographed image to flicker.

Conventional projection mechanisms proved too unsteady for process work because the slightest "jiggle" or movement becomes obvious when a projected scene is juxtaposed with solid foreground objects. Other problems included *hot-spot,* the noticeably brighter light at the centre of a projected image, and *fall-off,* the resultant diminishing of illumination at the edges and corners of the frame.

Previous rear projection screens were made of sand-blasted glass. Aside from the fact that they were necessarily small, these screens produced a middle-grey image with no sparkling highlights or rich blacks. The images were dulled further by the necessity of using filters to control *hot-spot* and *fall-off.* They were fragile, non-insurable and hard to replace. Breakage of glass screens resulted in serious injuries at two studios.

The Saunders screen, however, was flexible, non-breakable and impervious to any heat other than an open flame. It measured sixteen by twenty feet, being more than two feet greater in each direction than any other process screen then in use. Stretched tightly on a frame, the Saunders screen resembled a large sheet of waterproof canvas. Initial tests proved that brilliancy of image was increased by more than twenty percent while *hot spot* was reduced by more than fifty percent. True white highlights and intense blacks were achieved in rear projection for the first time and the overall tonal range was broadened greatly. The projector was re-built with the usual *Maltese Cross* projection mechanism being replaced with the pilot-pin movement of a production camera, thus insuring a rock-steady picture.

The first scenes to utilise Saunders' screen are those in *Kong* which show Fay Wray in a tree-top (live foreground) being menaced by the tyrannosaurus (projected background) and observing the subsequent battle between the reptile and Kong. The animation footage of the beasts was weeks in the making, but Fay Wray's scenes could have been filmed in only a few hours had all the "bugs" peculiar to the process been known.

Shutter synchronisation was achieved by use of the then-new Selsyn interlock motors on both camera and projector. These 220-volt, three-phase motors turn at exactly the same rate of speed, assuring perfect synchronism of both sets of shutters, pilot pins and pull-down mechanisms.

Considerable difficulty was encountered in matching the intensity and direction of lighting in the separate elements so they would appear to

A sketch by Mario Larrinaga suggesting content and composition for full-scale rear projection

Larrinaga's sketch realised

Fay Wray reacts to the "reel" thing

Mario Larrinaga in a moment of relaxation

have been photographed at the same time in a single location. One thorny problem was the necessity of keeping reflected light and spill-light from the foreground from leaking onto the screen, causing flare or washouts. All lighting had to be controlled with *barn doors* (flat extensions on light units used to direct or narrow light beams) and *gobos* (black flats used to shield areas from unwanted light).

Mastering the intricacies of the new process required days of shooting, including one non-stop session of twenty-two hours that left everybody exhausted. Fay Wray recalls being sore all over from crouching in the tree-top for long periods of time. The finished shots—which remain in the final cut of *King Kong*—suffer not in the least when compared to process work done years later

A complicated test for the dramatic ledge sequence made to study miniature animation, rear projection, and matte problems

with vastly improved equipment and know-how. A more striking demonstration of the possibilities of rear projection can hardly be imagined: the Tyrannosaurus, a forty-odd-inch refugee from *Creation,* appears large enough to swallow the actress in one gulp. The success of these scenes earned Saunders a special award from the Academy of Motion Picture Arts and Sciences for his part in "the development and effective use of the translucent cellulose screen in composite photography."*

The taking of these scenes was a memorable occasion for one of the technicians because it was his job to carry Miss Wray to and from the treetop for each take. The man was selected for the

Model of Fay Wray with unfinished glass painting in the foreground

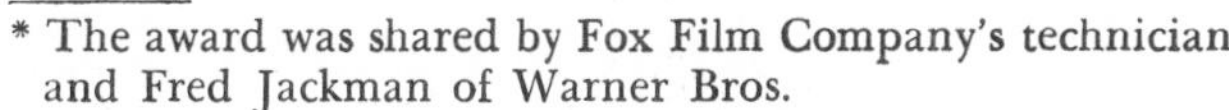

* The award was shared by Fox Film Company's technicians and Fred Jackman of Warner Bros.

A lush, dramatic vista. Miniature trees, foliage and log with painted glass and backing

In this side angle of miniature and glass surrounding the Arsinoitherium the surface of the animation table "explains" how the beasts were clamped in place

Styracosaurus in a verdant scene not used

A typical reaction

"chore" because he knew the locations of various objects that might trip up the actress had she travelled about the set in the customary manner. The man recalls that the task was not an unpleasant one.

The success of the Saunders shots led Cooper to suggest that the principle could be adapted to achieve a corollary effect, i.e., the placing of actors into the miniature settings with the prehistoric monsters. The idea was a sound one, although a great deal more complex than it sounds, and O'Brien set himself to the task of developing it as a practical method. Miniature rear projection when perfected proved to be indispensable to the making of the film, being in many instances a more flexible and satisfying technique than the unwieldy stationary mattes by which actors had been placed into the miniature tableaux of *The Lost World*.

The initial problem was to find a suitable material from which to make the transparency screens. The spray-painted cellulose of the big screen was too grainy to be photographed at close range as part of the miniature set-ups. Ground glass, tracing cloth, tracing paper and other materials were tested with similarly unsatisfactory results. The little screens were eventually made of surgical rubber sheeting—the material then used in the manufacture of surgeons' gloves and baby pants—and stretched tightly on wooden frames. Not only was the material free of grain but *hot-spot* and *fall-off* could be controlled by varying the tension of the screens. The one insoluble problem was that the rubber tended to deteriorate rapidly under the heat of studio lights and had to be frequently replaced.

The major problem encountered in miniature projection was the critical matching of scale, textures, lighting and perspective, all of which would be exaggerated mercilessly when projected on theater screens. These considerations required the most intricate calculations in preparing both the full-scale action and the elements of the miniature.

Among the first scenes using miniature projection are those in which Cabot hides from Kong in a shallow cave. The actor, image filmed pre-

Top: Cabot and the cave projected into the miniature. Centre: Cabot in the small cave surrounded by glass painting. Bottom: matte without the miniature

viously in a matching set of the cave, was rear-projected on a screen set several inches back from the cave opening. The image had to be positioned in this way because light used to illuminate the miniature would wash out the rear-projected image if it struck the screen. Each frame of Cabot was projected and re-photographed as a "still" with each change of Kong's position. Glass painting was used to add surrounding rocks and foliage to the full-scale close views of the cave.

A gigantic hand of Kong was constructed for close shots in which Kong reaches into the cave and Cabot slashes the huge fingers with his knife. This hand was not articulated, being merely a hastily-made ramrod affair that could be thrust into the scene and withdrawn.

Zoe Porter, Cooper's secretary, one day received a call to report to one of the stages. There she found Cooper examining another giant hand and arm, unfinished and covered roughly with sponge-rubber "flesh." Cooper told her to sit in the open palm. When she did so, she was shocked to find herself being lifted high into the air. Cooper was delighted with this first test of his latest gadget and Mrs. Porter still prizes a photo of the occasion. Delgado, who later added the intricately detailed skin, nails and hair to the articulated armature, was dissatisfied with the design of the paw because it could not be made to "cup" in the manner of a true hand. It was nevertheless an impressive prop with properly jointed digits and would prove invaluable in the staging of many important scenes.

The main function of Delgado's giant hand was to hold Fay Wray, who described the experience in her by-lined article, "How Fay Met Kong, Or the Scream That Shook the World":

"Then I saw the figure of Kong. He was in a *miniature* jungle habitat, and was less than two feet tall! It was only the great furry paw, in which

Cabot in matte watches the miniature Kong

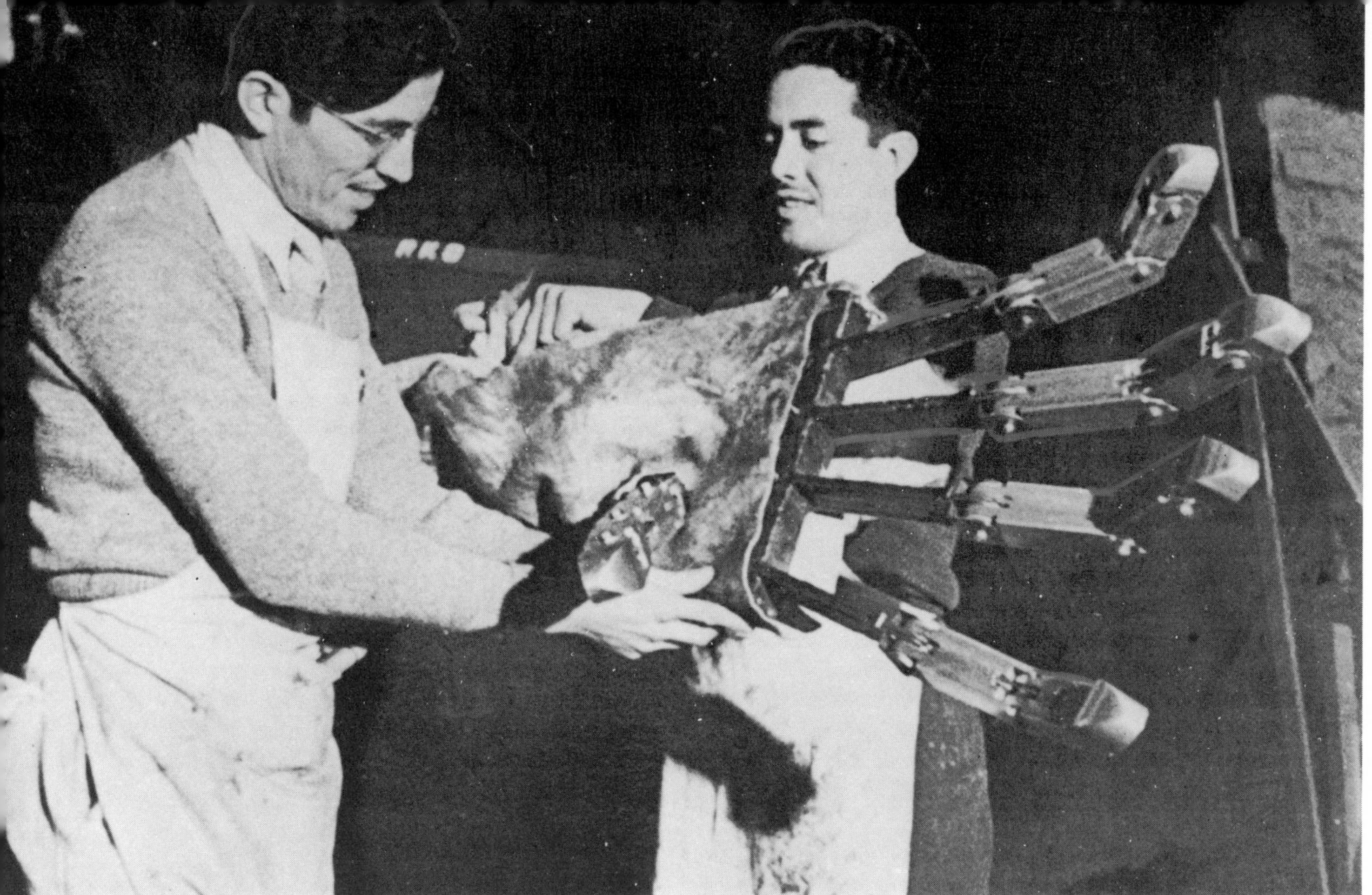

Armature for the full-scale hand being worked on by Victor (left) and Marcel (right) Delgado

I would spend the next ten months, that was absolutely *enormous*. . . . The hand and arm in which my close-up scenes were made was about eight feet in length. Inside the furry arm, there was a steel bar and the whole contraption (with me in the hand) could be raised or lowered like a crane. The fingers would be pressed around my waist while I was in a standing position. I would then be raised about ten feet into the air to be in line with an elevated camera. As I kicked and squirmed and struggled in the ape's hand, his fingers would gradually loosen and begin to open. My fear was real as I grabbed onto his wrist, his thumb, wherever I could, to keep from slipping out of that paw! When I could sense that the moment of minimum safety had arrived, I would call imploringly to the director and ask to be lowered to the floor of the stage. Happily, this was never denied for a second too long! I would have a few moments rest, be re-secured in the paw and the ordeal would begin all over again . . . a kind of pleasurable torment!*

By means of projected backgrounds, the hand and Miss Wray appeared to be nearly a thousand feet in the air when Kong examined his captive while perched atop the Empire State Building. In another memorable shot the arm was combined with the miniature in an over-the-shoulder view as Kong lifted the girl from the jungle floor. The most unusual use of the arm was for scenes devised by O'Brien in which Kong, comfortably seated near the summit of his mountain stronghold, tears away pieces of the actress's dress, gently strokes her body with his fingertips and sniffs the feminine scent that lingers there. Here miniature projection was used to make Miss Wray and the arm appear to be a part of the miniature Kong.

* "The New York Times," September 21, 1969. The story was reprinted in the "San Francisco Chronicle" under the title, "King Kong and Me."

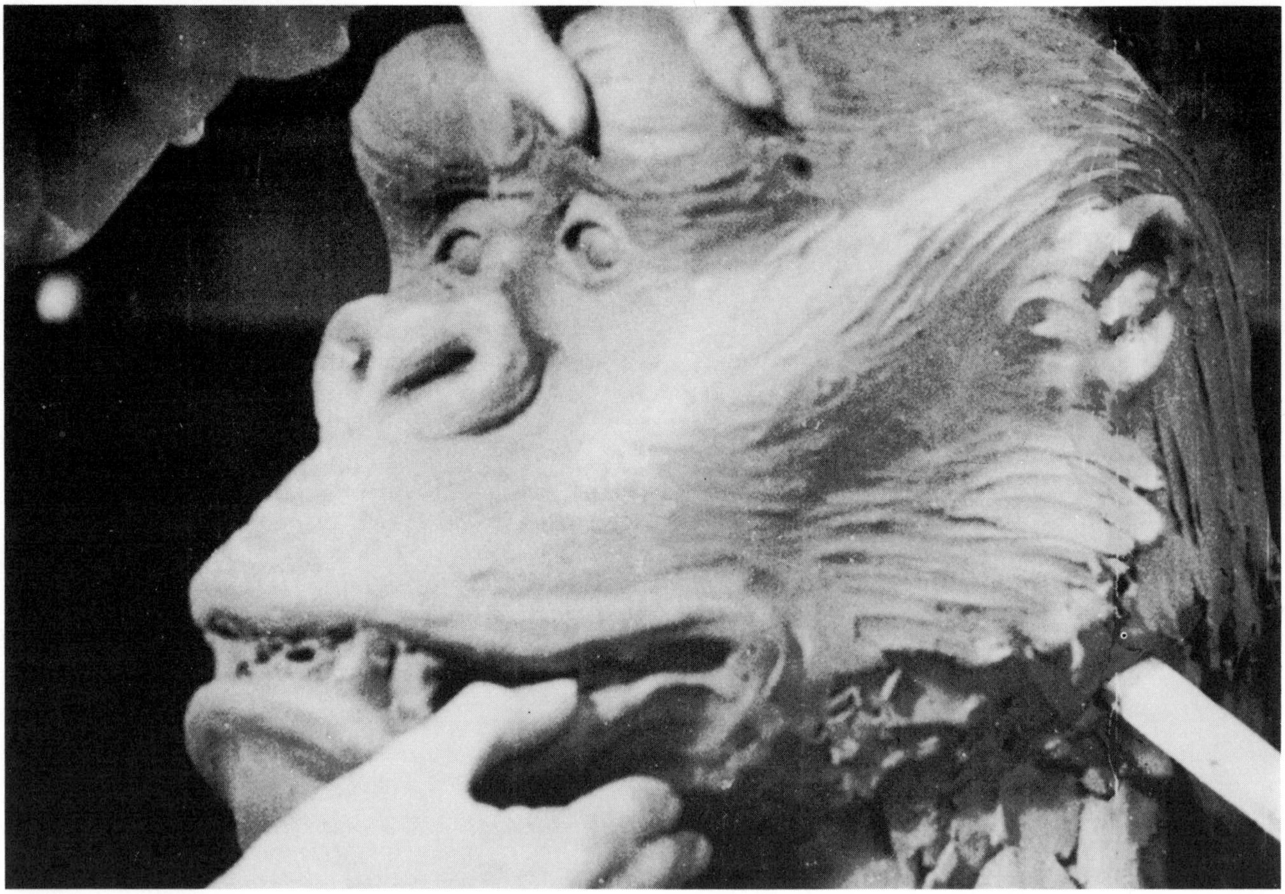

The clay model that guided construction

Scale of the head becomes apparent

Intricate construction to achieve realistic action

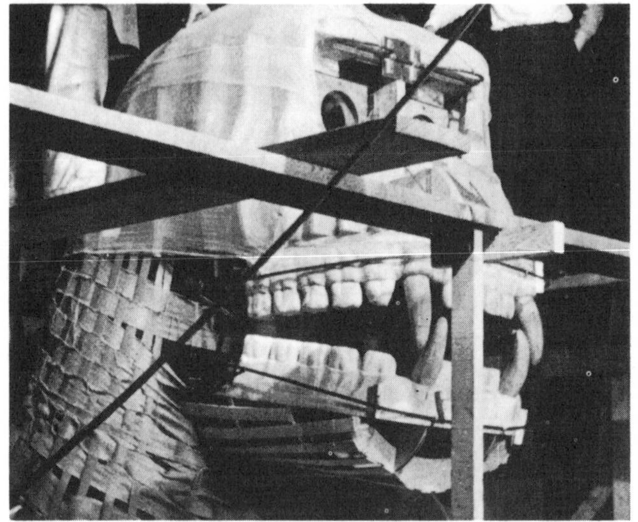

This sequence ran into censorship trouble several years later, although it was considerably less erotic than envisioned originally; she was expected to finish the scene in the near-nude. The actress was adamant in her refusal to carry the scene beyond the limits of decency and insisted on being covered under the scanty garments she was permitted to retain. O'Brien conceived the celebrated "strip scene" and animated it personally.

Other full-size properties included a foot and lower leg of Kong to permit close-ups of men being trampled into the ground and the lower body of a pteranodon (or flying lizard) that tries to carry Miss Wray away from Kong's mountaintop home.

The most spectacular prop of all was a huge head, chest and shoulders of Kong to be used in close-ups. Technicians constructed the frame of wood, wire, cloth and metal and covered it with rubber and pruned bearskin. As many as three men could huddle inside and by means of ingeniously designed levers and a compressed air device operate the mouth, lips, nose, eyes, eyelids and brows so that they moved in an astonishingly lifelike manner. It was capable of achieving a wider range of expression than can be summoned by many a professional actor.

The balsa-and-plaster eyes of this behemoth were about twelve inches in diameter. The balsa wood eye-teeth were ten inches long and the molars were four inches high and fourteen inches in circumference. The ears were one foot long. The mouth was capable of stretching to a six-foot smile or grimace and could be opened wide enough to accommodate the bodies of actors who portrayed victims of Kong. The nose, which dilated and twitched with the stress of various passions, was two feet across. The heavy brows, which

Fred Reese watches progress on the colossal head

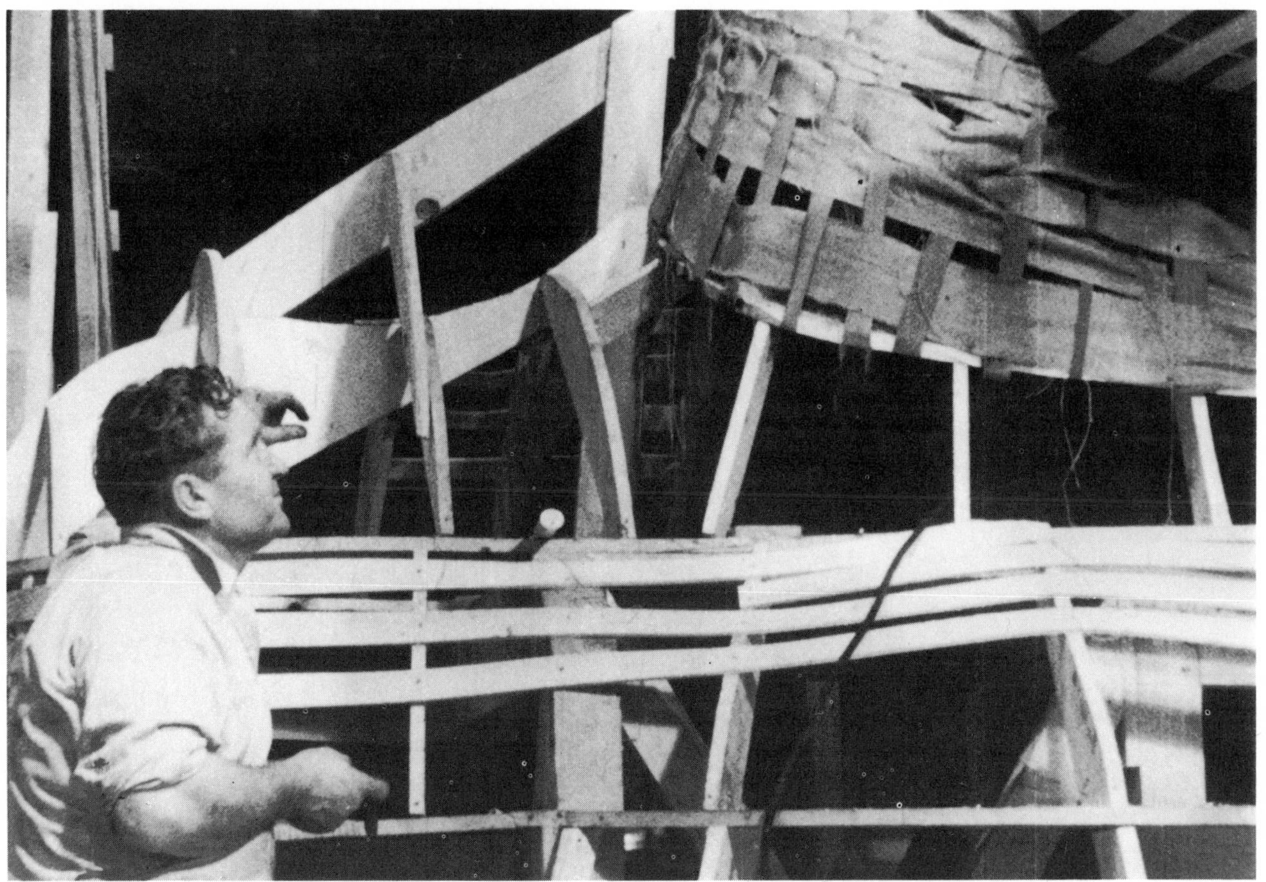

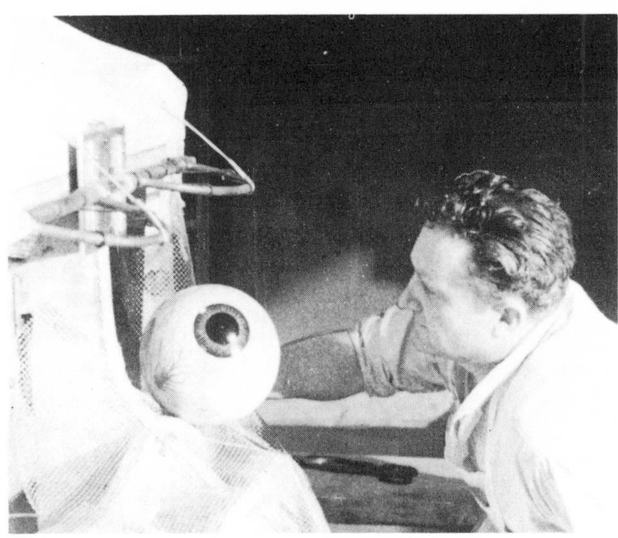

Fred Reese thinks, "What big eyes you have!"

could be wagged in the Barrymore manner, were more than four feet across. The contraption was mounted on a heavy, rubber-wheeled flatcar so that it could be moved about.

Delgado tried to convince Cooper that the full-scale head would not be worth the effort for the limited use it would receive. Forty years later, at a screening of the film at the Motion Picture Hall of Fame in Anaheim, Cooper gleefully pointed out to Delgado each scene in which the big head appeared. Delgado had to admit that the scenes were tremendously effective.

Some scenes in which foreground and background action had to be photographed at different times and places were combined through the Dunning travelling matte process, which permitted filming of greater scope than could be achieved with rear projection. This process had been used with great success at several studios during 1930/31. Columbia, for example, was able to show explorer Paul Hoefler seeming to photograph action

The "big one" nearly finished. (From a badly damaged print in the collection of Marcel Delgado)

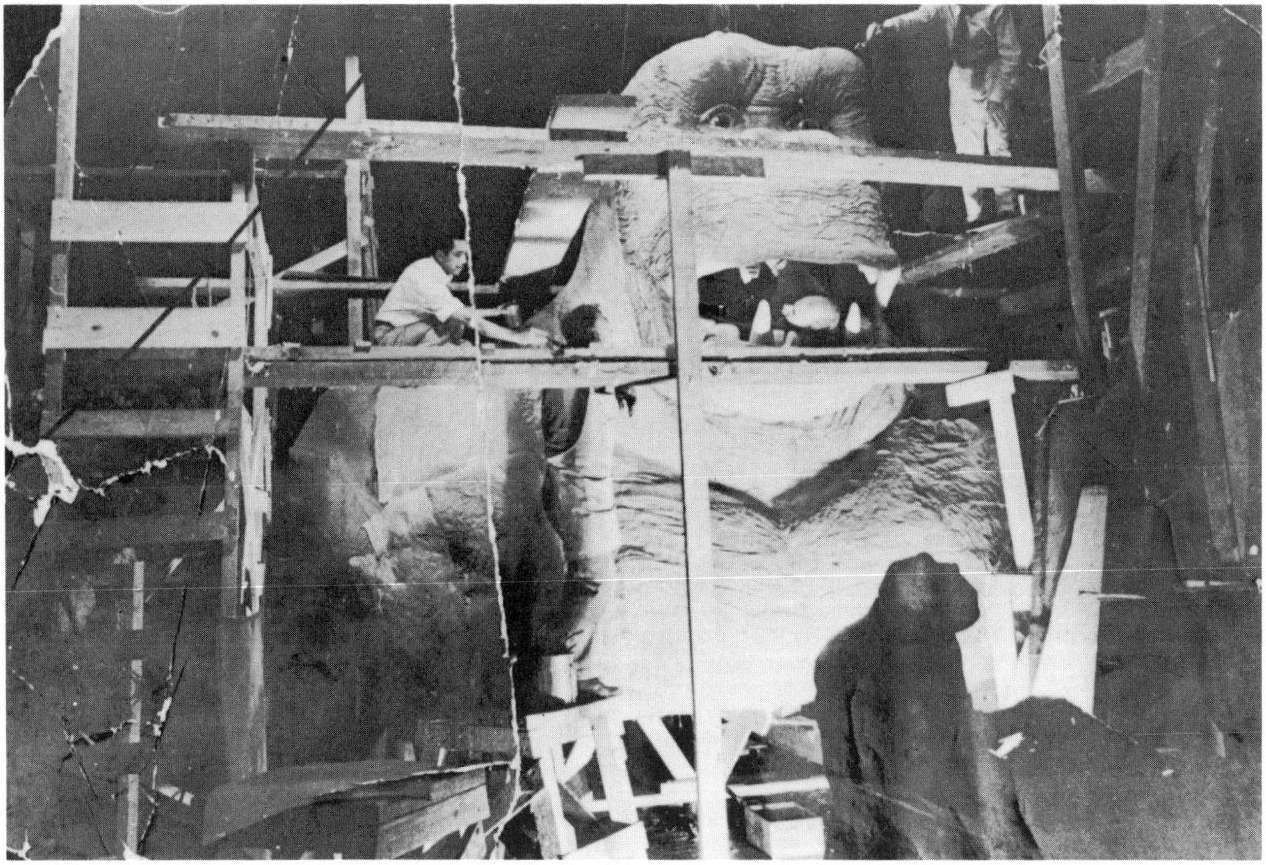

he had shot in Africa months earlier in *Africa Speaks.* M-G-M, in *Anna Christie,* combined scenes filmed in New York Harbour with new action involving Greta Garbo and Charles Bickford which was filmed entirely on a Culver City sound stage. The most famous moment in *Trader Horn,* which shows Mutia Omoolu spearing a charging lion, is a Dunning shot, as are numerous scenes of *Tarzan, the Ape Man.* At RKO, Carroll Dunning screened for all the company's directors a film showing how the trick work in *Tarzan* was done. O'Brien, who already had accomplished some excellent Dunning shots in *Creation,* used the process in *Kong* for scenes such as one in which a dinosaur attacks Denham and his men.

The Dunning system was patented in 1927 by a seventeen-year-old schoolboy, C. Dodge Dunning, son of Carroll Dunning, vice-president of the Prizma Color Process Company. It took the elder Dunning two years to convince the patent office that his son's invention would work. The basic idea, which combines new photography with contact printing in a single operation, hinges on the principle that an object of a certain colour becomes invisible when viewed through a filter of the same colour. The object becomes distinct when viewed through a filter of a contrasting colour.

After a negative of the background action has been made, a positive transparency is prepared in which the silver particles that make up the black-and-white image are bleached away and replaced by a yellow-orange dye. This toned print is loaded into a specially designed camera magazine with a reel of raw negative stock, the latter passing through the camera behind and in contact with the orange positive print. If a brightly lighted blue backdrop of the hue complementary to the orange dye is photographed by the production camera through the orange print and onto the raw stock, the result is a duplicate black-and-white negative of the scene from the orange positive film, which has been printed onto the raw stock by exposure to the blue backdrop. The blue backing functions as a printing light.

If actors and/or props are placed between the camera and the backdrop and are lighted with lamps screened with orange filters identical to the dye on the orange print, these objects are combined on the new negative with the background action. The background does not print through the actors (as a double exposure) because the orange-lighted actors mask out the blue printing light with their own bodies. The raw film records a completed composite negative showing the actors seemingly in the environment previously photographed, the backgrounds being printed around (and, to all appearances, *behind*) the players.

Some other scenes were achieved with the more complicated Williams Travelling Matte Process, which also utilised two films and a blue backing but permitted the use of "hard" (white) light in foreground action. This feature was particularly useful in filming vast scenes with complex lighting, such as Kong's first appearance in the native village. The inventor, Frank D. Williams, pioneered the principle of the travelling matte, patenting the first such process in 1916. Refinements of the original Williams system made possible the scenes of the brontosaur's rampage in London in *The Lost World* and the fantastic flying carpet scenes of Douglas Fairbanks' *The Thief of Bagdad.* Williams, a true genius of the motion picture, also helped devise the special techniques used by his former assistant, John P. Fulton, in photographing *The Invisible Man.* His improved double-matting system was introduced in mid-1932, just in time to play an important role in the production of *Kong.*

A key member of Vern Walker's camera effects department was Linwood Dunn, a leading expert in the then-new art of optical printing. Dunn and his assistant, Cecil Love, and engineer Bill Leeds, had developed for RKO an optical printer. It seems primitive in comparison with some of the sophisticated printers Dunn now employs at his independent effects studio, Film Effects of Hollywood, but was at the time the most efficient in existence. Dunn and Love later designed the Acme-Dunn Optical Printer, the first special effects printer to be manufactured for the trade and that earned for them a 1944 Academy Award for "technical achievement and important contribution to the motion picture industry." This printer remains in use the world over.

"OBie was trying to do everything in the camera," Dunn recalls of his work on *Kong.* "That meant that when things didn't match up in intensity they had to do it over until they got it right. This involved a great deal of testing. About halfway through the production I managed to talk him into letting us match the composites in the optical printer, where we could see what we were doing and get it right the first time. We only had one optical printer and the thing was constantly in use for duping, making trick matting shots, fades, dissolves, split-screen effects and multiple exposure work. We also made all registration prints for Vern's process-background work so he could secure perfect registration in his process composites."

Although the optical printer used for *Kong* is no longer in use, Dunn bought and kept it as a sentimental item. It consists of a standard motion picture camera fitted with a pilotpin registering movement, which faces a printer head also equipped with a registering device, and mounted on a rigid lathe-bed six feet long. The camera re-photographs motion pictures at various magnifications. There are many refinements to permit zooming in, reduced aperture printing, hold-frames, transitional effects (fades, dissolves and wipes), adding rocking movements to boat and aircraft scenes, levelling of badly framed shots and other useful effects.

The ingenuity and hard work of the remarkable technical crew responsible for bringing Merian Cooper's brainchild to realisation on the screen was summed up by Relman Morin in his review in the "Los Angeles Record":

"*King Kong* is a supreme product of the co-ordination of human imagination and human skill."

9. The Skull Island Expedition

The cost of filming a picture over such a long period of time would have been prohibitive had it been necessary to keep the cast on salary during the entire fifty-five weeks of work. In those pre-Screen Actors Guild days it was possible to use actors only when they were needed, re-hiring them later for additional shooting. Schoedsack, a fast director who seldom called for a re-take, was able to keep the live action moving at a rapid pace, but the special effects work was agonisingly slow, requiring an abnormal amount of patience from everybody concerned.

The actors worked on the picture for several weeks at a time, then were given time off for as much as two months while the animation work caught up with the live action. During these periods they worked in other films, some of which were released before *Kong* was finished. Cabot made his official *début* in *Roadhouse Murder,* filmed during one such hiatus. Fay Wray worked in First National's *Dr. X* and *Mystery of the Wax Museum* during 1932. Schoedsack took time out to direct two sequences for Wesley Ruggles' *The Monkey's Paw.*

Schoedsack directed most of the live action at the RKO-Pathe Studio, south of Washington Boulevard in Culver City. The studio was built in 1918 by Thomas H. Ince. After his death the lot was purchased by Pathe Exchange, Inc., which filmed many serials, features and the early Hal Roach comedies. Harold Lloyd, Will Rogers, Laurel and Hardy, serial lovers Walter Miller and Allene Ray, Bill Boyd and numerous other popular stars appeared under the aegis of the Pathe rooster. Cecil B. DeMille, after breaking with Paramount in 1925, established his own production company on the Pathe lot. There he produced several features and personally directed four "specials," including his favourite, *The King of Kings.* By 1929 the studio was heavily in debt and both DeMille and Roach decided to make arrangements to produce for their wealthy neighbour, Metro-Goldwyn-Mayer.

RKO, which had been operating in cramped quarters at the thirteen-and-a-half acre Radio Studio (built in 1920 by the British firm Robertson-Cole), bought the Pathe lot in January, 1931. The stock market collapse and the necessary conversion to "talkie" production left RKO in financial straits and there was among the company officials considerable dissension regarding the wisdom of operating a second studio.

Pathe was an impressive forty-acre layout which included eleven sound stages, superb drapery and property departments, some spectacular standing sets, a meandering ravine and a segment of Baldwin Hills. Conspicuous among the available sets were those representing old

The wall, the gate, and the altar. (From a badly damaged print)

The Great Wall set unfinished

Jerusalem *à la mode* DeMille that were built in August, 1926, for *The King of Kings.* Some of the big artificial cliffs and boulders from the Place of the Skull set already had been used on the jungle set for *The Most Dangerous Game.* A colossal wall about seventy-five feet high, several tiers of broad steps, a flagstone floor and some massive Romanesque columns remained of the Council House interior, which actually was an outdoor set without a ceiling. In the centre of the wall was a rectangular opening sixty feet high and twenty feet wide which was originally hung with gigantic drapes. This remnant of DeMille's Holy Land became the site of Skull Island's ruined city.

Unit art director Al Herman had his craftsmen cover the wall with weird carvings and jungle undergrowth. In the opening was placed a massive double door constructed of vertical planking and equipped with a gigantic wooden bolt. A tocsin gong about twelve feet high was mounted on top above the opening. The pillars were reduced to ruin and partially buried under vines and moss. Wooden scaffoldings and scaling towers were erected along the wall to suggest that the natives kept the structure in repair to protect them from the jungle.

When King Vidor's *Bird of Paradise* expedition returned from the Hawaiian Islands early in 1932, it was decided that the scenes of native dancing were unsuitable and re-takes would be staged by Busby Berkeley with music by Max Steiner and dancing by thirty-five Hollywood chorus girls. For this purpose an authentic-looking Polynesian village was erected at Pathe. These grass houses later were moved to the Council House set to

become part of the village of the Skull Islanders.

Three spectacular sequences involving hundreds of "natives" were filmed at the Council House site: the first encounter with the natives during the ceremony in which a black girl is supposed to become "the bride of Kong," the night ritual in which Ann is sacrificed and the long sequence in which the lovers return from the jungle with Kong following to ravage the village. The sacrificial altar was built full-scale outside the gate and duplicated in miniature for scenes with Kong.

The night scenes are especially impressive. Sixty-five electricians were employed to handle the 350 lamps required to light the set and the horde of weirdly costumed extras. Schoedsack was ready to begin shooting at nightfall on August 11 when a heavy fog rolled in from the west. Enormous amounts of food and soda pop were served out to the milling extras to keep them from becoming restless while the director and his crew waited and worried. Fortunately, the fog lifted at midnight and shooting began. The fire department was on hand because of the torches carried by the "natives."

The jungle side of the wall was built in miniature, its "stone" surface intricately textured in glue mixed with sand and corn meal. Through a *split screen* effect the live actors were shown standing along the top. To get the necessary elevation, the players were lined up atop Sound Stage 10, near the front gate on Washington Boulevard. Scores of blazing torches lighted the sky and soon a large crowd gathered, thinking the studio was on fire. One studio official who had opposed the purchase of Pathe and knew it was

Opposite: before the shooting starts. This page, below: night scene at the wall with Kong matted in

The Great Wall reproduced in miniature with the native torchlight parade matted in

Milling natives prepare for the sacrifice

Below: sacrificed to Kong!

One of the tests for the first appearance of Kong

heavily insured was reported to have shouted, "I'll give somebody $10,000 to burn the place down!"

The scenes in which Ann becomes "the bride of Kong" are pictorially the most exquisite in the film. The lighting effects are dazzling and the cameras move through the massed players with virtuosity worthy of D. W. Griffith. After Ann has been taken outside and bound to the altar, the closing of the gates is shown in a series of monumental, formalised compositions that make her utter isolation seem more terrifying than her plight when she was in the hands of the savages. The ceremony is accompanied by some of Max Steiner's most impassioned music, the wildness of which is heightened by the pagan cries of the villagers.

The later episode in which Kong breaks the bolt of the gates and rampages through the village is the stuff of an inspired nightmare. The doors were pulled open by four concealed tractors and Kong later was matted into the opening by the Williams process. Schoedsack encountered difficulty in getting the extras to react properly to the situation when all they saw beyond the gates was a bright blue backdrop.

Although most of the action in the village was directed by Schoedsack, Cooper staged the scenes in which a native is bitten to death by the great ape, for which he used the life-size bust of Kong. He also directed two scenes in which natives are crushed under Kong's foot. This too was accomplished using a full-scale prop. The actors chosen for these roles were terrified when the gigantic foot, which was mounted on a crane, was lowered onto them, pressing them into the muddy earth. One of them, eyes bulging from his muddy face as the foot was lifted away, leaped to his feet and fled from the stage.

Both directors worked on the scenes in which Kong is overcome by gas bombs on the beach, but for the most part they worked separately. So divergent were their methods that they found close collaboration in the studio to be difficult. It was quite a different matter from their work on expeditions, where nature and circumstances called the tune.

Some of the shipboard scenes were made

An early sacrificial altar test. One effect is still burning through the other in this unfinished trial

Another test for an early appearance of Kong

Foreground glass and miniature unfinished in a test that shows details of the model carved altar

aboard a freighter out of San Pedro while others were done at the studio using mock-up portions of the ship. Several diffused shots of the crew at work as the steamer gets under way in the early dawn are beautifully atmospheric and are matched perfectly to the studio shots. The men portraying seamen are genuinely salty types. Schoedsack even secured a bearded and bow-legged English tar to cast the leadline during the fog sequence.

The sequence of Ann's screen test aboard ship was filmed at the studio on a stage equipped with a plain backdrop. The effect of a distant sea-horizon was simulated by painting the drop in two tones of blue and having it raised and lowered by stagehands.

During the screen test sequence, Armstrong was supposed to adjust the lenses of his camera and insert a rectangular filter into the matte box while explaining that he always cranks his own camera because a cameraman he hired for a jungle film fled when a rhinoceros charged the camera. On each take the actor was unable to fit the filter into place—much to the merriment of the camera crew. Schoedsack finally cut from the scene at the crucial moment to a shot of sailors watching the action. Later the remainder of Ann's test was filmed, including the famed scene in which the girl, under Denham's direction, covers her eyes and screams at the top of her lungs. This time only one take was necessary—much to Fay Wray's relief.

While the scenes of the shipboard search for the kidnapped girl were being set up, Cabot disappeared. At last he emerged from a gear locker where he had hidden some whisky. It was obvious that he was in no condition to play the scene. When Schoedsack reprimanded him, Cabot tried to kid him out of his anger by breaking into a comical dance. Schoedsack, normally the least temperamental of directors, slapped Cabot hard—twice. The chastened and sobered actor, although badly shaken, finished the day's shooting without further mishap. Schoedsack regretted the incident. It was the only time he ever struck one of his players, although he was sorely tempted when working with such hard drinkers as John Barrymore, Alan Mowbray and Louis Calhern.

A model of the "Venture" twelve feet in length was used to show the ship in the fog. It duplicated faithfully all external details of the real steamer, the studio shipboard mock-ups and the personnel on deck. The human figures, carved from wood by Cerisoli, were superbly detailed, even to the pipes being "smoked" by Denham and Englehorn. The plates of the ship's hull were constructed from illustration board and painted to resemble metal long exposed to the sea. The thousands of rivets were brass escutcheon pins. The effect of the ship on the ocean was achieved without actually launching the model into the water.

A test with dowels where the altar will be

Beach scenes at Skull Island were filmed near San Pedro. The long shot of the initial landing shows the actual ocean in the foreground, the players and the boats on the beach in the middle distance and, via a glass painting, the great wall and Skull Mountain appear to be in the far distance. The glass art actually was within a few feet of the camera. Flying gulls were superimposed to add depth and movement to the scene. The closer views of the landing were photographed from a high angle to eliminate the necessity of a background. For the reverse angles of Denham

Another view of the "Venture"

Cardboard plates and brass escutcheon pins!

The non-floatable model of the "Venture"

and his party on the beach after Kong has been subdued, a glass shot was employed to place the "Venture" offshore against a night sky. This shot then was projected in miniature behind the unconscious figure of Kong lying on the beach.

Schoedsack's camera technique in the "live" scenes is far different from the photography of his expedition films. Availing himself of the cranes and dollies at the studio he kept the camera moving most of the time, whether out of doors or on the sound stage. The fluidity of these shots is complementary to the necessary rigidity of the majority of the scenes that involve animation.

Even in the Dunning and Williams composite shots the camera is surprisingly mobile. Careful shooting of separate elements to be combined and perfect timing of the ultimate shot were required for scenes such as the one wherein the camera follows the players as they approach a fallen stegosaurus.

A new technique which became standard procedure in rear projection work was employed to show Armstrong and Cabot walking past the writhing body of the stegosaurus. The players

On the way to the gate. Miniature and glass

walked on a treadmill in front of a screen on which was projected a scene wherein the camera moved along the seemingly gigantic carcass.

Equally intricate was the planning of full scale-scenes to be combined with animation via miniature projection. O'Brien was usually on hand to assist in establishing proper lighting and spatial relationships for the ultimate matching. The live portions were photographed well in advance of the animation, preceding the final combination shot by weeks or even months.

Another Larrinaga master drawing that sets the scene (see overleaf)

10. People, Primroses and Other Problems

The production of *Kong* made unusual demands on the assigned personnel, who in numerous instances were required to step out of their normal roles and call on talents of which they may have been unaware.

Archie Marshek, who came to the studio in 1924 as an assistant projectionist, was a first-rate film editor. During the early summer of 1932 he cut two Cooper productions, *The Most Dangerous Game* and *Phantom of Crestwood.* Cooper, after viewing rushes from the latter, told Marshek to remove a long stretch of dialogue he felt slowed the action of the film. Later, Cooper and the director, J. Walter Ruben, screened the sequence.

"Hey!" Ruben cried, "There's a page-and-a-half of dialogue missing! What happened to our dialogue?" Cooper turned innocently to the editor.

"Archie, what happened to all that dialogue?"

"Why, you said to cut it out," was the reply. It was the wrong answer.

"Don't tell me that, you son-of-a-bitch!" Cooper said furiously, pointing at Marshek with his pipe.

"You can go ---- in your hat!" Marshek retorted as he stamped out of the room. He went to his office and told his colleagues, "I guess I've just been fired." Then the 'phone rang. The voice was Cooper's.

"Can you come back to the projection room and put that dialogue back in?" Nothing more was said of the incident.

Two weeks later, Cooper summoned Marshek to his office.

"Cooper was sitting over in one corner, chewing on his pipe," Marshek recalls. "Finally, he said, 'How would you like to be my assistant?' It was quite a shock to a guy expecting to be canned. I guess he liked the way I stood up for myself, as *he* would have done. I said yes and was put to work on *Kong.*

"When I started they were taking tests of the ape, working on his facial expressions and so on. Coop's pipe was always going out and he never had any matches. I didn't even smoke, but I soon learned to have a pocket full of kitchen matches on the set because he was constantly saying, 'Archie, have you got a match?' Dorothy, his wife, always got a kick out of that.

"I spent a lot of time running back and forth between RKO and the Williams lab, where they made most of our composite shots. It was a little pie-shaped building on Santa Monica and I don't think it's there any more. I'd have to see that they got those little bleed lines out and explain what Coop wanted and they'd have to do it over until it was right. I worked on the stage with O'Brien, ran the dailies with Cooper and O'Brien

From the "Hollywood Reporter" presentation issue on KING KONG

Another montage from the same issue

More personalities featured in the special KONG issue of the "Hollywood Reporter"

Another montage from the same issue

and worked on the editing, although I didn't actually cut the picture—Ted Cheesman did that."

Marshek found working for Cooper to be a lively chore. He continued as Cooper's assistant for several years, contributing to the production of such films as *The Son of Kong* and *The Last Days of Pompeii*. Eventually, he returned to his former profession, editing many films at Paramount. Now retired, he often chuckles over his many experiences with Cooper.

Twenty-seven-year-old Walter Daniels was assigned to Schoedsack as production assistant. Like the director, he was both artistic and rugged, having been a lithographer and a rancher in Colorado before entering movies as Will Rogers' prop man. He also shared the Schoedsack sense of humour and the two got on well.

In addition to his work on the set, Daniels functioned as unit business manager and even secured a yacht so that Schoedsack could throw a weekend party for his cast and crew. Daniels became assistant production manager of RKO in 1935 and was appointed studio manager six years later. He continued in the same capacity when the studio was purchased by Desilu Productions. When he died, in 1969, he had been at the studio for forty-six years during many changes of ownership.

Willis O'Brien said that "The miniature technician cannot bring his set to the screen singlehanded. It is fundamentally an artist's conception but requires the united efforts of many craftsmen, its success depending entirely upon the combination of artistic, photographic and mechanical effects, each person being a specialist in his field but also having a general knowledge of the whole.

"When making *King Kong* it was necessary to have a large staff of experienced men to carry on the work. A group of men were kept busy building and repairing the animals or executing any mechanical necessity that was required. Another group built the miniatures, which included a New York Elevated Railway recreated in detail, and jungle settings on a tropical island. Mario Larrinaga and Byron Crabbe made the sketches and later painted the backings and glasses for the sets after the miniatures were drawn up and put to work. Besides these men, others were necessary for the actual working of the miniature."*

The members of O'Brien's technical staff were men who just happened to be in the right place with the right skills at the right time. The heads of the various departments from which they were recruited resented having to furnish personnel without having any authority over the work they were doing. Most of them worked on *Creation* and by the time *Kong* was put into production the curiously assorted group was able to contribute a variety of skills learned during the previous year.

O'Brien selected as his first assistant a burly studio grip, E. B. "Buz" Gibson, who, typical of men of his calling, was able to do a multitude of jobs on the set. O'Brien and Gibson shared several outside interests, including archery and boxing. While working on the Kong-tyrannosaurus fight sequence, O'Brien and Gibson attended boxing and wrestling matches regularly, noting bits of action which might be applicable to Kong's semihuman methods of fighting. Animation was something new to Gibson, but with O'Brien's help he learned rapidly. He helped with the animation as well as supervising the construction of some large properties, such as the large bust of Kong. Although O'Brien preferred to work alone on animation that was particularly subtle or "touchy," Gibson participated in staging such complicated scenes as the fights between prehistoric monsters. He also animated several key scenes alone, most notably Kong's climb up the Empire State Building.

Husky Fred Reefe was an expert builder and a master at improvising mechanical devices. A beefy and affable man, Reefe was responsible for many of the contrivances used in the full-scale Kong. Frequently he helped O'Brien and Gibson in animation when the "under the table" fastening job became difficult and when animals had to be held in jumping attitudes by concealed devices.

Orville "Goldy" Goldner worked in Don Jahraus' miniature shop where he specialised in creating special effects properties and in matching textures for scenes involving miniature and full-scale composites. A background in fine arts and experience in puppetry and puppet animation made him a "natural" for O'Brien's unit. For *Creation* and *Kong* he built miniature trees and

* O'Brien: "Miniature Effect Shots" in "International Photographer," May, 1933, pp. 38–39.

Detail of Mario Larrinaga's splendid drawing of KONG fighting the reptile outside his cave

sets, matched foliage and rock textures, animated birds and aircraft, worked with live animals and devised special trick riggings.

John Cerisoli, an elderly Italian who spoke little English, was the studio's master sculptor. Working alone in a little shop adjoining the sound department, he carved the wooden prototypes (and stand-ins) of the animals as well as the dozens of articulated wooden models of the human characters. He also fashioned the skulls of some of the working animals (the Tyrannosaurus, for example, had a wooden skull covered with thin copper).

W. G. "Gus" White, a studio grip, became a jack-of-all-trades for the unit. In addition to making props and rigging sets, the stocky Texan became so adept at miniature construction that he continued in this field. One noteworthy achievement was the building of the city of Pompeii that was systematically destroyed for the 1935 epic, *The Last Days of Pompeii.*

Carroll Shepphird was employed in the art department but had a desire to work in photographic effects. O'Brien gave him the highly technical job of laying out construction plans for the effects sequences, even to the exact placement of characters and the position of the camera. "Shep" also determined what lenses would be used, preparing for this purpose charts showing the sizes of screen images at various distances when photographed with lenses of different focal lengths. Thirteen lenses were used, ranging from a focal length of forty millimeters to a moderate telephoto of five inches. One chart was a perspective diagram showing the relative sizes of a man as seen by a forty millimeter lens at distances from the camera of ten to one hundred feet. Shepphird never returned to the art department. At the time of his retirement he was head of visual effects at M-G-M.

There were others who worked on *Kong* as a part of their regular studio jobs. Van Nest Pol-

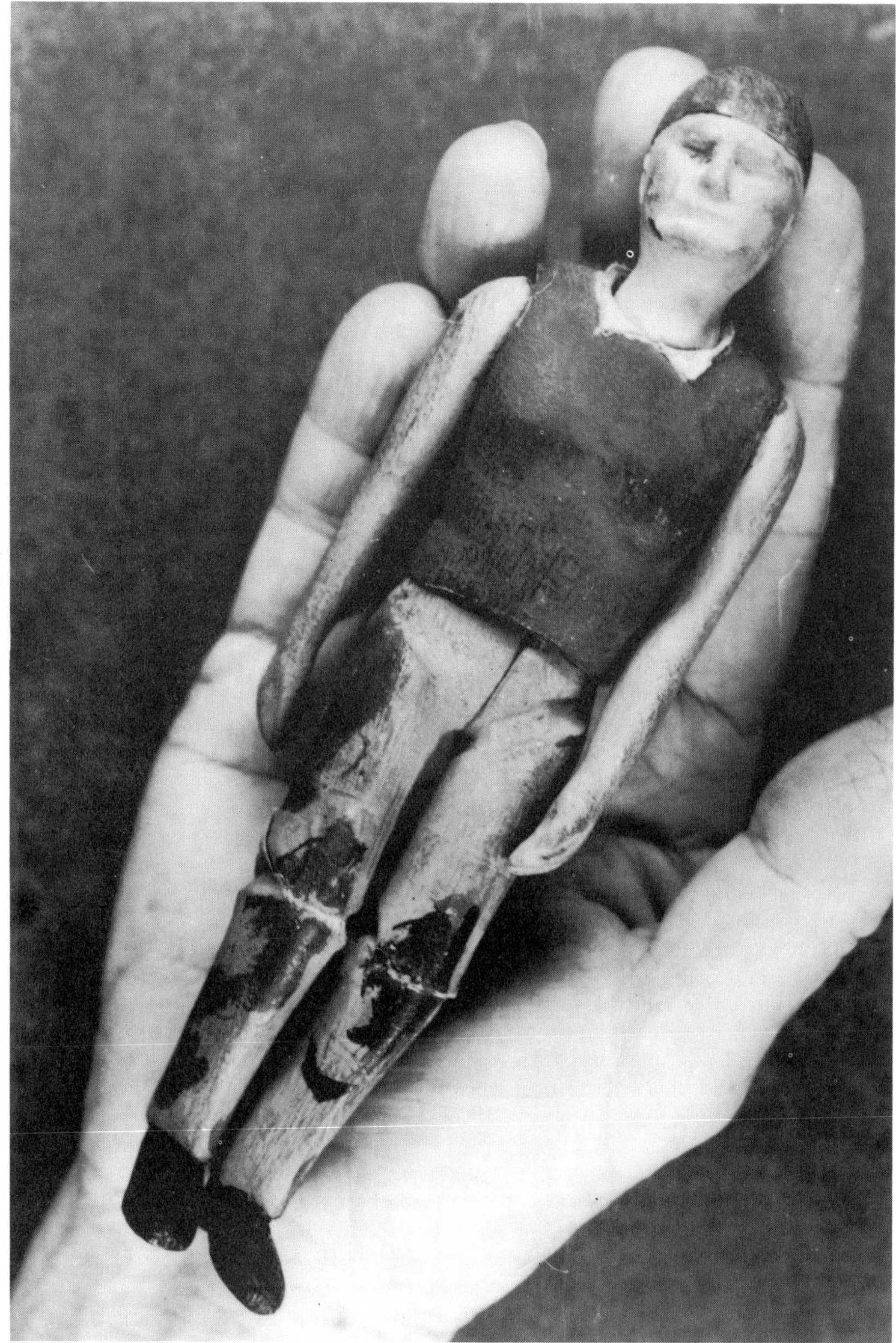

An articulated wooden figure used in many KONG scenes

OBie animates the fight scene in the great cave

glase, Art Director, made preliminary plans for the full-scale sets and assigned the unit art direction to Carroll Clark and Al Herman. Thomas Little, head of the property department, supplied set decorators and property masters to dress the Clark-Herman sets. Costume designer Walter Plunkett contributed Fay Wray's "beauty and the beast" costume and the fantastic attire of the Skull Islanders. Harry Redmond Jr. was responsible for the realistic fog effects in two sequences. There were others—many others.

The studio's top cameramen were not available for a picture that would tie them up for many months. RKO's aces—men like Henry Gerrard, Lucien Andriot and Edward Cronjager—were needed to handle the glamorous assignments, the star vehicles with Constance Bennett, Richard Dix, Dolores del Rio and Irene Dunne. O'Brien settled for Edwin G. "Eddie" Linden as chief cameraman in charge of all photography, both live action and miniature. Linden, who had been relegated for years to Westerns and low-budget features, most of them for the independent producers, had the patience and temperament necessary for coping with the many problems of a picture like *Kong*. As many as ten cameramen worked under Linden during certain stages of production, most of them young fellows on their way up. His first assistant was Bert Willis. It is a curious fact that after earning an enviable reputation for his work on *Kong* and two other Cooper-Schoedsack-O'Brien productions, *The Son of Kong* and *The Last Days of Pompeii,* Linden returned to the "poverty row" companies. After grinding out scores of "quickies" for little companies like Regal and PRC, Linden regained some prestige at Columbia in the last few months of his life.

J. O. Taylor had gained repute as a documentary cameraman before becoming a lighting cinematographer. He followed Pancho Villa throughout the Mexican Revolution, shooting spectacular footage that is still used as stock footage. His ability in handling mass action is much in evidence

A view of the cave. Testing the rear-projected image of Fay Wray

in the New York street scenes of *Kong*.

Vernon L. "Vern" Walker assisted Fred Jackman in the camera effects department at First National before coming to RKO as assistant to camera effects supervisor Lloyd Knechtel. Shortly after *Kong* went into production Knechtel left the studio and Walker succeeded him. A big, hearty man with a thorough knowledge of all phases of trick photography, Walker continued in this capacity until his death in 1948.

Among the assistant and operative cameramen involved in *Kong* was the youthful William Clothier, today one of the industry's top colour cinematographers. Clifford Stine, who was a talented member of Linden's team in lighting and testing intricate miniature composite shots, also rose to fame as a director of photography and for five years was in charge of the special effects department at Universal. Linwood G. Dunn, who operated a camera for miniature scenes in *Creation,* became Vern Walker's assistant in charge of optical photography while *Kong* was in production. William Reinhold, an assistant cameraman, received recognition in the documentary field.

G. Felix Schoedsack, brother of the director, not only worked as a camera operator but started something of a trend in motion picture "still" photography during production. Production stills at that time were made with large format cameras on sheet film, but the difficulty of shooting the miniature setups with bulky cameras proved to

Previous pages: one of the original key drawings by Byron Crabbe to illustrate the high drama of the great fight sequence

be a problem. Felix Schoedsack, who was the proud owner of the latest Leica 35 mm. camera and all its precise accessories, convinced his superiors that the small negative was practical for "stills" in many instances. This was one of the first times the "candid" camera was used for the production of movie "stills."

All the crew members wore rubber-soled shoes because of a studio rule born with the sound-film era. They quickly learned that Cooper's visits were heralded by the clacking of his hard-heeled English walking shoes, a useful warning at times when everybody was taking a rest.

"Eventually we became aware that Mr. Cooper walked harder than usual when he came to see us," one of the technicians recalls. "The fact is that he was very much a gentleman and didn't want to catch us unawares."

The animation required an abnormal amount of skill, patience, and attention to subtle details and conditions. It had to be done under incandescent light. All light-bulbs were replaced at the beginning of each scene because a burn-out would spoil it (the intensity of the replacement bulb would not be the same).

"Experience is the only teacher," O'Brien had said. "Each new set is an individual problem and requires separate treatment. There is no set rule or method by which you can classify all miniatures."

It soon became evident that an animation scene, once begun, must be carried through to

Another angle of the cave with the projected images of Fay Wray and Bruce Cabot (lower right)

The Arsinoitherium deep in lush jungle. Many varieties of small plants and moss were used in such scenes

completion without lengthy interruption. Some of the early scenes were ruined because they were abandoned before completion at the end of the work day and finished the next day. When screened these scenes betrayed sudden startling changes during the action because the live plants used in miniatures tended to grow, die or in other ways become noticeably different. Lamps would not relight at the same intensity due to variations in voltage or normal deterioration.

Real plants used in miniature sets had to be watered frequently because of the heat of lamps. The resulting highly humid condition caused some plants to grow much faster than usual. When animation of a scene was continuous such growth was normally imperceptible but any delay in time during the animation process would show up on the screen as a disturbing "jump."

The thin copper palm fronds and ferns made with great skill and patience for the miniature jungles were sometimes ruffled into different positions or completely collapsed as the result of the inrush of air when stage doors were opened by departing and returning personnel. This was a practice severely frowned on during critical animation sequences except in the greatest necessity. Large, hot incandescent lamps could be caused to blow up from a sudden inrush of cold air.

On one occasion a certain miniature scene was in work for an entire day (not an unusual circumstance). In this instance a primrose plant used to represent large-leaved jungle foliage came into bloom. Nobody noticed this slowly developing phenomenon until the rushes were projected the next morning. Then it was found that the scene contained a perfect time-lapse study of the pure white flower opening! In the miniature set the white blossom appeared gigantic and, of course, made re-shooting of the entire scene unavoidable!

On another occasion involving several days of work the crew lined up the various elements of a complicated scene with three planes of glass art and mattes, a painted backing and miniatures in

Exterior of cave entrance with wooden Kong stand-in and model figure

Fay Wray in relation to the miniature Kong. Side angle

At the entrance to the cave

Miss Wray swoons for the composite test

An unfinished carved stand-in for the boat sequence

between. After many photographic tests the set was at last considered camera-ready about noon of the third day. Everybody went to lunch and while they were eating a slight earthquake occurred. It was only a minor tremor and nobody gave it more than a passing thought. When the crew returned to work and made a last test before shooting they found that the different elements of the set had shifted just enough to require a new, tedious re-matching job.

At one point in the work on this same set, technicians Stich and Goldner were knocked to the floor with a tremendous bang when the hose of an acetylene tank (used for heating paint materials) exploded. The tank fell over and started to burn the wooden floor of the stage and the huge black "daisy cloth" that separated this set from others. Regaining their footing, both men tried to douse the flames, which could get out of control quickly. Studio fireman "Fat" Burns had been summoned immediately, but before he could arrive Mario Larrinaga, who had spent many hours painting the glass elements of the set, grabbed the large bottle of water from a nearby water cooler and smashed it into the fire. The flames were quenched by Larrinaga's spontaneous action which, because of his rather small stature, was considered by all hands as a remarkable feat. Some painful injuries and a temporary loss of hearing put Pete Stich under a doctor's care for several days.

Other strange things could happen in animation. An animator worked for several hours on a difficult scene when he discovered that he had left a pair of pliers lying so that one of the handles was within camera range in the foreground. Due to the low camera angle it was unidentifiable, but appeared only as an elongated gray mass. Unable to bear the thought of starting afresh, the animator slowly and carefully moved the tool out of the scene frame by frame as he animated the dinosaur featured in the particular action. Anyone seeing the undistinguished form moving along the bottom edge of the frame would consider it a snake or other reptile escaping. But it is safe to say that few people would be diverted from the main story line unfolding on the screen to the extent of giving the animated pliers a second thought.

Kong's fur, as Delgado had predicted, proved to be a problem in animation. Cooper and Schoedsack were appalled when some RKO executives joined them in viewing animation rushes. Their hearts sank as they watched the hair of Kong's head and shoulders ripple with each touch of the animator's fingers. The unwelcome effect was emphasised by artful backlighting.

"Hey, Kong is mad!" one of the officials cried delightedly as Kong roared his defiance. "Look at him bristle!"

Above: the miniature reptile snaps at the projected Fay Wray. Below: Kong and the reptile struggle

11. It Wasn't Easy

"He was a holy terror and I was scared to death," Zoe Porter said in recalling a day in October, 1931 when she became Merian Cooper's secretary at RKO. Very soon she was to realise that her employer's gruff manner masked a gallant and sympathetic nature and a consuming loyalty to his friends. She continued to work for Cooper until his death more than forty years later. "He was a real genius," Mrs. Porter says. "I don't think there's more than one mind like his in any generation."

"It wasn't easy working for Coop," camera ace Linwood Dunn recalls. "He was such a perfectionist. Sometimes it was very frustrating. He'd look at a scene we'd worked on for a long time and say something like, 'I think it would be better if he scratched with his *left* hand.' "

One scene Cooper had second thoughts about was a part of the test film in which the Arsinoitherium chased the sailors onto the log bridge. He ordered the action to be re-filmed using a Styracosaurus, a bulky reptile possessing a highly ornate, multi-horned skull. In the new version the dinosaur tried to dislodge the log with its long nasal horn. Both versions eventually were thrown out because they captured too much audience attention, creating a diversion from the main story. At this point in the film the action is moving so swiftly that viewers haven't time to stop and wonder why the men stay on the log instead of retreating to the jungle. The Styracosaurus made its public *début* in *The Son of Kong,* a sequel.

Scenes of the sailors falling into the gorge and being devoured by gigantic spiders, lizards and insects proved even more of a show-stopper. The fate of the sailors was so horrifying that the viewer tended to forget what he was supposed to be thinking about—the plight of Fay Wray. The sequence was changed so that the men were seen falling to instant death in a rocky chasm. Jointed dummies six inches high were dropped into the canyon and photographed with a camera running at eight times normal speed to produce the slow-motion effect necessary to create the illusion of bulk. The dummies refused stubbornly to react as real bodies would. Experiments proved that weights placed in various parts of the figures caused them to bounce properly when they struck the canyon floor. Even without spiders the scenes are horrifying enough to create audience shudders. The anguished screams of the falling men were supplied by sound effects man Murray Spivack, whose distinctive voice was also heard during the shipwreck sequence of *The Most Dangerous Game.* A giant lizard was substituted for the spider that climbed up to Cabot's hideaway in the first filming. Also jettisoned from the chase were

the scenes featuring a Triceratops and the huge snake that menaced Fay Wray during the action at the gorge.

The first version of Kong's initial appearance as he arrives at the wall to claim his "bride" also got a "thumbs down" reaction from both Cooper and Schoedsack. The animation of Kong and of the trees as they are pushed aside lacked the smoothness of other key scenes. Kong's entrance was filmed again with minor changes, and again and again. By the end of the production schedule, no less than sixteen different versions of the scene were completed. The one used in the final release is the first version filmed. Despite its shortcomings it was judged more effective than any of the others.

The inimitable visual style of *Kong* was attained largely through the imaginative drawings of Mario Larrinaga and Byron Crabbe. Working from O'Brien's action outlines and following his order to strive for the dramatic lighting and mood of Gustave Doré, these men in the course of production made hundreds of drawings and sketches. Not only were the artists responsible for the design of the film but they also rendered the glass and background paintings that were an integral part of the miniature settings. The men who crafted the three-dimensional elements of the sets followed as closely as possible the details and textures delineated in the Larrinaga-Crabbe art. To assure that the original drawings would be reproduced accurately in the technical art, O'Brien had an ingenious opaque projector designed so the drawings could be projected on glass as a guide to the painting. The projector was duly constructed, but Larrinaga preferred to work without it, in fact did not need it.

O'Brien's idea of emulating Doré as a basis for cinematographic lighting and atmosphere may have originated with the pioneer cameraman and special effects expert, Louis W. Physioc, who in 1930 stated that "if there is one man's work that can be taken as the cinematographer's text, it is that of Doré. His stories are told in our own language of 'black and white,' are highly imaginative and dramatic and should stimulate anybody's ideas."*

* Physioc: "Cinematography an Art Form," from "Cinematographer's Annual Volume I," Hollywood, 1930.

The Doré influence is strikingly evident in the island scenes. Aside from the lighting effects, other elements of Doré illustrations are easily discernible. The affinity of the jungle clearings to those in Doré's "The First Approach of the Serpent" from Milton's "Paradise Lost," "Dante in the Gloomy Wood" from Dante's "The Divine Comedy," "Approach to the Enchanted Palace" from Perrault's "Fairy Tales" and "Manz" from Chateaubriand's "Atala" is readily apparent. The gorge and its log bridge bear more than a slight similarity to "The Two Goats" from "The Fables" of La Fontaine, while the lower region of the gorge may well have been designed after the pit in the Biblical illustration of "Daniel in the Lion's Den." The wonderful scene in which Kong surveys his domain from the "balcony" of his mountaintop home high above the claustrophobic jungles is suggestive of two superb Doré engravings, "Satan Overlooking Paradise" from "Paradise Lost" and "The Hermit on the Mountain" from "Atala."

O'Brien appears to have invented the three-dimensional glass-and-miniature settings he pioneered in *Creation* and brought to public view in *Kong*. This technique was too time-consuming to be popular with producers although O'Brien was able to use it to a lesser extent in several later pictures and Walt Disney did something rather similar without the added solid forms in his celebrated Multiplane cartoons. Marcel Delgado bemoans the fact that the producers of most films using animated models "never take any pains with the sets. They just use a few trees and rocks. In *Kong* the sets have depth; you can see into them for miles, it seems."

The scenes in Kong's Skull Mountain cavern were particularly complicated, requiring an unusual number of special processes. The setting itself is a complex amalgam of glass art and miniature construction. The pool from which the snake-like Elasmosaurus emerges is real water, photographed separately and matted into the scene. Another matte was necessary to introduce a pool of bubbling lava into the foreground. Rising steam, filmed backlighted against a black velvet background, was superimposed. Two separately photographed and projected images were necessary to place Fay Wray on a ledge at the left of the screen and to show Cabot hiding among the

Previous pages: Kong fights the Pteranodon in the key drawing by Crabbe. (Drawing courtesy Merian C. Cooper)

Miniature foreground with cardboard cut-out to establish proportion in the test

rocks in other parts of the cave. Kong, the reptile and the models of the actors (necessary for certain portions of the scenes) were animated by O'Brien while assistants manipulated the projected images. The absolute synchronisation necessary to the successful combining of all of these processes was a formidable undertaking.

Although miniature projection replaced the old stationary matte process in most instances, a variation of split-screen matting was useful in putting certain "live" elements into such animated scenes as the ones just described. These mattes were executed similarly to glass shots, the artist matting out the desired portions of the scene by applying opaque black paint to a sheet of glass mounted in front of the camera. When the first shot was made through the glass, the black area (neither transmitting nor reflecting light) permitted the portions of the negative which recorded the matted areas to remain unexposed. The "live" portions were then filmed through a glass containing a counter-matte that covered the exact area that was exposed on the film in the first shot. In certain scenes, such as those showing architectural features, it was necessary to use a hard-edged matte. Those using jungle foliage permitted use of a soft-edge "match," that was somewhat easier to control. Overlapping of the two components resulted in white masses or lines at the points of match, while any space left between the components resulted in black areas.* Avoiding these deficiencies (called *plusses* and *minuses*) was most important.

Running water was matted into other scenes. The Los Angeles River flows by in the foreground as Kong carries Fay Wray through the jungle

* This was the negative condition and the positive print would then be the opposite.

Kong at his lair in an early test

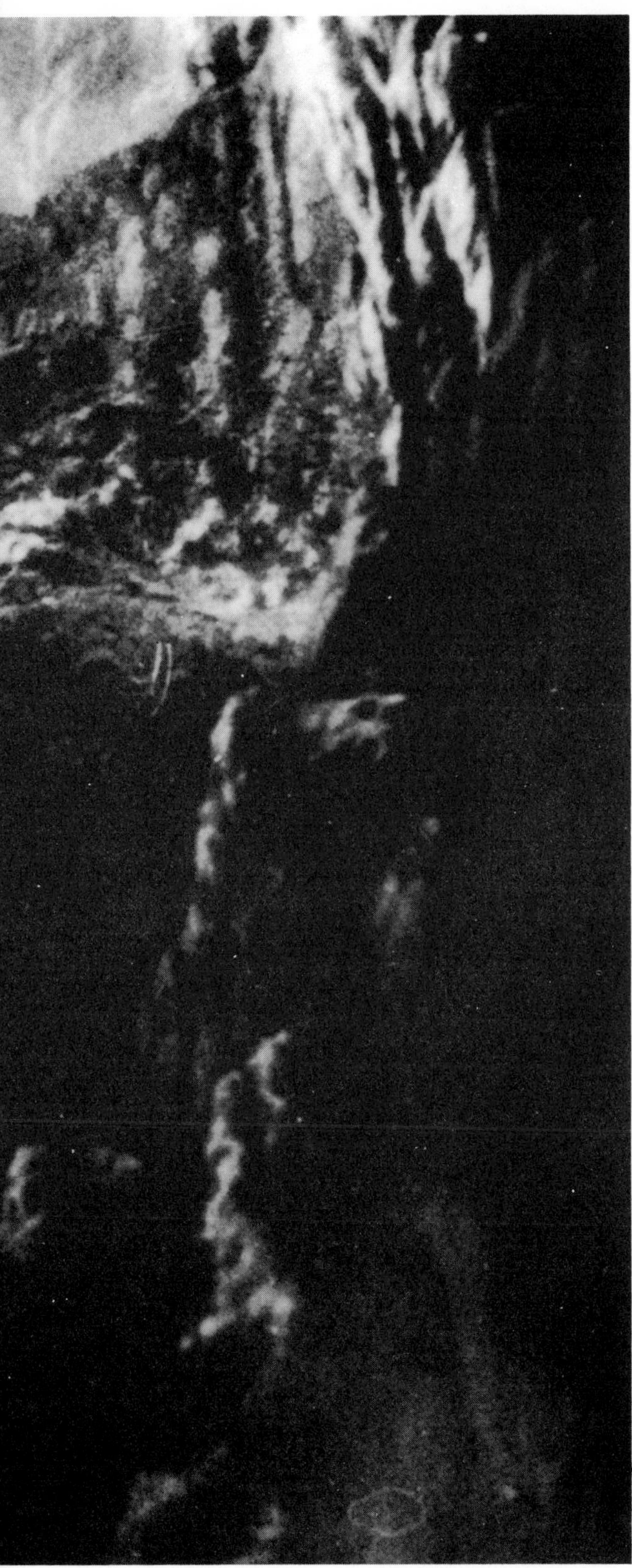

after vanquishing the Tyrannosaurus. The waterfall that tumbles from the lake at the base of Skull Mountain was photographed in the Sierra Nevada Mountains and is also seen in *The Most Dangerous Game.* The effect of combining "live" water with animated beasts is an O'Brien "touch" first seen in *The Lost World* and repeated in *The Son of Kong* and *Mighty Joe Young* as well as in the surviving footage of *Creation.*

O'Brien has said that the most difficult scenes in *King Kong* are those in which Kong fights a Pteranodon on the mountaintop after the flying reptile has attempted to carry away the girl. The sequence was in work for seven weeks. O'Brien has been accused of putting a mouthful of sharp teeth in the jaws of a creature known to have been toothless in real life, but the teeth the critics think they saw in the picture are only in the stills, the work of an over-zealous re-touch artist. It is unlikely, however, that a real Pteranodon could carry a human being for, although the wingspread of a Pteranodon was as great as twenty-seven feet, the hollow-boned creature was very lightweight. Some paleontologists insist that Pteranodons could not fly but merely glided down from high crags to skim over Kansas' inland seas to capture fish. It hasn't been explained how such a non-flying monstrosity could return to its lofty perch. At any rate, O'Brien's winged reptile not only flies but flaps about as furiously as a captive bird when it falls into the grasp of Kong. Keeping the Pteranodon suspended aloft and animating the beating wings made the staging of this sequence unusually difficult. Further problems were added by the movements of the actors, it being necessary to use animated mannikins in certain portions of the frame and projected figures in others.

All the prehistoric animals are depicted with a certain amount of dramatic licence. The Elasmosaurus, for example, is more slender than the ones known to science and its swimming limbs are less prominent. The stegosaur in *Kong* combines the features of two different members of the genus, the well-known *Stegosaurus ungulatus,* which bore two rows of spectacular bony plates along its back and two pairs of long spines on its tail, and the relatively unfamiliar *Kentrosaurus,* the tail of which held numerous paired spines. The beast of the film has the spectacular features

Kong slays the Pteranodon

of both species. At the time of filming most scientists were divided as to whether the back plates of *S. ungulatus* were paired or alternately spaced. O'Brien, noting that few vertebrates have an alternate arrangement of dermal appendages, had the plates organised in pairs—to the dismay of some experts and the approval of others. An argument as to the arrangements of the dorsal plates of the Stegosaurus continues to be debated by paleontologists. The *Kong* version is considerably larger than known specimens, which are less than thirty feet in length.

The great sauropod dinosaur, Brontosaurus (or, more correctly, *Apatosaurus*), is depicted properly in the film as an amphibious creature seventy feet in length. For dramatic purposes the head is somewhat exaggerated and the ferocity of the animal as depicted is at variance with scientific opinion. Because both stegosaurs and sauropods were herbivorous and stupid it is not considered likely that they would attack men (if, indeed, there had been men at the time they existed). It could, of course, be argued that a paleontologist of the future might make the same statement about elephants, rhinoceroces and hippopotami—all of which are highly dangerous even though they do not eat flesh. The Brontosaur in Kong uses its mouth as a weapon but it is never suggested that it feeds upon its victims, which are dropped or cast aside after being bitten to death.

The three-horned Triceratops and its young (none of which appears in the release version) conform to scientific opinion in most particulars except scale, the adult of the film being much larger than the known specimens, which were about twenty-five feet in length. The same is true of the Styracosaurus, a horned dinosaur closely related to the Triceratops, which also was edited from the film.

The Arsinoitherium, another casualty of the cutting room, was not a dinosaur but a gigantic mammal that lived in Egypt long after the dinosaurs became extinct. The legs of this Oligocene beast were similar in size and shape to those of an elephant, the body was somewhat rhinoceros-like and the skull was adorned with two massive horns set side by side on the face. It is entirely probable that the animal was as belligerent and awesome in life as it is on film. The giant spiders and insects of the gorge were wholly imaginary, although some arthropods and insects of the Carboniferous period were much larger than those of today. A large reptile shown in the excised version of the gorge sequence appears to be one of the very ancient mammal-like reptiles found in the Permian deposits of Africa, *Cynognathus.*

The huge serpent that appeared in one scene and was later cut out of the film had its living prototype in Egypt during the early part of the Age of Mammals. The Egyptian snake was about sixty feet long. A curious reptile that menaces Driscoll during the gorge episode is largely imaginary, although it exhibits some of the known features of the Desmatosuchus, of which only fragmentary remains have been found in the Triassic beds of the Texas Panhandle. The giant vulture, Teratornis, and flying reptiles, Rhamphorynchus, are authentic.

A certain amount of mystery surrounds even such a well-known dinosaur as *Tyrannosaurus rex,* the largest flesh-eater ever to walk the earth. The Tyrannosaurus that battles Kong conforms to the known facts. In life the "tyrant lizard king" was about fifty feet in length and was more heavily constructed than other carnosaurs. Its skull was approximately four feet long and armed with curved, dagger-like, six-inch teeth. The hind legs were massive and possessed of tremendous strength while the forelimbs were so degenerated as to be useless. These tiny "arms" are the only part of the animal's skeletal structure not completely known and therefore have been a subject of speculation among scientists, some of whom contend that each manus held only two digits (as in the related Gorgosaurus) while others opt for three digits (as per the somewhat similar Allosaurus). O'Brien and Delgado followed the advice of the famed paleontologist Barnum Brown, who, in restoring the celebrated Tyrannosaurus at the American Museum of Natural History, gave three digits to each "hand."

Such are the fauna of Skull Island: a mixing

The lovers escape the beast momentarily

Stegosaurus in the middle distance

The Brontosaurus splashes through the foggy swamp

Emerging from the swamp, the Brontosaurus pursues a sailor

Just before the big fight

Just after the big fight. The composite scene is unfinished with Eddie Linden "sitting" in for the test

of giants from various eras of earth's history reconstructed with regard to dramatic necessity. As for the "star" of the show, Kong was purely a product of the imagination. Cooper used a giant ape as his hero because, in his words, "Dinosaurs and pterodactyls of the Jurassic Age were all right as menacing influences on our imaginary Skull Island, but they were clumsy and inhuman whereas apes are similar to man." Cooper made clear that he "had no intention of making a 'plausible' picture. In fact, I couldn't imagine anything more implausible."

The idea of an ape as large as a dinosaur may be somewhat less fantastic than it seemed at the time, inasmuch as the Leakey African expeditions have recently unearthed the remains of a baboon so large as to dwarf the largest living gorilla. Even the oversized dinosaurs, so depicted as a consequence of Cooper's oft-repeated demand to "make it bigger," have been vindicated by recent discoveries of dinosaurs in Baja, California much larger than any previously known to science. One of these is a type of trachodon more than one hundred feet in length (the maximum length of this most prolific of dinosaurs had been established as thirty-eight feet). Living prehistoric survivals have come to light in the years since *Kong* was conceived, the most spectacular example being the large Devonian bony fish *Coelacanth,* captured alive off the Madagascar coast in 1938. It must be admitted, however, that in the case of *Kong,* truth is *not* stranger than fiction.

"*King Kong* represents the goal of more than twenty years," Willis O'Brien said in 1933. "For that long a time—and that is a long time in motion pictures—I have delved into bygone periods,

The Stegosaurus enters the scene on the farthest animation table

Skull Island on glass with a "live" California beach foreground

studied the life of animals long before the descent of man, preparing myself for the day when someone would dare to reproduce on the screen the giant beasts that once ruled the world. Without knowing it, I was waiting for *King Kong.* That is the picture for which I have studied twenty years. I feel it has been worth the long years of research . . ."

David Selznick recommended to the Academy of Motion Picture Arts and Sciences that O'Brien be given a special award for his unique work on *King Kong.* O'Brien insisted that the names of eight of his key men be included in the nomination. The Academy informed Selznick that it had no intention of presenting awards for special effects work. Honours in this category were not initiated until 1940.

There is little doubt that, with Kong, O'Brien created a performance ranking with the finest characterisations of the screen. No other artificially created film monster, however skilfully executed and cleverly manoeuvred, has engendered a comparable degree of audience empathy. O'Brien's *Mighty Joe Young,* actually a better designed and more expressive giant ape, is too lovable to achieve the dramatic qualities he was able to give Kong. Such later O'Brien monsters as the titular characters of *The Black Scorpion* and *The Giant Behemoth* are horrifying enough but create little audience rapport. Spectators cannot respond so warmly to them as they can to Kong, with his many human characteristics. The same is true of the technically excellent but cold-blooded reptilian monsters of Ray Harryhausen's fantasy films such as *The Beast from 20,000 Fathoms* and *The Valley of Gwangi,* Clifford Stine's *Tarantula* and other prehistoric or legendary monsters of the movies.

The truly great hero-villains of literature and film, however mis-shapen in mind or body, have in common certain qualities above and beyond the ability to menace or terrify. We are touched by their aloneness, their frustrated longings, their foredoomed struggles against the inexorable workings of fate. The cruelties of Heathcliff, Hamlet and Long John Silver make their personal tragedies all the more poignant. The Invisible Man and Dr. Jekyll became monsters because they were trying to benefit humanity and were betrayed. Vampires and werewolves, for all their evil, are even more to be pitied than are their innocent victims, for they are condemned to everlasting torment. The Golem, the Monster of Frankenstein and the crazy-quilt Quasimodo, cut off as they are from love or companionship (or understanding, even) , inspire our sympathy rather than hatred. Even Satan, the king of all villains, was an angel before his fall from grace.

Only the most gifted actors are able to convey such complexities in a manner to evoke the desired emotional response in an audience. Such an ability made stars of William S. Hart, Lon Chaney, John Barrymore, Emil Jannings, James Cagney, Edward G. Robinson and Boris Karloff—players whose abilities transcend mere physical effectiveness. That O'Brien was able to invest a creature made of metal, rubber, glass and fur with a personality and "acting" sufficient to rival the most memorable performances of the finest character actors of the screen must be considered one of the real miracles of cinematic achievement.

The foreground glass with the artist's marks for foliage rendition in painting

The black area is on a foreground glass

Here the glass painting is almost completed and is tested for matching

Full-scale tree and foliage textures are tested for the composite

Miss Wray in a full-scale test

Walter Daniels sits for a test

Reverse angle in the finished composite

Fay Wray in the big hand in juxtaposition to the miniature Kong. Top shot

12. The King in New York

"It isn't *big* enough!" Cooper howled when he screened the first tests showing Kong in New York City. Schoedsack agreed: however awesome the gigantic gorilla appeared while fighting dinosaurs and carrying Fay Wray through the jungle, he was dwarfed by the towering stone cliffs of the big city.

Although Kong was referred to in the publicity as being fifty feet high, he was actually represented as being much smaller than that. His proportion was originally selected to provide an effective dramatic relationship between Kong and the players. That an inordinately big monster is as impersonal as a hurricane has been demonstrated by those dreadful Japanese films of the Sixties featuring a five-hundred-foot whatsit called "Godzilla." It was rightly deemed that Kong must be thought of as a personality capable of pathetic yearnings rather than as a natural disaster.

For the jungle scenes, technicians worked on a basic scale of one inch equals one foot, making Kong appear to be eighteen feet tall. For some scenes Cooper ordered the scale adjusted to suit the dramatic needs of the scene. It was his conception of the beast that he must always appear gigantic, but never so large as to destroy his interest in the human players.

"We realised we'd never get much drama out of a fly crawling up the tallest building in the world," Schoedsack says. Too much of the picture had been done to permit a new start. After much gnashing of teeth, the producers decided they would film the city scenes in a different scale, making Kong appear twenty-four feet high, and hope that audiences would be too engrossed in the action to notice.

Schoedsack and Linden went to New York City to photograph the night-effect shot of New York Harbour and the Hoboken Docks that opens the film, the early morning scene of the ship leaving the harbour, views of the Empire State Building and action involving the Navy aircraft. None of the actors made the trip, all of their city scenes being shot in the studio. Kong also did all of his New York scenes in California—in sets duplicating in miniature the streets of the city.

The night exterior of the theatre in which Kong makes his Broadway *début* is a combination of art and a busy street scene. The interiors were filmed in the old Shrine Auditorium in Los Angeles, which Schoedsack rented for one day's use. The principals acted their scenes on a stage before an audience of dress extras. Kong, photographed separately in a miniature stage, was matted in.

The leading players and the actors appearing as newspapermen are shown in the wings of the stage when Kong leaps down from the platform

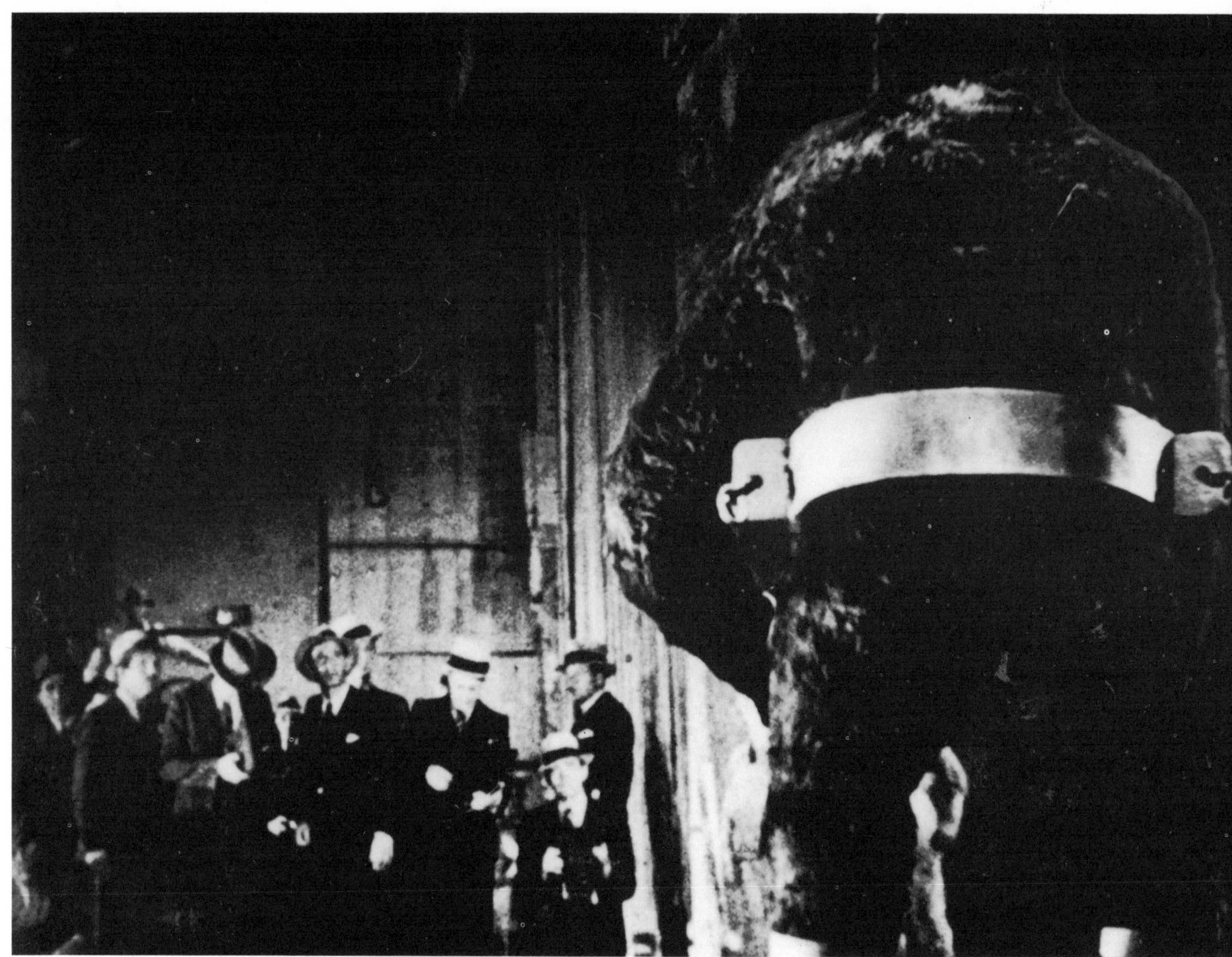

Press photographers and flashbulbs anger Kong

after breaking free. In reality, Kong was lowered in barely perceptible steps of animation. The actors were introduced through miniature projection in this and a subsequent scene wherein Kong smashes the stage door (made of thin copper for animation purposes) at the back of the theatre and emerges into the alley as the players in the background race toward a hotel across the street.

The lower level of the hotel was executed in full-scale and miniature. Miss Wray and Cabot were filmed hurrying into the lobby of the large set just as a real car crashed into the *façade* near the doors. The driver then leapt out and ran inside while the passenger—a man in evening dress—lay on the sidewalk as though stunned. The actor's next scene shows him writhing and dying between the massive jaws of the full-size head of Kong. A scene done in miniature animation, intercut between these shots, shows Kong approach the building, grab up the struggling man and bite him. After the close shot, Kong flings the man to the ground, tears off the hotel marquee and hurls it onto the fleeing crowd of extras on the street. The stampeding extras were superimposed in the foreground of the miniature shots and the full-scale marquee was dropped on them after the miniature marquee had been thrown (animated) out of the top of the frame. A masterful touch typical of Cooper-O'Brien perfectionism is the cloud of dust (superimposed) that emanates from the marquee as Kong rips it from the building.

Kong's climb up the miniature hotel building was photographed from various angles with spotlights from below providing a garish lighting effect. The beams of light were animated so they appeared to sweep over the grotesque figure of Kong.

The film's most nightmarish moment has Kong peering into a high window at a sleeping woman, then smashing his paw through another window to snatch her from her bed. The screaming woman is borne through the window, head down, and held far above the street as Kong examines her. When the monster realises that she is not Ann, he disdainfully opens his fingers and the woman falls headlong to her death. Here is the ultimate nightmare, shattering in its evocation of nocturnal terror and brutality.

Madness in the street

Above: the break away. Below: full-scale scene of the wrecked car to be reproduced in miniature

Another original concept by Crabbe changed in the film. (From the "Hollywood Reporter" presentation issue on KING KONG)

Previous pages: As Byron Crabbe saw the bedroom scene. (Drawing courtesy of Merian C. Cooper)

Kong's face which looks into the window in this and other scenes is that of one of the eighteen-inch models. The large head proved unsatisfactory for these scenes because it was too inflexible to convey the idea that the ape was hanging onto the side of the building and moving about. The unbilled actress who so effectively portrayed the victim is shown in the grasp of the huge paw both in the room and as she is held over the process background of the street. An animated figure was used for the more distant views when she is held and then dropped by Kong. Delgado's articulated giant hand released the victim convincingly in the close shot. The last part of the sequence consists of a dizzying downshot toward the spotlights below in which the kicking and shrieking woman (superimposed) plummets to her doom.

A different version, which was abandoned, had the woman talking on the telephone when the monster hand reached for her. Also not used was a scene in which Kong's appearance at a window broke up a poker game.

Kong's re-capture of Fay Wray was photographed in the same technique as the earlier scene with the unfortunate woman. Miss Wray and Cabot are shown in the room as the monster face rises into view at the window behind them and expresses recognition. The face withdraws and Kong's full-scale arm crashes in through another window. The arm is withdrawn and Kong looks in again to see Miss Wray swooning across the bed as Cabot snatches a chair as a weapon. Again the great hand is thrust into the room, tumbling Cabot, and draws the bed to the window. It lifts Fay carefully and holds her over the background

Kong at the bedroom window!

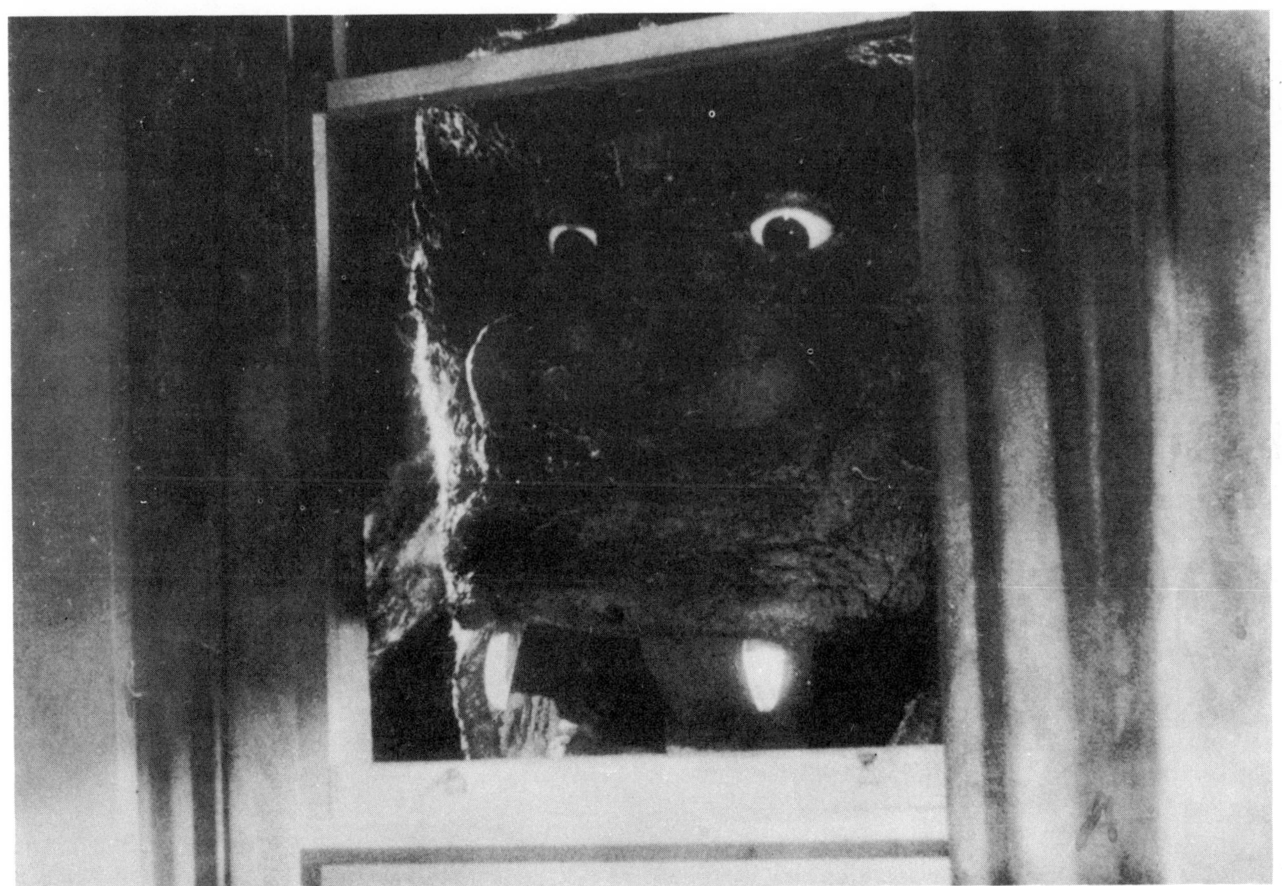

Another Crabbe concept somewhat altered in the definitive version. (From the "Hollywood Reporter" presentation issue on KING KONG)

of the distant street with its sweeping spotlights. The miniature Kong ascends, carrying the miniature girl.

Original plans called for Kong to be shown leaping from roof to roof, for which several buildings were constructed to scale. These structures, although not used as intended, are seen in the background when Kong and the girl are on the hotel roof. Miss Wray, via miniature projection, took the place of the animated figure when Kong set her down on the roof for a moment before grabbing her up again and clambering over the side. More of the buildings are shown in a reverse angle as a process background when Armstrong and Cabot appear on the roof.

"Buz" Gibson animated Kong's climb up the Empire State Building, wiring the model into position with each step of the ascent up a ladder of dowels. Kong was positioned on the side of the real edifice in two scenes and on a miniature building in others by means of the blue-backing process.

The four Navy biplanes and their pilots were obtained from Floyd Bennett Field. Schoedsack contributed $100 to the Officers' Mess fund and the pilots were detailed ". . . to cooperate with the producer of *Kong* in the making of certain scenes involving Naval aircraft in flight over New York City." The pilots each received $10 "under the table" and were so elated (this, remember, was during the Depression) they decided to do "something special" for the director to show their appreciation. Schoedsack was shooting the approach of the aircraft when he realised they were linked together by lines decorated with flags! After the decorations were jettisoned, he and Linden got good ground and aerial scenes. The latter were shot from a Curtiss-Wright Travel Air camera plane from Roosevelt Field.

The biplanes were basic training craft, Curtiss

Ready to smash the marquee

Buz Gibson starts Kong up the Empire State Building

Schoedsack (left) with his flight commander at Floyd Bennett field, planning the attack on the Empire State Building

02C-2 and Navy NY models. They were photographed flying in formation, peeling off and diving at their imaginary target then looping and attacking from the other direction. Twenty-eight scenes of the genuine aircraft were intercut with scenes filmed in miniature and in process. The commander of the flight was killed in a crash only a few weeks after he led the attack on the imaginary target.

The cityscapes seen behind Kong as he perches on the miniature mooring mast were painted in three planes of depth by the Larrinaga brothers and Crabbe. The illusion is far superior to that achieved in some test shots wherein a projected photographic background was used. The glass paintings and backing were unusually large in this instance, being about twelve feet wide. This was necessary for the staging of an unusual effect in which Kong is seen as though through the eyes of the pilots of the attacking aircraft. The camera was made to "dive" toward the madly gesticulating monster by being animated down a long wooden ramp. These are the most elaborate examples to date of animating the camera itself, an effect O'Brien pioneered more than a dozen years earlier in *The Ghost of Slumber Mountain.* The tracking ramp was about twenty-four feet long, making possible the effect of a diving approach.

The illusion of aircraft swooping around the building was difficult to achieve because of the forced perspective of the set. This made the use of model aircraft of various sizes necessary, each scale being chosen to represent a different dis-

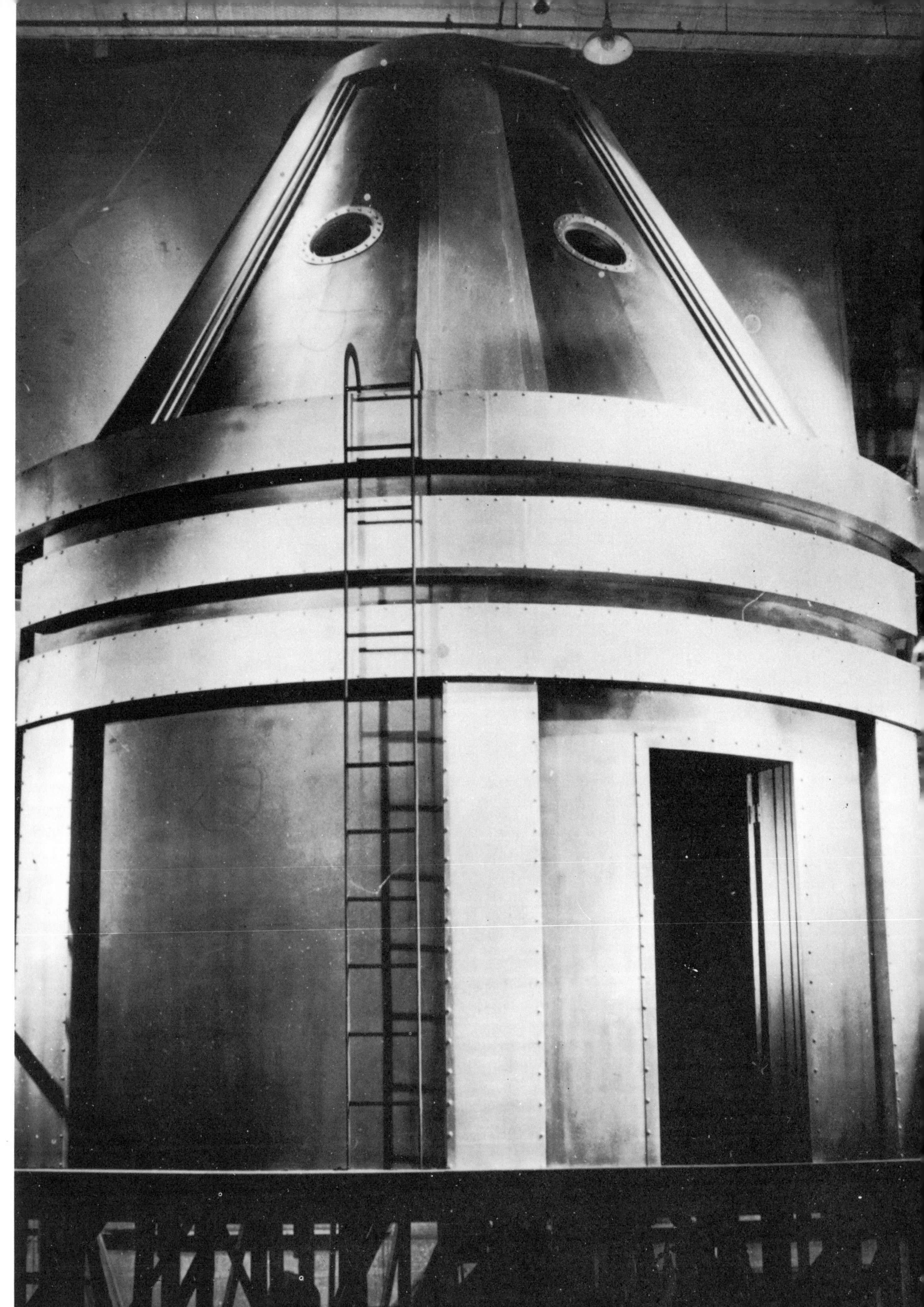

tance. The aircraft ranged in size from four inches up to about fifteen inches in wingspan. It was also necessary for Shepphird to calculate the speed at which the airplanes would appear to be moving at various simulated distances from the camera. The speed was regulated by the distance traversed with each frame exposed, i.e., if a four-inch model were moved in steps of one-quarter of an inch, a twelve-inch model would be advanced in three-quarter-inch steps, for example.

The airplanes were suspended on hair-thin piano wire stretched tightly between pulleys situated outside of camera range. The wires had to be kept taut because piano wire "kinks" if tautness is not maintained. The models moved *with* the wires rather than *along* them, the wires being weighted at the forward end and released from the other end in carefully controlled steps. To facilitate accuracy in measuring the increments of movement a hook at the control end was engaged in the mesh of quarter-inch hardware cloth (the galvanised steel wire screen used in small animal cages) with each step forward. This method was also used in animating birds in the jungle scenes.

While the airplane sequence was being planned, Cooper invited one of the animators to join him at lunch. When they were eating, Cooper asked: "Can you do a peel-off with little airplanes behind the Empire State Building?"

The technician talked about the problems of rigging four tiny balsa aircraft and taking them smoothly through the manoeuvre in quarter-inch steps. Finally, however he told Cooper he thought he could do it, although secretly he dreaded the idea. After laying out a system and rigging for doing the scene the technician was relieved to learn that it would not be needed because Schoed-

An incomplete process shot using a studio mock-up

Full-scale top of the Building

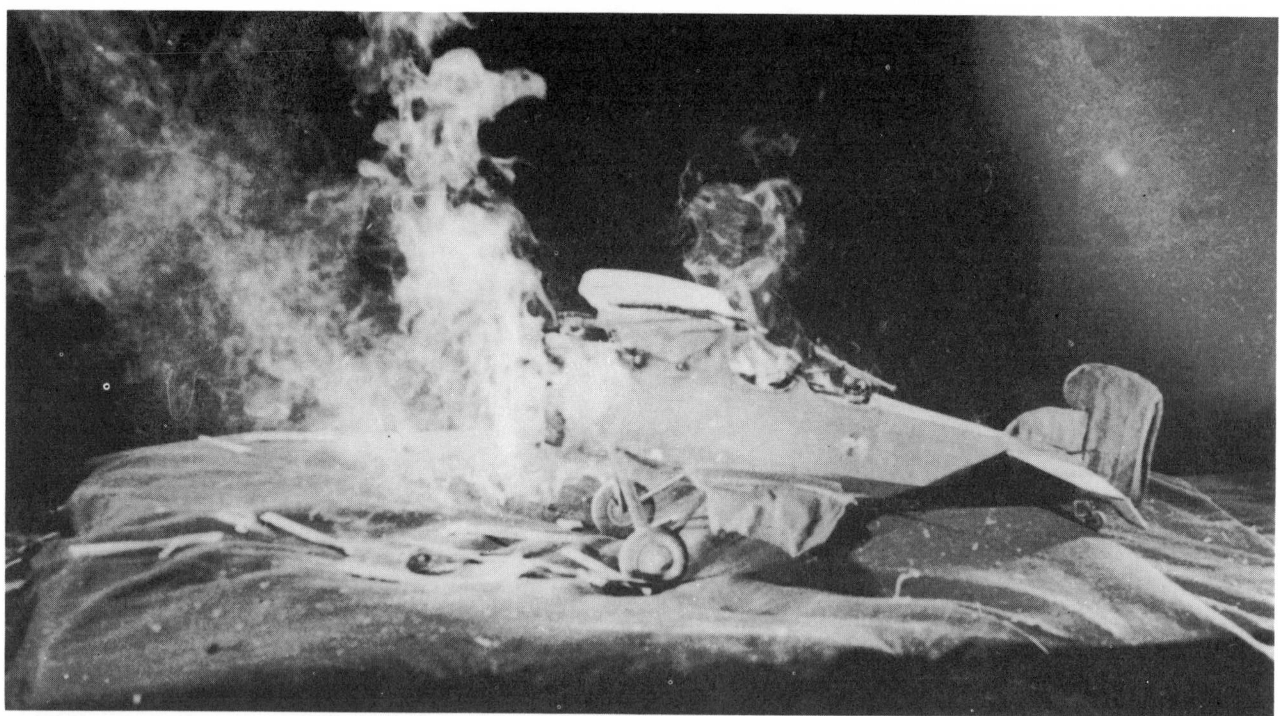

A miniature plane is crashed in flames for doubling-in

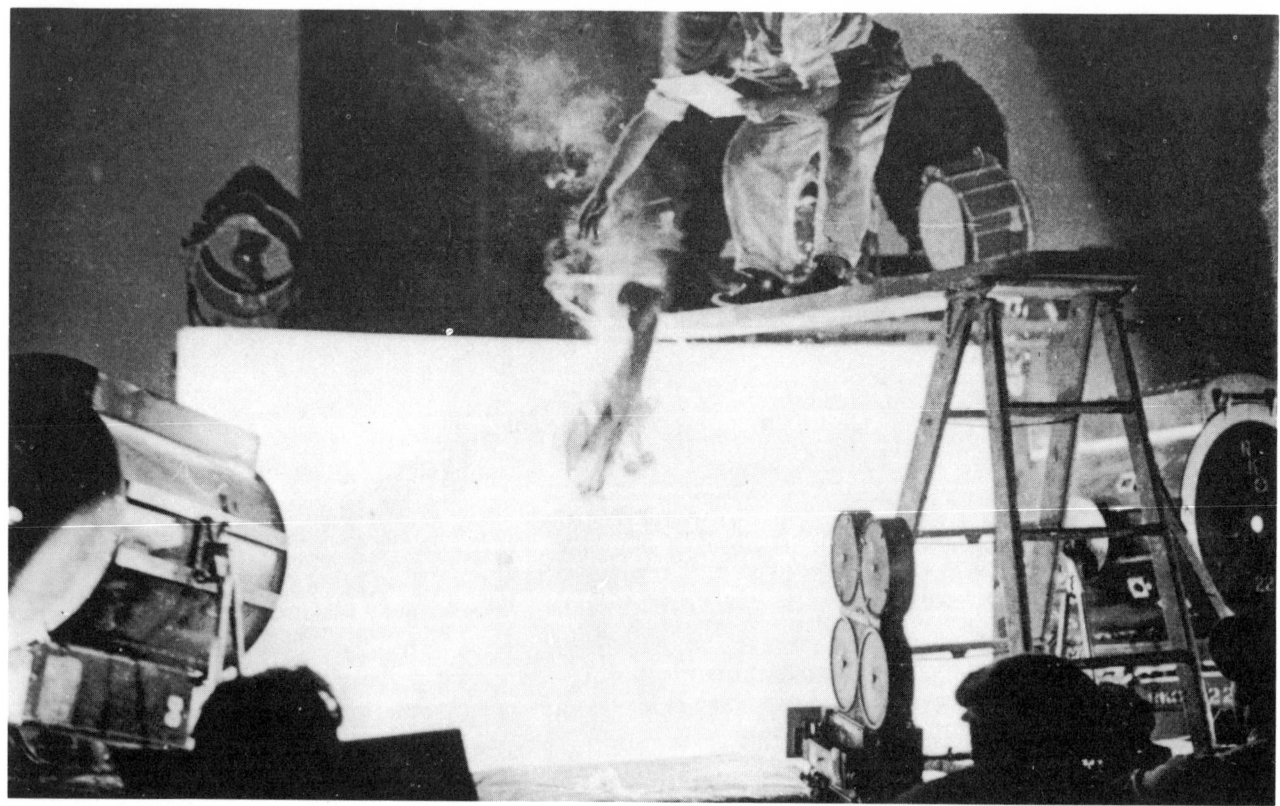

The plane lands on a pad to be saved for re-takes

At the top, with Fay Wray projected in

sack's New York footage included the peel-off shots.

The scene in which an airplane crashes down the face of the building is a composite. As "Gus" White dropped the burning model from a scaffolding past a blue backing, the falling craft was combined in the camera with a previously-made shot of the building. In this and most of the other scenes a miniature building was used, but the genuine building appears briefly in two scenes as the airplanes approach.

Fay Wray appears on a ledge of the mooring mast via miniature projection. An animated dummy substitutes for her when Kong holds her in his hand. She is also seen in the full-scale hand against a vertigo-producing process shot of the city as seen from what was then its highest elevation.

During his New York trip, Schoedsack secured details and measurements of the pinnacle of the building to guide the art department in constructing an actual-size replica. The large prop was built on a sound stage and, by mid-summer of 1932, was ready for use in filming close-ups of Miss Wray and the scenes in which Armstrong and Cabot hurry to her rescue.

Close-shots of the pilots and gunners were made at the studio with mock-up aircraft and composite backgrounds. The stalwart flight commander and his handsome chief observer in these scenes are none other than Cooper and Schoedsack, performing under Schoedsack's direction. This unusual bit of casting was the result of Cooper's remark that "We should kill the sonofabitch ourselves."

A highly dramatic version of Kong's fall from the building was filmed in composite with the body hurtling away from the camera toward the street nearly a thousand feet below. Unfortunately,

The animation as it appeared in the composite

Machine guns weaken Kong

the scene was spoiled by a "phantom image" effect —the building showed dimly through Kong's body. It was decided to use a more conventional view in which a loosely jointed dummy would plunge down the profile of the building. Because the scale model of a 102-storey building was necessarily small, the problem of camera speed appeared insuperable. Sheppird's calculations indicated that the proper degree of slow-motion required to make the fall appear sufficiently ponderous was beyond the capability of the high-speed cameras being produced at that time.

A special mounting was built to hold a Bell and Howell camera and a drive motor that were connected with a rubber hose. The plan was for the rubber hose to shear off in case the camera jammed. The set was flooded with blinding light, which was necessary to get an exposure at an abnormally high shutter speed. The motor was revved to its maximum possibility, exposing the frames of film at more than eight times the normal speed. The camera screamed as though in agony as the technicians wondered if it might be torn apart under the unnatural stresses to which it was being subjected. The dummy toppled from its perch—and the film stuck. The rubber hose failed to shear and before switches could be thrown the film accordioned in all the gates. Several camera gates were sprung and the film was crammed in so tightly that the cameramen had to cut it out of the mechanism bit by bit with a pen knife. Several days later the camera was

Overleaf: a passing shot for the final sequence

Kong falls to the street. This scene was not used

"It was beauty killed the beast"

again ready for operation and, after a few tests, the scene was successfully filmed.

In the final scene the crushed body of Kong is viewed by spectators when Armstrong appears and makes the famous closing speech. The head, arm and upper torso of the fallen giant lie in the foreground (one of the eighteen-inch models) and the crowd is seen beyond (in miniature projection). The effect is splendidly tragic.

"It's in thirteen reels," Archie Marshek said when he brought Cooper the news that Ted Cheesman had finished editing *Kong*.

"No picture of mine is going out in thirteen reels!" Cooper exclaimed. "I'll shoot an extra sequence to bring it up to fourteen reels."

"We can recut it so the reels aren't so full and make it a fourteen reeler," Marshek suggested, but Cooper was adamant in his insistence that he would add extra footage. Movie studios are notable for harbouring superstitions—there is no such thing as a sound stage 13 or a dressing room 13. Marshek believes, however, that Cooper wasn't all that superstitious. "He really wanted an excuse to film another sequence he had in mind."

O'Brien's men soon were at work on one of the most elaborate miniature sets of all, a detailed reproduction in three-fourths-inch scale of New York's elevated streetcar tracks, trains and streets. Here Cooper and O'Brien staged the memorable scenes in which Kong wrecks an elevated train just before he begins his ascent up the Empire State Building. A large number of players were used in the thirty new scenes.

The realistic buildings bear signs such as "Gibson & Co.," "Delgado Building," "Goldner's Chocolates" and the like—artist signatures on a monumental piece of work. Artists created tiny posters advertising *Chang* and "Denham's Monster" as well as building minute lighting fixtures, railings, switch boxes, mazda and neon signs, autos, fire

Miniature details. Note the "passengers"

escapes, traffic signals, trash receptacles and innumerable other details necessary for realism. Live actors, superimposed, seem to flee along the streets and watch from the windows of adjacent buildings. A man on crutches hobbles out of Kong's path. After the train crash, animated figures scramble out of coach windows and scurry to safety.

The effect of Kong as seen from the engineer's cab of the approaching train was achieved by mounting a camera and a spotlight on a dolly and moving them in stop-motion along the rails toward the rampaging monster. These scenes are so smoothly animated that many writers have assumed them to be live-action shots with an ape-suited actor appearing as Kong. While this might seem at first thought to be the logical way to accomplish the scene, in the manner of the Japanese monster films, it would have necessitated building the set four times as large as the one used in the film. The set was scaled to accommodate an eighteen-inch Kong.

J. O. Taylor's camera caught memorable scenes of panic as the extras and stunt artists tumbled about in the full-scale set of the doomed train. A number of minor injuries resulted, but the sequence is superb.

Neither Cooper nor his superiors were satisfied with the fourteen-reel version. It was too long to suit the New York office as there was at that time a virtual tabu on features running more than one hundred minutes. There were too many lapses of pace to please Cooper, who joined Ted Cheesman in the cutting room and, after much sweating and cursing, emerged with a feature of eleven reels. Even the credit titles were shortened considerably before the film was considered ready for public view. The final cut consists of 846

More miniature details. Holes in the "street" show where Kong will work

Reverse angle. As Kong sees the elevated

scenes, eleven art titles, twenty-three dissolves and nine in-out fades.

Gone were several of Delgado's best monsters—the Triceratops, the Arsinoitherium, the Styracosaurus and "the great crawling things of the pit." Gone was the journey of Ann and Jack down the river and Kong climbing down the side of Skull Mountain, roaring in frustration and rage. Gone were numerous bits-of-business and gags and snips of dialogue—painful but necessary sacrifices.

O'Brien and his men, as they viewed the final release version, mourned the hundreds of man-hours lost. The *cinéphile* may well shed a tear for the *intrinsic* value of what was thrown away, just as he must regret the loss of *Creation* and Schoedsack's "natural drama" version of *The Lives of a Bengal Lancer* and the Abyssinian films of 1923 that would have become the first Cooper-Schoedsack production but for the burning of the ship "Wisdom II." Here, indeed, is a classic example of the spilled milk one mustn't cry over.

For Cooper was right, of course. He set his jaw and cut his own ideas with a ruthlessness that must have given him nightmares. In doing this he delivered to the public a movie that holds the attention during every one of its scenes, each second of its one-hundred minutes. It is one of the few films that builds its suspense deliberately and then holds it until the last fade-out because there is no useless action, no waste of words, no side-plots to detract from the main stream of the story it tells—a show without fat or padding. Cooper's skill as an editor is no less remarkable than any of his other accomplishments.

How the elevated was photographed

Kong waits for the train

Schoedsack did not participate in the editing or post-production work on *Kong,* having been sent to the Syrian Desert in December to film backgrounds for a proposed film story by Philip MacDonald, *Arabia.* When he returned, in mid-February of 1933, important changes had taken place at the studio.*

* The Arabian film, later scheduled as *The Uncrowned King* and *A Fugitive from Glory,* was intended as a starring vehicle for John Barrymore. It was never completed, although some of the expedition footage eventually was used in a 1943 release, *Action in Arabia.*

David Selznick, disturbed by increasing interference from the New York office, had announced his resignation on February 3 and accepted a position at Metro-Goldwyn-Mayer. Merian Cooper was named as Selznick's successor.

The studio heads never had liked the title of the Cooper-Schoedsack production. *Kong,* they believed, sounded too much like *Chang* and *Rango;* the public might mistake it for another expeditionary film. Selznick, in one of his last executive acts before leaving RKO, provided the final title for the forthcoming release: *King Kong.*

13. The Finishing Touches

Murray Spivack, RKO's thirty-one year old director of sound effects, had prepared on July 19, 1932, a cost estimate for his department's contributions to Production 601, which had just been re-titled *Kong*. With only a hazy idea of how some of the effects could be accomplished (the "talkie" era not having previously brought forth anything comparable), Spivack studied the script and itemised the unusual sounds he was expected to provide. His notes reveal a great deal about the concept of the film at that stage of production.*

All sound effects were added after filming was completed, including Fay Wray's celebrated screams, which were recorded in one session and dubbed in where they were needed.

"*Kong* presented many problems," Spivack says. "I worked on it for about nine months and we had to come up with a lot of new ideas. Sound equipment was very limited then, although we no longer had to record music, effects and dialogue all at the same time the way we did a couple of years earlier."

In his native New York City Spivack had been percussionist in a symphonic orchestra that specialised in recording music for silent pictures. The group was made up of first-chair musicians from the best symphony orchestras in the East and its conductors included Hugo Riesenfeld, Erno Rapée, David Mendoza and Josiah Zuro. Spivack says this all-star orchestra had one flaw:

"In the strings we had sixteen concert masters and this caused us a lot of trouble because they were individuals rather than ensemble players." Spivack's recognition of the desirability of proper ensemble work makes his soundtracks distinctive. To date his work has earned for various studios eight "Oscars" and fourteen Academy nominations.

He entered the infant sound-film recording field in New York and in 1929 came to Los Angeles as recording technician and assistant musical director for Film Booking Offices (FBO Pictures), which shortly after became RKO-Radio. The studio used the Richard Dix film *Seven Keys to Baldpate* as a testing ground for sound effects and Spivack created wind and thunder effects that were considered sensational at the time.

The creation of a voice for Kong was a unique task because nothing like it had been attempted before. The sound department had amassed a library of sounds made by living animals comprising about 500,000 feet of roars, barks, growls, snarls and hisses. Spivack knew that any of these sounds would be too familiar as well as too brief for a monster of Kong's proportions. Even an elephant's roar lasts only eight or nine seconds,

* See Appendix 9.

whereas Kong was shown silently roaring for as long as thirty seconds at a time.

"I went to the Selig Zoo and arranged to record some lion and tiger roars at feeding time," Spivack recalls. "The handlers would make gestures as though they were going to take the food away from them and we got some pretty wild sounds. Then I took some of these roars back to the studio and put them together and played them backward. I slowed them down, sort of like playing a 78 r.p.m. record at 33, until the tone was lowered one octave, then I re-recorded it. From this we took the peaks and pieced them together. We had to put several of these together in turn to sustain the sound until Kong shut his mouth, because Kong's roars were many times longer than those of any living animal. Then we added a sound tail to the end so it would die down naturally instead of coming to an abrupt stop. That's how I conceived the roar of Kong."

There was no precedent to guide the sounds made by Kong when he tried to express his affection for Fay Wray. For these scenes the voice of Kong was that of Spivack, who uttered low, gutteral grunts of varying duration into a megaphone. By slowing the track and re-recording it, he achieved a depth of tone suitable for a simian seven times as tall as a living gorilla.

"I wrote to the curator at the Lincoln Park Zoo in Chicago and asked for advice regarding the voices of dinosaurs," Spivack says. "When the reply came I had to translate his scientific language into English. It seemed to be saying, 'You fool! Those animals didn't have vocal chords and therefore they didn't have voices.' Well, I couldn't tell that to Mr. Cooper. We couldn't show a fifty-foot-long monster and not have it roar—it would be laughed off the screen!"

Dr. J. W. Lytle, curator of vertebrate paleontology at the Los Angeles County Museum, told him that various degrees of hissing sounds would be appropriate for the dinosaurs. Because the brontosaurus was amphibious, Spivack added some croaking sounds to the reptilian hisses of the gigantic sauropod.

"For the screeches of the tyrannosaurus I made most of the sounds with my mouth and then slowed the track down," Spivack says. "Most of the animal cries were made this way. The pterodactyl squawks were those of some bird—I forget which kind—which were slowed 'way down for depth. Almost all of our animal sounds were slowed down because we wanted a 'big' sound."

The heavy breathing of the monsters was sometimes simulated by use of a bellows. Compressed air and unusual noises such as a panther's purr were combined in certain instances with the voice of Spivack or of his assistant, Walter G. Elliott. The bellowing of the triceratops was simulated by grunting and growling through a double gourd. The death-rattle of the dying tyrannosaurus was recorded as Elliott, with a mouthful of water, gurgled through a megaphone.

"The sound of Kong beating his breast proved to be one of our most difficult problems," Spivack says. "I simulated that by hitting Elliott on the chest with a tymp-stick while an assistant held a microphone to Elliott's back. Kong's footsteps were made by walking plumber's friends covered with sponge rubber across gravel and recording the sound with plenty of bass.

"We had trouble with gunshots in those days because the loud noise would sort of 'paralyse' the mike. A lot of sound men had to simulate them with slapsticks. I discovered I could record real shots by using a .22 bullet and removing half of the powder. In *Kong,* the rifle shots are real."

"When we were doing the train sequence I had such a confusion of sounds the noise was terrific. When Cooper saw it he said, 'Murray, there's a car going by; he should honk his horn.' We only had three tracks at the studio then—one for dialogue, one for music and one for effects—which is pretty primitive when you consider that I had 77 channels in the parade sequence of *Hello, Dolly!* Our equipment was so limited that if we needed additional sounds we had to go through another generation of recording. I told him it would lower the quality of the recording. He got mad. I said, 'Be sensible, Merian; you couldn't hear a car horn in all that noise if we did it.' He insisted he wanted it. Pretty soon we were shouting at each other, and right in the worst part of it I started to laugh. He looked surprised and asked, 'What are you laughing at?' I told him, 'Do you know that when you get mad your forehead turns a bright red?' He started laughing then and finally he said, 'Okay, have it your way,' and left."

Working closely with the musical director,

Rampaging through the native village

Spivack developed an unusual "first" for *Kong*: the harmonising of sound effects with music. After the score had been prepared the sound effects were altered in pitch to conform to the music. This unprecedented technique made bearable the almost uninterrupted cacophony of roars, shrieks, crashes and thunderous music heard during the last two-thirds of the movie. Murray Spivack spared millions of moviegoers from headaches when he conceived this idea.

The head of RKO's music department was an energetic little Austrian whose father and grandfather were the biggest impresarios in Vienna. Richard Strauss was his godfather and his youth was spent in the company of Jacques Offenbach, Johann Strauss and Gustav Mahler. A musical career was inevitable for a man with such a heritage and a name like Maximilian Raoul Walter Steiner.

The musical world took note of Max Steiner when, at the age of fifteen, he won the Emperor's Gold Medal for completing the four-year course of study at the Imperial Academy of Music in one year. The following year he was conducting "The Beautiful Greek Girl," an operetta composed by himself, which ran for a year at Vienna's Orpheum Theatre. Several of his compositions were published and a symphonic suite was performed by the Vienna Philharmonic. In 1906, at the age of eighteen, he went to England, where he established himself as a composer, concert pianist and conductor of the 110-man orchestra of the London Opera House.

In 1914, he was declared an enemy alien and subject to deportation. Through the intervention of the Duke of Westminster he was able to go to America. He practically starved during his first weeks in New York City, but in a surprisingly short time he rose from vaudeville pianist to orchestrator and conductor for the chain of theatres owned by William Fox. During the next fourteen years he orchestrated and conducted for the "Ziegfeld Follies," "George White's Scandals," and shows by Victor Herbert, Jerome Kern, George Gershwin, Harry Tierney and Vincent Youmans.

While he was conducting Jack Donohue's "Sons O' Guns" in Boston, Steiner was approached by William LeBaron, then production chief of RKO, who wanted him to come to work at the studio at $450 per week. Steiner arrived at RKO in 1929 and orchestrated Tierney's music for the film version of *Rio Rita* and another musical, *Dixiana*.

Studios at that time were steering away from background music because of recording problems and a prevailing theory that dramatic scoring was a *passé* hangover from non-dialogue films. Nevertheless, when the spectacular *Cimarron* was filmed, LeBaron decided an impressive score was needed. W. Franke Harling was supposed to do the music, but was occupied at Paramount and couldn't accept. Steiner, as musical director, was instructed to hire a "name" composer for the film, which was scheduled to open in four weeks. Accordingly, he approached George Gershwin, Leopold Stokowski and Percy Grainger, all of whom asked for a year's time and from $250,000 to $350,000 to do the job. Steiner composed the music eventually and his work was so highly praised by reviewers that he was given a raise of $50-per-week.

By 1932 Steiner made innovations in film scoring that gave RKO's soundtracks a distinctive sound. He liked to use leit-motifs for the major characters somewhat in the manner of Wagnerian opera. His most unusual practice was the accenting and enhancing of film visuals with music cues, underscoring each bit of action instead of providing merely an overall mood for scenes or sequences. While there are many who express distaste for this approach (known derisively as "mickey-mousing"), several important films would doubtless have been far less impressive without the dramatic emphasis provided by Steiner's intricately conceived scores.

RKO President B. B. Kahane had his doubts about *Kong* and was sceptical that the public would accept an animated ape as a film hero. "We've spent so much money in the year-and-a-half we've worked on it, so please don't spend any additional money on music," he told Steiner, instructing him to put together some music from existing tracks. Steiner was disappointed, because he saw tremendous musical possibilities in *Kong*. Cooper, realising that proper scoring would lend a greater semblance of life to the animation, told Steiner to get an original score under way. "Don't worry about the cost because I'll pay for the orchestra or any extra charges," Cooper said. Steiner set to work with enthusiasm and the close collaboration of Cooper and Spivack.

"Maxie, that music isn't right for *Kong*," Cooper said when he heard part of the proposed music. "It sounds too much like something out of a Broadway stage show." Steiner, appalled, replied that he didn't understand what Cooper wanted. "I mean that we can't use that damned stage music for this picture," Cooper said. "This is a movie. Now I don't know anything about music, but I do know we need movie music, not stage music. That stuff might be all right for those pictures everybody's making where the camera's in an icebox and everybody is standing around in those little sets, but this picture is made out in the open with the camera moving."

It was true that Cooper knew what he wanted, and he spent many hours consulting with the composer during the eight weeks the score was being written. Steiner has said, "I write what I see on the screen," and he became excited by what he saw in *Kong*. He timed each scene with a stop-watch so that his musical phrases would complement each nuance of action. He worked day and night, until he was near collapse. Finally, he conducted an eighty-man orchestra for the music track, which was recorded by Spivack. The music added $50,000 to the budget, and a good investment it was, for no wedding of music, sound effects and pictures has ever produced a more stunning offspring. Cooper arranged a bonus for Steiner, stating that 25 percent of the effectiveness of the film could be credited to the music.

It is difficult to imagine such an impassioned, often dissonant, hair-raising score coming from the genial composer of "The Beautiful Greek Girl." Steiner called it one of his few "modernistic" scores and said that it "worried" some of his friends in Vienna and America but won him new admirers in France and Russia.

The music is built largely upon three motifs: "King Kong," a descending three-note figure that is the leitmotif of the title character; "Jungle Dance," which symbolises the natives of Skull

Island; and "Stolen Love," a plaintive melody used to suggest the "beauty and the beast" longing of Kong for Ann. These themes are paraphrased and deployed throughout the film in numerous variations. Among other compositions are "The Forgotten Island," "A Boat in the Fog" and "Sea at Night," all of which have about them a suggestion of Debussy tone poems. "The Sailors," introduced as a march as the men plod through the jungle, is developed as exciting chase music during several episodes. "Aboriginal Sacrifice Dance," scored for orchestra and male chorus, is played during the first native ceremony. Kong's arrival on Broadway is heralded by the "King Kong March," which is done in the style of a theatrical overture.

Music is present through most of the film, the exceptions being during the New York and shipboard scenes prior to the arrival at the island, the fight with the Tyrannosaurus (which is so filled with furious sounds as to make music superfluous) and the battle with the airplanes.

The earnestness of Steiner is transmitted to the subconsciousness of the viewer, contributing immeasurably to the suspension of audience disbelief in an entirely fantastic tale. The precise conformity of the music to the flow of images results in a unity seldom achieved in the combining of visual and sound arts. The growing love of Ann and Jack is emphasised by waltz-like string passages in a lush Romantic style, the mystery of an uncharted sea by softly ominous chords with the disturbing rhythm of distant drums in the background, the frantic terror of pursuit by cyclopean giants by *scherzi* calculated to accelerate the beating of one's heart. Music accompanying the native ceremonies conveys the frenzy of barbaric religious passion.

It is in the delineation of the complex emotions and personality of Kong, himself, that the music achieves its greatest expressiveness. His savage brutality is accented by brassy, dissonant variations on the King Kong theme. The "Stolen Love" motif subtly underlines the tragic side of his nature, portraying his loneliness and the painful bewilderment inherent in unrequited love. This theme is developed to its apogee of power and finally resolved in the finale as Kong mutely bids Ann farewell and gives himself up to the sacrifice that was, from the beginning, inevitable. It would be difficult to overestimate Steiner's share in creating a classic tragic figure from what could have been just another monster.

Four selections were published as sheet music by Sam Fox Music Company: "The Forgotten Island," "A Boat in the Fog," "Aboriginal Sacrifice Dance" and "King Kong March." A concert suite comprising the main themes was published and recorded much later.

All this music proved extremely durable and was used by Steiner's successors at RKO—Roy Webb, Nathaniel Shilkret and Constantine Bakaleinikoff—for dozens of subsequent features and innumerable editions of *RKO-Pathe News.* Among the soundtracks containing sizeable chunks of the Kong music are *The Last Days of Pompeii, The Last of the Mohicans, Muss 'Em Up, We're Only Human, Back to Bataan, and Michael Strogoff*. Steiner, himself, reprised portions of this material in several of his much later works for Warner Brothers. "A Boat in the Fog" builds suspense as admirably for Bette Davis in *A Stolen Life* as it did for the passengers on the "S. S. Venture" fourteen years earlier. Shortly before his death, in 1972, Steiner said that *King Kong* was one of his personal favourites.

The late Oscar Levant, who was employed by RKO at the time *King Kong* was produced, said of this score:

"Full of weird chords, strident background noises, rumblings and heavings, it was one of the most enthusiastically written scores ever to be composed in Hollywood. Indeed, it was always my feeling that it should have been advertised as a concert of Steiner's music with accompanying pictures on the screen."

By March 1933, *King Kong* was ready to be shown to the exhibitors. Insiders predicted it would be a sensation and even the die-hard dissenters in New York gave in, authorising preparation of the biggest selling campaign in the studio's history. A large, garishly coloured press book contained a message to exhibitors that is worthy of preservation:

"Into a show-world grown weary of namby pamby plots stalks the gigantic figure of KONG! The very name conjures up visions of a realm crowded with strange sights! If ever there was a show sired by the spirit of P. T. Barnum it's this Hippodrome of thrills and daring adventure staged in the Arena of Earth's creation. KING KONG comes like a gift from a showman's heaven . . . a picture . . . big . . . original . . . startling . . . to blast away with its dramatic dynamite the lethargy that now holds show business in its grip! For the first time in months comes a SHOWMAN'S PICTURE . . ."

The national magazine ads, featuring Mario Larrinaga's drawing of the Empire State Building climax, used only one line: THE PICTURE DESTINED TO STARTLE THE WORLD!

S. L. "Roxy" Rothafel, impresario of New York's two largest theatres, Radio City Music Hall and the New Roxy, knew an audience-grabber when he saw it. Against the advice of his associates he decided on an unprecedented plan: he would open the film at both houses (total seating, ten thousand) on the same day. A large newspaper ad heralded the event on opening day, March 2, and included a description of the accompanying stage presentations:

"JUNGLE RHYTHMS—brilliant musical production. Entire singing and dancing ensemble of Music Hall and New Roxy—Spectacular dance rhythms by ballet corps and Roxyettes—Soloists—Chorus—Symphony Orchestras—Company of 500 —Novel features."

Even with tickets selling at Depression prices, Roxy's gamble paid off handsomely. Crowds queued up four abreast at both theatres and in the first four days of its run *King Kong* set a new all-time world attendance record for any indoor attraction, bringing in $89,931 in hard-earned coin. To accommodate the crowds it was necessary to run ten shows daily. "Ten thousand seats weren't enough," Rothafel reported joyously.

Sid Grauman, the West Coast's answer to "Roxy," was not to be outdone, although he had to wait until March 24 to stage the official *première* in Hollywood at the Chinese Theatre. A special *King Kong* edition of "The Hollywood Reporter" announced the coming event on March 6 with a unique twenty-eight-page insert printed in four colours on two kinds of heavy stock with parchment end sheets and covers stamped from pure sheet copper. The layout was by Keye Luke, the Chinese artist-actor.

"This is a Grauman opening in the full sense of the word," Louella Parsons reported in the Los Angeles "Examiner." First-nighters had plenty to gape at; in addition to the customary spotlights and celebrity interviews, the life-size head and shoulders of Kong greeted the patrons in the forecourt. On stage, Jimmy Savo hosted a spectacular prologue that included a fifty-voice African choral ensemble and a dance troupe of black girls performing "The Dance to the Sacred Ape" and sixteen other musical numbers. Reviewers on both coasts were extravagant with praise for the film.

National release followed on April 10. The resulting flood of badly needed money brought a temporary end to RKO's financial problems, lifting the studio out of debt for the first time.

"We brought that picture in for only $430,000," Cooper revealed later. "That was the actual cost, but those bookkeepers tacked on the cost of *Creation* and a lot of so-called 'overhead.' The 'official' cost was $650,000."

A commanding view of the city

III. Postlude

"So great is its impact that I venture to predict it will not be forgotten even in 1960—destined to become a living legend, part and parcel of American filmlore . . ."
—Lloyd Arthur Ashbuck, 1933

"If we'd had a percentage deal we wouldn't be such nice people. We'd be rich."
—Fay Wray, 1973

14. The Inevitable Sequel

By the time *King Kong* made its New York *début* Selznick had departed from RKO and Cooper had reorganised many of the studio departments and was busily living up to a vow that he would have eleven features under way by April 15. Early in March, Cooper announced that one of the pictures already started was *Jamboree,* which would be filmed under strict security. Schoedsack's Arabian film was announced for a later date for completion in the studio and on desert locations near Yuma. Of the mysterious *Jamboree,* Cooper would reveal nothing except that "it will be produced on the same elaborate scale that attended the making of *King Kong,*" and that it was "well under way" with Schoedsack directing from a script by his wife.

"We called it *Jamboree* to keep people from visiting the set," Schoedsack says. "If they'd known we were making another Kong picture they'd have driven us crazy trying to find out how it was done." The film, of course, was *The Son of Kong,* the inevitable sequel to a hit film. Cooper had approached the New York office with the idea and was told to "go ahead with it and make it even bigger." His enthusiasm was dampened somewhat when he learned the budget would be $250,000.

"It was a case of 'if you can't make it bigger you'd better make it funnier,'" says Ruth Rose, borrowing an old Broadway axiom. To combat budget restrictions Cooper arranged royalties for key personnel in lieu of part of their salaries. Filming was done at the Radio lot, at the nearby Warner Ranch, at sea and on Santa Catalina Island. Most of the production crew of *King Kong* worked on it. Shooting was completed in October.

The Son of Kong has suffered the fate of most sequels: virtual eclipse in the shadow of a bigger and more exciting predecessor. Certainly it cannot compete in terms of spectacle or horror, but it is a fascinating creation in its own right and provides some interesting footnotes to the original. More importantly, it provided director and crew with an opportunity to polish and improve their pioneering techniques. The animation compares favourably to that of *King Kong* and the composite work, in which an improved double-matting process was used, is considerably better.

Also superior are some of the characterisations, particularly in the instance of Denham, as played again by Armstrong. The Denham of *King Kong* was a strong but only semi-sympathetic individual who could tell a hungry waif, "I'm not bothering with you just out of kindness." There is much more to the character than could be brought forth in a single picture and additional facets of his personality are more fully explored in the sequel.

"For me, personally, the role was better than

SON OF KONG. The ape expresses concern over his wounded finger

SON OF KONG. Denham bandages Kong's finger. Miniature ape in foreground, miniature background with full-size arm and players projected

before," Armstrong said. "It gave me a great deal more character, swell dialogue and love scenes. Denham was a character audiences could identify me with; many actors work all their lives without getting that."

Reicher, Wong, Johnson and Clemente were also retained to re-create their original roles. In the cases of Reicher and Wong the roles were expanded considerably (Wong's role again was added after the completion of the official shooting script). Johnson and Clemente appear only briefly because some planned action involving the natives was eliminated.

Armstrong's leading lady, Helen Mack, is appealing as a typical Ruth Rose heroine not unlike Ann Darrow. Human villainy is represented by the most cowardly, snivelling blackguard imaginable, as portrayed by John Marston, and a mutinous crew led by Ed Brady as a surly Marxist.

The titular character is a wholly sympathetic monster despite his awesome potential for destruction. Scaled to appear twelve feet high, the young Kong has blond hair and a remarkably expressive countenance. As apes will do, he often imitates the actions of his human companions with amusing results. He is, however, suitably ferocious when the occasion demands. The hair is virtually free of the unwanted animation that plagued the animators of Kong Sr.

Three baby Kongs were constructed over the skeletons of original Kongs. Close-ups were made without the use of a large mechanical head but the articulated Kong hand, re-designed in some particulars, is shown in two key sequences. Schoedsack used a similarly designed *human* hand in his *Dr. Cyclops* in 1939. The voice of Kong Jr.

SON OF KONG. The fight with the cave bear

was built upon the chattering of baby gorillas recorded at the San Diego Municipal Zoo. The roar of the ape as he fought a giant bear and a dragon was taken from the battle cries of tigers and elephants that were combined, played backward and slowed down to achieve depth of tone.

Except for the Brontosaurus, which surfaces briefly, the monsters are new. The Styracosaurus which failed previously to survive the cutting room belatedly appears, with smoother animation than that accorded the quadrupeds of the earlier work. A bear, scaled to appear fifteen feet tall when standing on his hind legs, chases Denham and the girl, tumbles and shakes his head when stunned by a shotgun blast and engages in a rough-house battle with the ape. Because bears are both frightening and comical he is an ideal foil for a fight sequence played equally for thrills and laughs. A dragon-like reptile, created by Delgado to O'Brien's order to "build something nobody has ever seen before," is the ape's opponent in another fight. This singularly evil-looking monstrosity has large, clear eyes that appear almost luminescent. A sea monster, another Delgado original, is the film's most terrifying denizen and appears in four shots wherein he rises from the depths to devour the villain. Except for a hair-raising animated close-up this monster was operated mechanically exactly as the brontosaurus was handled in *King Kong*.

Miniature rear-projection was used extensively to place Armstrong and Miss Mack in scenes with the ape and in a sequence in which players are pursued and cornered by the styracosaurus. A nine-inch animated figure of Armstrong was used to make it possible for Kong to lift Denham to safety from a collapsing cave, for scenes of Denham and the ape climbing up Skull Mountain as it sinks into the sea, and for the long shots of Kong holding Denham above the water at the climax.

Marston is shown in composite with the sea monster as it rises from the water. The snake-necked creature is then shown from a different angle seizing a miniature dummy which it shakes in a terrier-rat manner before dragging it under. The earthquake that destroys the island, as accomplished in a combination of miniature and full-scale work, is an exciting spectacle although the schedule did not permit O'Brien to stage the

SON OF KONG. Animated close-up of the sea monster

stampede of dinosaurs envisioned by the script. Some unusual composite work was necessitated by scenes in which the animated figures of Kong and Denham are seen in the same frames with raging ocean waters, landslides and rain.

The Pathé lot was sold shortly after production was started, obliging Schoedsack to find a new jungle for the full-scale shots, hence the location work at Catalina. The Larrinaga-Crabbe glass art and the malevolently detailed miniature jungles are as intricately beautiful as those of the original. The native village is kept in the distance (glass art). A vast cave temple containing a gigantic idol is an impressive miniature set.

Steiner's score is apparently the first done in the style he used a decade later for *Casablanca* and which film composers designate as "the *Casablanca* technique." Dramatic variations are worked out from the melody of a plaintive song called "Runaway Blues," which Helen Mack introduces early in the film. The paraphrased theme is especially effective in a sequence involving a murder and fire, and also during the fight with the bear, each instance being a remarkable example of what a skilled composer can develop from simple

SON OF KONG. Players in lifeboat during storm sequence, filmed in front of a blue backing. Turbulent background of water and falling boulders will be introduced via the Williams travelling matte process

SON OF KONG. Helen Mack, Robert Armstrong, and Little Kong in the lost temple

SON OF KONG. Robert Armstrong, projected, with the eighteen-inch-high Little Kong

SON OF KONG. Little Kong in quicksand, with Robert Armstrong and Helen Mack introduced via projection behind miniature tree. Rippling water in foreground is matted in

thematic matter. The lyrics are by Edward Eliscu, author-producer-actor, whose songs include "More Than You Know," "Without a Song," "Flying Down to Rio," "Orchids in the Moonlight" and "The Carioca." A three-note theme for Kong Jr. is used extensively and key themes from *King Kong* are woven into certain scenes. There are many humorous touches, such as a quotation from the traditional Hebrew *Mazeltof* when Kong Jr. makes a gesture associated with Old World Jewry.

The Son of Kong is rather slow in getting under way. Again all story elements are established early so there will be no interruption once the action starts. The ship arrives at the island at about the halfway point.

The first half contains an outstanding sequence which Schoedsack staged with consummate skill. It depicts the striking down of the girl's drunken father by the villain, the subsequent fire that destroys the show tent in which the victim and his daughter live, the freeing of the endangered monkeys and seals by the girl and her desperate attempt to rescue the dying man. The camera moves along beside the girl through the blazing rooms as, kicking obstructions from her path, she drags the unconscious man into the open, then hurries back to retrieve her dress and wardrobe trunk seconds before the tent collapses. Steiner's emotion-charged music, Miss Mack's intense performance and Schoedsack's attention to detail and adroit use of the camera to take the spectator into the scene add up to a highly dramatic episode. The action was filmed quickly and without mishap on the Warner Ranch, near Hollywood.

Equally remarkable is an unusually long scene in which the camera follows the players and their lifeboat through a narrow channel between towering miniature cliffs. Flawlessly executed in composite using a method devised by Schoedsack, the scene betrays no sign of fakery. The effect is repeated with the addition of storm effects as the boat is shown retreating through the same passage, now buffeted by water turbulence as boulders splash into the sea.

O'Brien provided a number of those extra touches that distinguish his work from that of any other man in his field. Water ripples around the quicksand in which the ape is caught. A bubbling spring and running stream are included in the scenes showing the Styracosaurus. Animated birds fly across the foreground in some shots and flit among distant branches in others.

More than one hundred and fifty off-stage workers were required for the production. The location shots of the five principals at sea and on Catalina required the services of the director, three assistants, eight grips and property men, two labourers, seven sound recordists, eight electricians, two wardrobe women, one script girl, three cameramen, a makeup artist, a hair dresser, a doctor, two carpenters, two horticulturists, and twenty sailors. Schoedsack recalled with nostalgia the days when he and Cooper worked alone in the jungles of Asia.

The Son of Kong was profitable in the United States, but it was in the foreign market that it really paid off. It did especially well in the Orient and in Malaysia, being one of the few Hollywood-made films depicting that part of the world that looked sufficiently authentic to be accepted there.

O'Brien is said to have been unhappy with the "tongue-in-cheek" approach to *The Son of Kong* and was reluctant to discuss it in later years.

SON OF KONG. A monster enters the temple

15. Remember Cavalcade?

King Kong's most celebrated set, the Great Wall, saw further use in several other films before it went out (literally!) in a blaze of glory.

Pathé was sold in April 1933, to a syndicate that rented its facilities to independent producers. Through the use of Pathe's excellent sets, stages, properties and equipment, small companies such as Sol Lesser's Principal Productions, Nat Levine's Mascot Pictures, Edward Small's Reliance Pictures and George R. Batchellor's Invincible-Chesterfield Corporation were able to achieve a major studio "look" in their films.

Lesser's Bela Lugosi serial, *The Return of Chandu,* which was filmed at Pathe during the Summer of 1934, made good use of what remained of Skull Island, now represented as the legendary island of Lemuria. Each of the twelve episodes opened with a Lemurian striking the very gong with which Noble Johnson had summoned Kong to the sacrifice. There was much action shot around the wall and in the village.

Cooper returned the following year to borrow the wall for his spectacular independent production for RKO, *She,* wherein the re-dressed set may be seen as the entrance to a legendary palace carved from the heart of a Siberian mountain.

Selznick leased Pathé in 1936 as the home of Selznick-International Pictures and during the next dozen years produced his most famous films there.

The great wall expired in a spectacular manner on December 10, 1938, when special effects expert Lee Zavitz staged the burning of Atlanta for Selznick's *magnum opus, Gone with the Wind.* Suitably camouflaged to resemble background buildings, the wall was laced with pipes through which was fed to atomizers a mixture of twenty percent rock gas and eighty percent distillate. The fuel flow was controlled electrically from a pumping station that permitted all atomizers to be turned on or off instantly. Another control fed a flow of oil or water into the pipes, so that the fire could be started and extinguished on cue. More than one thousand gallons of fuel per minute were used, sending tongues of flame two hundred feet into the air. Within about six minutes the wall crumbled into ashes. As in 1932, Washington Boulevard and the Baldwin Hills were crowded with spectators. Among the guests inside the walls was the British actress Vivien Leigh, and it is said that Selznick that night decided that it was she who would play Scarlett O'Hara in his epic film.

The studio mock-ups of the "S. S. Venture" made countless film journeys after the Skull Island expeditions. The day and night shots of the

Bob Armstrong, Bruce Cabot and stuntmen in a Kong scene using the Pathe jungle

ocean from *The Son of Kong* were likewise subjected to much use to provide process plates for many a romantic movie voyage. One beautiful glass-miniature animation scene from *Son,* showing birds flying among the distinctive trees of Skull Island, provided an appropriately fantastic process background for a sequence of Orson Welles' *Citizen Kane.*

King Kong did its bit for the solvency of RKO again in 1938, when it was reissued to heavy grosses. Kong fans were shocked to find that the Hays Office had ordered drastic cuts of scenes deemed too strong for the stricter censorship code enacted in 1934. Even so, Kong seemed a virile fellow at a time when the leading box-office stars were Deanna Durbin, Sonja Henie, Shirley Temple and Gene Autry.

Only about three minutes were removed, totalling twenty-nine scenes. Three scenes showed men being bitten to death by the Brontosaurus, who was now permitted to claim only three victims instead of five. Three more made up the sequence in which Kong tears away Fay Wray's dress. Eight were shots in the native village—the ones Schoedsack disliked—showing natives being bitten to death and crushed under foot along with the shot of Kong smashing down a scaffolding covered with spearsmen. Three showed Kong biting a New Yorker to death. A dozen made up the sequence in which Kong drops a woman from the hotel building, although portions of this action were retained in the trailer.

Another reissue in 1942 was a great financial success. All new posters and a more modern-style trailer heralded the release and Willis O'Brien's name was added to the advertising material (although his middle initial was incorrectly shown as *J*). The 1942 prints appear to have been made from a release copy rather than the original negatives and the entire Empire State Building sequence was printed out of frame. The same was true of the prints reissued by RKO in 1952 and 1956. New posters were prepared for these versions and the film was offered as a double bill with, in each instance, a Val Lewton horror film (*The Leopard Man* in 1952, *I Walked with a Zombie* in 1956).

After the demise of RKO as a producing company, *King Kong* became a television favourite as a C & C Television release. Its phenomenal success in that medium has been exceeded only by the perennial *The Wizard of Oz,* which has the advantage of being in Technicolor.

In 1956, censorship having relaxed somewhat, RKO had announced that it would restore the scenes removed in 1938. A search of the studio vaults failed to unearth the missing footage, however, and it was believed lost forever. It was not until 1971 that the missing scenes were restored by the new holders of the feature, Janus Films. The footage was found in an attic in Philadelphia and all but the first three shots appear in Janus prints. The original main and end titles are missing, however.

In each incarnation *King Kong* has proved a great audience success, brought in a great deal of money and gained greater status as a classic film. Most of the critics loved it in 1933, but it wasn't a *prestige* picture by any means. There were no Academy Awards, no film festival medals, no decorations from the King of Belgium. But lo! (as Merian Cooper's Old Arabian Proverb writer might say) the beauty of the beast has become evident to film historians. Remember *Cavalcade*? Probably not, although it won the Academy Award as Best Picture of 1933—the year in which *King Kong* failed to be nominated in any category. Twenty years later, however, *King Kong* was cited when Charles Brackett presented a special "Oscar" to Merian Cooper for "his many innovations and contributions to the art of motion pictures," and again some months later when Jesse Lasky presented Cooper with a special award from the Hollywood Chamber of Commerce.

After the release of *The Son of Kong,* Cooper conceived a second sequel dealing with the misadventures of the Denham expedition in bringing Kong to New York, with the captive escaping ashore somewhere in the Malay Archipelago. Schoedsack talked him out of it. Much later, when Cooper was in charge of production for the Cinerama organisation, it was rumoured that *King Kong* would be re-made in the tri-camera process under its original working title, *The Eighth Wonder.* Cooper, however, withdrew from the company and such a venture was never initiated.

For the record, a Japanese company produced *King Kong Escapes* and *King Kong Vs. Godzilla* in the late Sixties. Kong and the dinosaurs were portrayed by actors wearing ill-fitting costumes. The less said about these films and a TV cartoon series the better.

Two unusual parodies deserve mention, however. Walter Lantz's cartoon, *King Klunk* (Universal, 1933), condensed the theme into one reel as a *Pooch the Pup* adventure. The tyrannosaurus fight and the Empire State Building finale were the highlights of the show, which was cleverly animated and directed by Lantz and William Nolan. Another parody, *The Lost Island,* was never finished and hence was not seen by the public.

Produced at the Christie Studio, *The Lost Island* was begun early in 1934 as one of the first live-action short films to be made in the new Technicolor three-colour process. It was an imaginative musical-comedy treatment of the *Kong* theme done with considerable scope. The "human" actors were marionettes designed and constructed by Blanding Sloan, Wah Ming Chang, Charles Cristadoro and Mickey O'Rourke. Wah Chang will be remembered for his extraordinary dragons and other animation effects for the George Pal features *The Wonderful World of the Brothers Grimm, Circus of Dr. Lao* and *The Time Machine.* Characters in *The Lost Island* included Mae West and the Marx Brothers. Kong, this time, *was* Charles Gemora in his ape suit. Other monsters were played by actors in ingenious costumes. Orville Goldner, co-author of the present book, was production manager. Original music was written by Eddie Ward. The director was LeRoy Prinz, Paramount's ace choreographer-director. The cameraman was Ray Rennahan.

Unfortunately, *The Lost Island* had to be

THE LOST ISLAND. The puppet of Mae West plays the part of Fay Wray in this Technicolor parody. Charles Gemora plays Kong

Leroy Prinz (left) and Sid Grauman on one of the sets of THE LOST ISLAND

abandoned when financial backing ran out. It was an expensive production due to the use of the tri-film Technicolor system, which was much more costly than the single-film systems now in use. Ironically, when the three-colour process made its live-action *début* later that year in *La Cucuracha,* a two-reeler made by Pioneer Pictures for RKO, the short won awards and high praise for everybody connected with it—including the production chief of Pioneer, Merian C. Cooper.

Although it is the most popular of the films made by the Cooper-Schoedsack team, *King Kong* is but one of many highlights in long and exciting careers. There followed many more films, flying adventures in another world war, travels to faraway lands and enough excitement for a hundred ordinary lifetimes. The partnership ended on the morning of April 21, 1973, with the death of Brigadier-General Merian Cooper at the age of seventy-eight, only a few hours after the passing of his old friend, Robert Armstrong. It would take a very large book to tell the Cooper-Schoedsack story in adequate terms.

O'Brien, although dogged by personal and financial problems to the last, continued to contribute his unique skills to the movie industry. There were many disappointments and unrealised projects. He was animating the complex miniatures for *It's a Mad, Mad, Mad, Mad World* for Lin Dunn when a heart attack ended his life at the age of seventy-six on November 8, 1962.

As for the technical staff that brought Cooper's wildest dream to the screen, there are a few who still work in what remains of the film industry. Others have retired or gone into different fields of work. Many are no longer living. For all of them *King Kong* was a unique experience, expressed eloquently in the words of Carroll Shepphird:

"I've always been glad I was allowed to be a part of that wonderful picture."

THE END

THE LOST ISLAND. Puppets in the great cave. The "dinosaur" is obviously a costumed human actor

A King Kong Portfolio

"Steady with those rifles, boys," Robert Armstrong warns his men after they have been discovered spying on the native ceremony. Frank Reicher, Fay Wray, and Bruce Cabot stand just behind Armstrong. The sailor in foreground with striped sleeves is veteran "heavy" Blackie Whiteford.

Ernest Schoedsack, on platform behind the three cameras, preparing to shoot a night scene at the great wall. Merian Cooper (wearing hat) stands at extreme left.

A studio artist's concept of Kong's first closeup, which was accomplished in the film using a giant bust.

This drawing by Byron Crabbe is one of the displays used by Merian Cooper to sell the idea of Kong *to the RKO board of directors. In the film the boat became a hastily constructed raft and Fay Wray wasn't aboard.*

A composite studio still made up of scenes from the swamp sequence. The background, including the brontosaurus and the man in the tree, combines miniature properties and glass art. The figures in the foreground are from an earlier scene aboard the raft. Robert Armstrong is the player third from right.

Heavily retouched still made from one of the actual process shots of the brontosaurus and a stunt actor.

A master production design by Mario Larrinaga for a scene filmed for the original test reel but deleted and replaced for the final product because, as Cooper said, "it stopped the show."

A studio artist's version of Kong's attack on the native village. The final version differed considerably.

Robert Armstrong as Denham and Fay Wray as Ann, as costumed for Skull Island.

Fay Wray as Ann and Bruce Cabot as Jack in costume for their escape from Skull Mountain.

At the great wall: Frank Reicher, Fay Wray, Bruce Cabot, and Robert Armstrong with some of the crew of the Venture.

A studio composite still reconstructing the action in which Kong approaches Denham and his men on the beach. Frank Reicher and Ethan Laidlaw are shown at extreme left and Robert Armstrong prepares to heave a gas bomb.

Publicity still symbolizing Kong's impact upon New York.

A composite still of Kong and Fay Wray that was used in advertisements.

Backstage with the reporters at Kong's Broadway debut are Bruce Cabot, Fay Wray, and Robert Armstrong. Lynton Brent and Frank Mills stand just behind Armstrong.

Kong's New York debut. The miniature Kong is matted into a scene photographed live at the Shrine Auditorium in Los Angeles.

One of the most widely published stills of all time. A studio artist added five airplanes and lost Fay Wray in preparing an otherwise authentic study of Kong on top of the Empire State Building. The city background was painted on glass and a backing by Mario Larrinaga, Juan Larrinaga, and Byron

IV. Appendices

Appendix 1

Grass

Year	1925
Releasing company	Paramount-Famous Players-Lasky Corporation
Produced by	Marguerite E. Harrison Merian C. Cooper Ernest B. Schoedsack
Musical Score	Dr. Hugo Riesenfeld Dr. Edward Kilenyi
Length at preview	10 reels
Length, general release	7 reels

The Cast

The American Woman	Marguerite E. Harrison
The Tribal Chief	Amir Jang

Synopsis

Mrs. Harrison, an American writer, sets forth from Turkey into the heart of Asia in search of a forgotten tribe. After considerable difficulty she finds the ancient Baba Ahmedi tribe of the Bakhtiari on the shores of the Persian Gulf, where they tend great herds of sheep and goats. This is their home in winter, but in the spring all vegetation is killed by intense heat and the tribe must migrate to the high mountain valleys at the edge of the central Persian plateau. Mrs. Harrison accompanies them on this dangerous journey across the awesome Zardeh Kuh range, a journey no white person has previously accomplished. Forty-six days after its beginning the migration ends as the tribes successfully bring their herds to the grasslands necessary to their survival.

Appendix 2

Chang

Year	1927
Distributing company	Paramount Pictures
Producers	Merian C. Cooper Ernest B. Schoedsack
Musical setting	Hugo Riesenfeld
Title writer	Captain Achmed Abdul-lah
Interpreter	Kru Muang
Chief trapper	Tahn
Length	8 reels

The Cast

The Man	Kru
The Woman	Chantui
The Boy	Nah
The Girl	Ladah
Himself	Mike
Himself	Bimbo

Synopsis

A Lao family is seen at their home in the jungle of northern Siam (Thailand). The family goat is attacked by a leopard and it is made clear that the family is in danger of being destroyed by various wild beasts. The father bands together with his neighbours to hunt down the tigers and leopards of the area. Various kinds of traps are built, including deadfalls, decoys and camouflaged pits. The great cunning of the beasts is demonstrated as many of them escape capture.

Eventually, the jungle is cleared of predatory cats and peace reigns—temporarily. The rice patch is ruined by a *chang*, the most feared beast of all. The *chang* is trapped in a pit and is revealed to be a baby elephant. The animal is tied to one of the poles that support the house. Soon the mother elephant comes and frees her young by demolishing the house.

The farmer and his family flee to the nearest village with the news that they have seen the Great Herd approaching. This is a band of some three hundred wild elephants which has not been seen in the area for fifty years. The herd rampages through the village, destroying it completely. Again the villagers assemble and, led by Kru, succeed in rounding up most of the elephants. The captured animals are trained to become allies of man in his fight against the jungle.

Notes

It would be difficult to overestimate the influence of *Chang* on the later Cooper-Schoedsack films, especially *King Kong*, for which it served as a model of construction. Chang, like Kong, is a mysterious element through much of the story, introduced and identified only after a suspenseful build-up. Tigers, leopards and snakes are secondary menaces like the dinosaurs of Skull Island. Audiences were requested not to reveal the meaning of the word *Chang* and the advertising and publicity kept faith with this promise. The mystery surrounding Kong, though admirably sustained in the movie itself, was diluted because the giant ape was exploited heavily in the advertising materials.

Equally perceptible is the impact of *Chang* on W. S. Van Dyke's *Trader Horn* and *Tarzan, the Ape Man*, which preceded *King Kong* as jungle spectacles. Van Dyke conferred with Schoedsack before embarking for Africa to film *Trader Horn*. The elephant stampede of the *Tarzan* film, although filmed in California with a tame herd and a great deal of process photography, very closely resembles the climax of *Chang*.

Stock footage from *Chang* may be seen in numerous jungle films. Most notably the Great Herd rampaged again in two Paramount pictures, *The Last Outpost* (1935) and *The Jungle Princess* (1937).

Appendix 3

The Four Feathers

Year	1929
Releasing Company	Paramount Publix Corp.
Producers	Merian C. Cooper Ernest B. Schoedsack
Associate producer	David O. Selznick
Directors	Merian C. Cooper Ernest B. Schoedsack
Additional direction	Lothar Mendes
Additional photography	Robert Kurrle
Based on the novel by	A. E. W. Mason
Screenplay	Howard Estabrook
Adaptation	Hope Loring
Titles	Julian Johnson, John Farrow
Music	William Frederick Peters
Sound supervision	Roy Pomeroy
Length	7,472 feet

The Cast

Lt. Harry Feversham	Richard Arlen
Lt. Durrance	Clive Brook
Ethne	Fay Wray
Capt. Trench	William Powell
Lt. Castleton	Theodore von Eltz
Sheik	Noah Beery
Ahmed	Noble Johnson

Other Players	Zack Williams Harold Hightower Philippe de Lacey Edward J. Radcliffe George Fawcett Augustin Symonds

THE FOUR FEATHERS. Clive Brook (left) and Richard Arlen (right)

Synopsis

Young Lt. Harry Feversham, scion of a family of soldiers in the service of England, has a morbid fear that he will besmirch the family name through cowardice. When he learns that his regiment is being sent to Africa to put down a revolt of dervish fanatics, Feversham resigns his commission. His three comrades, Captain Trench and Lieutenants Castleton and Durrance, each give him a white feather, symbol of cowardice. A fourth feather is presented him by his *fiancée*. When the three comrades fall into the hands of the enemy in Africa, a disguised Feversham, in a series of feats requiring incredible courage, rescues each of the men and returns the four feathers.

Notes

No camera or optical tricks were used to combine the African footage with that filmed at the studio and in the California desert. The result was so perfect that some of the critics took the producers to task for using such a small amount of "authentic" film. Some later re-editing by Selznick and the addition of some additional studio scenes after Schoedsack had completed the editing and returned to New York convinced Cooper and Schoedsack that they should personally edit all future productions.

Richard Arlen in THE FOUR FEATHERS

Appendix 4

Rango

Year	1931
Releasing company	Paramount Publix Corp.
Producer-director-author	Ernest B. Schoedsack
Assistant to producer	Ruth Rose
Cameraman	Alfred Williams
Sound supervision	Roy Pomeroy
Associate editor	Julian Johnson
Musical score	W. Franke Harling
Presented by	Adolph Zukor
	Jesse L. Lasky
Length	8 reels

The Cast

Uncle (in prologue)	Claude King
Boy (in prologue)	Douglas Scott
The Father	Ali
His Son	Bin
Himself	Tua
Himself	Rango

Synopsis

A talking prologue shows a little boy in the United States shooting down a cardboard tiger with his pop-gun. His uncle from India watches and then begins telling the story of a real tiger, whereupon the camera moves into the jungle to unfold the story, which is synchronised with music and sound effects.

Ali, an old hunter, and Bin, his little son, live in the upper jungle laying traps to protect the villages further down the mountain from marauding tigers. Bin makes a pet of Rango, a baby orang-utan, who later is freed by the father-ape, Tua. Grim jungle dangers are contrasted with comedy involving the apes and the monkeys that infest the trees. Eventually, Bin is chased through the forest by a tiger. Rango diverts the man-eater's attention and is killed. Bin frees his tethered water buffalo which, after a furious battle, kills the tiger. Ali rejoices in the fact that his son has been saved, but old Tua is seen watching from the trees, inconsolable in his grief.

Notes

Schoedsack deftly "humanised" the apes with humorous and pathetic touches. For years afterward he was accused of sacrificing Rango to the tiger for the climactic scene. Actually, he left the ape in the jungle alive and well. The charging tiger was filmed from a pit, in the front of which was installed an 18 x 24-inch plate glass an inch thick. Ruth held Rango on top of her head so that he appeared to be standing in front of the camera. When the tiger appeared on the trail, Schoedsack stepped out of the pit and sounded a noisy "Bronx cheer," his surefire method of infuriating a big cat. The beast charged and leaped —apparently on the ape, which was safely behind the glass. Later, Schoedsack filmed a scene of a tiger pouncing upon an ape-skin dummy and tearing it to shreds. That this harrowingly realistic bit of mayhem was conceived and staged in the jungle, without benefit of any kind of studio work, is typical of Schoedsack's ingenuity.

After the tiger has been killed by the buffalo an overburdened tree limb snaps, dumping a gallery of chattering monkeys on the corpse of their enemy. This has the look of a spontaneous "accident," but actually was carefully staged by Schoedsack. The idea came from something he saw in a Jewish community in Russia: a number of men were sitting in a tree watching troops march through when suddenly the limb broke and they were spilled into the street. The *modus operandi* of Cooper-Schoedsack demanded that most story elements be developed from within the realm of personal experience and, as it came to pass, the Sumatran expedition yielded a great deal of material that would be used in the making of *King Kong*.

"*Rango* was just a little picture—a trifle, really," Schoedsack says. Jesse Lasky had a different opinion and, for the first time in his career, wrote the copy for an unusual series of advertisements which ran in advance of the New York *première* (at the Rivoli, February 18). In each of these he called *Rango* "the greatest entertainment in the history of the screen." Most of the critics were nearly as enthusiastic, the "World" calling *Rango* "the best animal picture of them all" and the "Sun" stating it was "the most fascinating study of jungle life ever offered for popular entertainment." The "Times," hardly noted for indulging in superlatives, went so far as to suggest that "it tells a human story in terms so strong and so simple it seems this tale must have its page in the Bible. Its theme, the struggle of man and his brother ape against the manifold terrors of the jungle, is so close to nature, so free from guile in the telling, that by watching it the spectator may not notice the guiding intelligence behind the film and the care with which the story has been moulded from the materials of nature."

Appendix 5

The Ghost of Slumber Mountain

Year	1919
Releasing company	World Cinema Distributing Corp.
Presented by	Paul H. Cromelin
Produced by	Herbert M. Dawley
Directed by	Willis H. O'Brien
Technical Supervision	Dr. Barnum Brown
Length	520 feet

Synopsis

Uncle Jack, urged by some youngsters to tell them a true adventure, describes via flashback a camping trip through the depths of the forest to Slumber Mountain and Dream Valley, through which flows the River of Peace. Jack, his guide, Joe, and Jack's dog climb the mountain and make camp at the top. Next morning, on their way to the lake, they pass a reputedly haunted cabin once inhabited by a hermit known as Mad Dick. Joe says that he once saw the hermit leave the cabin at night and gaze intently into the valley through a strange optical instrument. Dick fled when he became aware of Joe's presence.

That night Uncle Jack sits by the fire, thinking about the crazed hermit. He hears a voice calling to him and the dog runs into the woods to investigate. Jack buckles on his pistol and follows. The voice leads him to the cabin. He forces the door open and discovers a room filled with books, fossil bones and statuettes of dinosaurs. He finds the instrument Joe told about and as he examines it the ghost of Mad Dick appears. The spectre tells Jack to bring the instrument to the edge of the mountain and look through the glasses.

To his amazement, Jack sees a Brontosaurus one hundred feet long grazing in the valley. The dinosaur disappears into the river. Then a gigantic flightless bird, Diatryma, enters the scene and devours a large snake. Jack next sees two Triceratopses engage in furious combat. The victor is attacked in turn by a flesh-eating Allosaurus, which kills and begins devouring the three-horned beast.

At this moment the ghost vanishes, leaving Jack alone. The Allosaurus sees Jack and rushes toward him. Jack's bullets strike the monster's face but fail to stop him, whereupon Jack flees toward the camp. Just as the monstrous jaws are about to seize him, Jack is awakened by his dog and Joe. He has been dreaming.

When the nephews realise that their uncle has not told a true story, they pummel him heartily.

Notes

The cast has not been identified. A legend tells that Uncle Jack was Willis O'Brien, and there is a physical resemblance. O'Brien never confirmed this, however, saying only that he had forgotten the names of the players. The ghost is shown in double exposure to give him a suitably wraith-like appearance. It has been said often that *The Ghost of Slumber Mountain* was re-made as *The Beast of Hollow Mountain* (1956). The latter film was based upon a story by O'Brien, who was not hired to produce the effects—unfortunately. It bears no great resemblance to the earlier work except that the hero is pursued by a flesh-eating dinosaur at the climax.

Technically, *Ghost* is a great step forward in the field of dimensional animation, easily surpassing any previous work by O'Brien or anybody else. Although it does not have the elaborate detail of setting that characterises *The Lost World, Creation* or *King Kong,* it clearly is the legitimate ancestor of these films. The animation of the animals is excellent, but O'Brien's use of the camera itself is unimaginative compared to his later work. Composition and editing are unremarkable, lighting is of the "natural" variety and O'Brien displays a reluctance to get in close to his subjects. The gulf between *Ghost* and *The Lost World* in these respects is very wide.

Appendix 6

The Lost World

Year	1925
Producing company	First National Pictures
By arrangement with	Watterson R. Rothacker
Produced under supervision of	Earl Hudson
Research and technical director	Willis H. O'Brien
Director of photography	Arthur Edeson
Director of settings and architecture	Milton Menasco
Film editor	George McGuire
Scenario and editorial direction	Marion Fairfax
Chief technician	Fred W. Jackman
Technical staff	Marcel Delgado
	Homer Scott
	J. Devereaux Jennings
	Vernon L. Walker
Dramatic direction	Harry O. Hoyt
Additional direction	William Dowling
Based on the novel by	Sir Arthur Conan Doyle
Length	10 reels (9,209 feet)

The Cast

Paula White	Bessie Love
Edward J. Malone	Lloyd Hughes
Sir John Roxton	Lewis Stone
Professor Challenger	Wallace Beery
Professor Summerlee	Arthur Hoyt

Mrs. Challenger	Margaret McWade
Austin, Challenger's Butler	Finch Smiles
Zambo, Roxton's Servant	Jules Cowles
Apeman	Bull Montana
Colin McArdle	George Bunny
Major Hibbard	Charles Wellesley
Gladys Hungerford	Alma Bennett
Half-Caste Girl	Virginia Browne Faire
Attorney	Nelson MacDowell

Synopsis

London newspaperman Ed Malone proposes to Gladys Hungerford, who tells him she can't marry him until he does something heroic. As a result, Malone manages to join Professor Challenger's expedition up the Amazon River, where Challenger believes a missing explorer named Maple White has discovered a plateau on which living dinosaurs exist. Other members of the expedition are Paula, daughter of White; Sir John Roxton, a big-game hunter who is in love with Paula; Professor Summerlee, a coleopterist, and two servants, Austin and Zambo. During the months of jungle travel, Malone and Paula become interested in one another. At last the party reaches the plateau, watching in amazement as a gigantic prehistoric reptile, a Pteranodon, flies overhead, carrying in its claws a large alligator. The servants are left below as Challenger and his associates climb a stone pinnacle adjacent to the sheer-walled plateau. They fell a tree across the chasm that separates the formations and cross over to the plateau, a dense jungle surmounted by a volcanic peak. An ape-like man watches from hiding.

The explorers encounter a "thunder lizard" (Brontosaurus), which Challenger says is "harmless—unless it happens to step on you." The two professors stalk the dinosaur to study its habits. Unfortunately, the Brontosaur dislodges the tree-bridge, which falls into the crevasse, leaving the party marooned. They are menaced by various monsters, particularly by the meat-eating Allosaurs that infest the jungle. These beasts are seen killing and feeding on Trachodons, Triceratopses, Monocloniuses and Stegosaurs. The Brontosaur is attacked by an allosaur and falls from the edge of the plateau into a pool. Crumbling earth from the cliff creates a quagmire in which the Brontosaur is trapped.

The explorers take refuge in some caves, where they find the skeletal remains of Paula's father. A volcanic eruption sets fire to the forest and the party appears doomed. Austin saves the day by sending Paula's pet monkey up the sheer cliff with a rope. As the last member of the group, Malone, is descending, the apeman seizes the rope and begins pulling the youth back up the precipice to certain doom. Roxton's unerring marksmanship accounts for the apeman and saves Malone. The Brontosaur that fell from the plateau is found half-buried in mud, but uninjured. With the aid of the Brazilian government, Challenger makes arrangements to float the dinosaur out and bring it to civilisation alive.

As the caged dinosaur is being unloaded in London, an accident causes the cage to be smashed, permitting the beast to escape. After destroying some well-known landmarks and terrorising London, the Brontosaur walks on to London Bridge, which collapses under its weight. The animal plunges into the Thames and swims out to sea. During the excitement Malone meets Gladys on the embankment and learns that she has tired of waiting and is married to a clerk named Percy Bumberry. This clears the path for Malone's romance with Paula. Sir John, hiding his heartbreak, offers his congratulations and walks away. A bystander sees him and tells another, "That's Sir John Roxton—sportsman."

Notes

From a purely spectacular standpoint, *The Lost World* easily surpasses any film of the *genre,* even including a wide-screen and colour re-make of the Fifties. In other respects, however, it is far less effective than *King Kong,* which has the advantages of a strong central character capable of evoking both sympathy and terror, a stronger love story, vastly better dramatic emphasis and—most importantly—the characteristic Cooper-Schoedsack pace. *The Lost World* rambles a lot and in many instances introduces the dinosaurs in a painfully matter-of-fact way as they amble through the jungle.

The settings are much more dramatic than those of *The Ghost of Slumber Mountain,* pointing the way to the still-unsurpassed jungles of *Creation, King Kong* and *The Son of Kong.* The animation, when projected at the proper speed, is superb. Dramatic lighting, which was lacking in earlier O'Brien films, adds tremendously to the effectiveness of the monsters, particularly in some fire-lit night scenes which anticipate the emphasis upon composition and chiaroscuro O'Brien brought to his later efforts.

Appendix 7

Creation

Year	1930–1931
Producing company	RKO-Radio Pictures, Inc.
Direction and Scenario	Willis H. O'Brien Harry O. Hoyt
Adaptation and dialogue	Beulah Marie Dix
Production artists	Mario Larrinaga Byron L. Crabbe Ernest Smythe Juan Larrinaga
Director of photography	Eddie Linden
Animal supervision	Olga Celeste
Technical staff	Marcel Delgado E. B. Gibson Orville Goldner Carroll Shepphird Fred Reefe

The Cast

Hallett	Ralf Harolde
Chimpanzee	Snooky

Synopsis

Steve, a penniless young intellectual, is in love with Elaine Armitage, a spoiled *débutante*. So he can be near her, he takes a job as tutor to her younger brother, Billy, and becomes a member of Mr. Armitage's yachting expedition to South America. Others on board are Elaine's aunt, Mrs.

Martin; Hallett, Elaine's wastrel suitor; Bennie, a likeable servant; and the ship's company. Elaine flirts with Steve, who is enraged when he learns that her interest in him is merely frivolous. Hallett tries jealously to discredit Steve. As tempers flare, a Chilean submarine approaches. The Captain tells everybody they must board the submarine immediately because a typhoon is approaching and the yacht cannot be expected to survive. Everybody crowds aboard the sub, which dives just as a waterspout hurls the yacht away and a terrific undersea earthquake sends a huge promontory rising from the sea-bottom. The submarine is drawn, twisting end over end, into the cavity along with millions of tons of water as the yacht is splintered into fragments on the newly risen island.

The stunned passengers awaken in the morning to find the vessel moving slowly through a long cavern. Through a porthole they see "green water and strange monsters." The craft grounds on a rocky shelf as water pours in through broken bulkheads. The occupants find themselves in a tropic lake. In a life raft they reach the shore of a jungle that is surrounded completely by the overhanging walls of a volcanic crater.

The group encounters several Brontosauri in and around the lake and sees two bull Triceratopses fighting. The party finds a narrow trail leading to a ledge above the treetops. From this camp Steve, the submarine captain and the sailors go into the forest to reconnoitre. They are attacked by an Arsinoitherium, a gigantic mammal resembling a giant rhinoceros. The beast kills two of the men, whereupon Pterodactyls swoop down like vultures to feed upon the victims. Only Steve is able to reach a place of safety as the monster harries the other men into a swift stream that carries them to certain doom in a deep chasm.

On Steve's return to the ledge he is forced into a fight with Hallett. Later, when Steve is injured in an encounter with a jaguar, Elaine realises that she is in love with him.

A month passes and still no way of escape has been found. The survivors have built a hut on the ledge. Hallett shoots at a passing Brontosaurus, which angrily destroys the hut and menaces everybody. Elaine saves the day when she thrusts a blazing torch into the monster's jaws, driving it away. Steve becomes leader of the group and Hallett angrily quits the camp.

In the jungle, Hallett kills a baby Triceratops and falls prey to the victim's mother, who topples a tree on the man and then gores him to death. Steve and Elaine retrieve the wireless from the sunken submarine. Searching for something from which to construct a necessary leyden jar, Steve, Elaine, Billy and Bennie go to the far side of the lake where they find the ruins of a pre-Incan temple and a fortune in precious jewels. Elaine is carried away by a Pteranodon, but Steve rescues her.

A Stegosaurus chases the party and they flee into the temple, only to be confronted by the largest of carnivorous reptiles, a Tyrannosaurus. When they attempt to hide in a burial niche they see several pairs of ghostly eyes in the darkness. The Tyrannosaur attacks the Stegosaur and the reptiles fight until the Stegosaur is mortally injured. In its death throes the armoured creature smashes a hole in the wall, through which the explorers escape. They look back to see numerous young tyrant lizards springing out of the burial niches to join in the feast.

It is discovered that the lake is beginning to boil and Steve reveals that the volcano is likely to erupt. Great monsters emerge from the water and stampede through the jungle. Steve manages to get the wireless into operation and is able to send out a call for help a moment before a fleeing monster topples the apparatus over the cliff. The forest bursts into flame and the cliffs begin to crumble. Just as death appears inevitable, rescue arrives in the form of two Chilean aircraft. Elaine, Steve, Armitage, Bill, Bennie and Mrs. Martin are carried to safety an instant before the volcano explodes and destroys the lost jungle.

Notes

Exactly which portions of *Creation* were filmed is not known except for the shipwreck sequence and a reel found among the effects of Willis O'Brien. The latter consists of a remarkable sequence that begins with a mother Triceratops and her two babies grazing in the jungle. A chimpanzee (Snooky) drops a limb on one of the babies, which then wanders away to follow, out of curiosity, a stork. The bird is seized by a jaguar. The little dinosaur next watches a lemur crawl into a cave. It then encounters Hallett (Ralf Harolde), who fires a rifle bullet into its eye. The mother Triceratops, hearing the death cries of her young, pursues Hallett.

The end of this sequence, in which the dinosaur pushes a tree on Hallett and then gores him to death, is missing—it was borrowed to use in the rough-cut of *Kong*. The live actor and animals are integrated with the animated reptiles flawlessly and the "acting" of the dinosaurs is as polished as that of Kong, the youngsters being as appealing as puppies. Troubles encountered with Snooky (a famous trained ape which had starred in his own comedy series at Universal), —and the jaguar, as well as Schoedsack's problems with a jaguar while making *The Most Dangerous Game,* resulted in the decision to avoid using live animals in *Kong*.

A technician in the set tree rigged the branch Snooky was supposed to drop on the dinosaur so that it would break free. In this precarious position the chimpanzee, who took a fancy to the man, wrestled him affectionately. On the first take, Snooky struggled desperately with the branch and was unable to pull it free. The technician climbed the tree again and loosened the branch, again handicapped by Snooky's fondling and whiskered kisses. A second take also failed because the branch was too firmly attached. The dishevelled man climbed the tree a third time wiring the branch so loosely it would come off at the slightest tug.

This time Snooky gave the branch a hard yank. It came away so easily that he was thrown off balance and almost fell from the tree. Snooky was infuriated, and there is nothing "cute" about an angry chimpanzee. Even a small chimp is stronger than a man and can deliver a vicious bite. Snooky leaped from vine to vine, screeching and snarling in rage as he swung across the set. Finally he came down to the floor, running around the stage and, in his fury, wrecking props and equipment. Encountering a tub of plaster of Paris used for mending sets, he thrust his face into the powder, emerging with a mouthful. The trainer was horror-struck; if Snooky swallowed the plaster it could prove fatal. The entire crew began chasing the ape around the stage, up and down ladders and through the trees to keep him too active to swallow. In good time he was cornered and captured and forced to spit out the plaster. Snooky was undaunted and unharmed!

Some of the existing production drawings for *Creation* were rendered in colours, indicating that at one time the use of colour photography was considered.

Although it was never shown to the public, *Creation* is important in that it is the film for which O'Brien developed the elaborate multiplane settings and composites that distinguish *King Kong,* provided the experimentation, produced the trained technical crew and contributed some of the actual physical properties that made possible the filming of *King Kong*.

Although the plot of *Creation* seems familiar in the light of the much later fantasies of the colour and wide-screen era, it was in the perspective of its time a novel and heady conception. There is little doubt that it could have become a noteworthy adventure spectacle, although lacking the suspenseful construction and strong central character of *King Kong*. Its demise was a heartbreaking blow to all concerned, but most particularly to Harry Hoyt, who never was able to regain his prestige in the industry. For the next several years he wrote and/or directed low-budget films for the independent companies while trying to find a backer for his prehistory epic. In November 1938, he began work on *Lost Atlantis,* using the *Creation* plot, in collaboration with producer Trem Carr and special effects expert Fred Jackman, of *The Lost World*. Twenty-five dinosaurs were built at a cost of about $600 each and Jackman photographed two reels of animation at his new independent laboratory before the sponsor, Harry Cohn, halted the production. *Lost Atlantis* was re-started two years later as a Technicolor production using new dinosaurs created by Walter Lantz, Universal's cartoon maestro, and Edward Nassour. Columbia again withdrew its support and the film was never completed. Hoyt later started a new career as producer of industrial and commercial films.

Appendix 8

The Most Dangerous Game

Year	1932
Producing company	RKO-Radio Pictures, Inc.
Executive producer	David O. Selznick
Produced by	Merian C. Cooper Ernest B. Schoedsack
Directed by	Ernest B. Schoedsack Irving Pichel
Screenplay by	James A. Creelman
Based on the short-story by	Richard Connell
Photographed by	Henry Gerrard
Music by	Max Steiner
Settings by	Carroll Clark
Sound recording	Clem Portman
Film editor	Archie S. Marshek
Make-up artist	Wally Westmore
Photographic effects	Lloyd Knechtel Vernon L. Walker
Optical effects	Linwood G. Dunn
Operative cameraman	Robert DeGrasse
Art technicians	Mario Larrinaga Byron L. Crabbe
Special effects	Harry Redmond, Jr.
Miniatures	Don Jahraus Orville Goldner
Special properties	Marcel Delgado John Cerisoli
Costumes	Walter Plunkett
Piano solos	Norma Boleslawski
Sound effects	Murray Spivack
Set decorations	Thomas Little
Sound system	RCA Photophone
Running time	63 minutes

The Cast

Bob Rainsford	Joel McCrea
Eve Trowbridge	Fay Wray
Martin Trowbridge	Robert Armstrong
Count Zaroff	Leslie Banks
Bill Woodman	Hale Hamilton
Ivan	Noble Johnson
Tartar	Steve Clemento (e)
Scar-face	Dutch Hendrian
Captain	William B. Davidson
Doc	Landers Stevens
First Mate	James Flavin

Musical Score

"The Iron Door"; "The Sea"; "The Wreck"; "Andante Quasi Mysterioso"; "Approach"; "Zaroff"; "Russian Waltz"; "Incidental Music"; "Molto Agitato"; "Emotions"; "Mysterioso Dramatico"; "The Flower"; "The Chase"; "The Fight."—Max Steiner. Song, "A Moment in the Dark"—Carmen Lombardo (music), Arthur Freed (lyrics).

Synopsis

Somewhere in the Caribbean, the captain of Bill Woodman's luxury yacht "Sylph" anxiously studies the buoy lights that mark the channel between Baranka Island and the mainland and decides that they are incorrectly positioned. In the ship's saloon, Bob Rainsford, American big-game hunter and author, is drawn into a discussion of hunting. When it is suggested that the pleasure is all on the side of the hunter, Rainsford insists that both hunter and hunted enjoy the same exhilaration. While the captain is trying to persuade Woodman to turn back and take a different course, the ship strikes a reef. Water rushes into the boiler room, scalding the crew and precipitating an explosion that hurls the men above into the sea. Only Rainsford, the captain and a few others survive the blast and marauding sharks soon account for all but Rainsford. Swimming toward a distant light, the lone survivor at length reaches Baranka Island. Walking toward the light he hears a dying animal scream and the sound of barking hounds. At length he reaches an ancient Portuguese castle. On the huge door is a door-knocker designed as a centaur, wounded by arrows, which holds in its arms the body of a woman. When Rainsford bangs down the knocker the door creaks open and Rainsford steps into an ornate and seemingly unoccupied hall. A bearded giant in the uniform of a Cossack is revealed when the door closes. Rainsford tries to talk to the man, who regards him with silence. The impasse is broken by the entrance from upstairs of a tall man in evening dress. He is Count Zaroff, owner of the castle, who explains that his servant is mute and "like all my fellow countrymen he is a bit of a savage." The Count shows his guest to an upstairs room and gives him a change of clothes. Rainsford observes that the centaur-woman motif of the door-knocker is repeated in the design of a wall tapestry.

Later Zaroff introduces Rainsford to his other guests, Eve Trowbridge and her brother, Martin, survivors of an earlier shipwreck. Eve is a beautiful woman in whom Zaroff obviously is interested. Martin is an amiable young man who drinks too much. Zaroff reveals that he is a great admirer of Rainsford and that he is himself devoted to hunting. The walls are covered with hunting trophies from all over the world. Zaroff tells of the cape buffalo that "gave me this," indicating a deep scar on his forehead. "My father was a very rich man, with a quarter of a million acres in the Crimea, and an ardent sportsman. When I was only stirrup high he gave me my first gun. My life has been one glorious hunt. It would be impossible for me to tell you how many animals I have killed. I escaped with most of my fortune. Naturally, I continued to hunt all over the world. One night, as I lay in my tent with this—this head of mine, a terrible thought crept like a snake into my brain: hunting was beginning to *bore* me." Eve asks if that thought is so terrible. "It is, my dear lady, when hunting has been the whip for all other passions. When I lost my love for hunting, I lost my love of life, of love." He says he tried to make the sport more challenging by hunting only with a Tartar war bow but finally realised that what he needed was "not a new weapon, but a new animal. Here on my island I hunt the most dangerous game." He refuses to divulge the identity of the animal or permit anyone to see his secret trophy room, which is concealed behind an iron door. "I keep it as a surprise for my guests against the rainy day of boredom."

While Zaroff plays the piano for his guests, Eve guardedly tells Rainsford that two sailors who were shipwrecked with her have disappeared after being taken to see the mysterious trophy room. After Eve and Rainsford have gone to their quarters, Zaroff invites Martin to visit the trophy room.

Shortly before dawn, Eve comes to Rainsford to say that her brother has disappeared. Together they go downstairs to find the trophy room unlocked. Entering, they see that the walls are decorated with mummified human heads. Another head floats in a jar of liquid. Hearing voices, Eve and Rainsford hide. Zaroff enters with his servants—the mute Ivan, a Mongol and a burly Russian—and the body of Martin. Eve screams and tries to strike Zaroff. When Rainsford leaps to her aid he is seized and strapped to the wall. Zaroff explains his set-up: fake channel lights lure ships onto the reefs, the survivors being kept as guests until they are to be hunted. To refuse to be hunted is to be tortured by Ivan. The "game" is given a hunting knife and a full day's start; Zaroff follows at dusk and if his quarry eludes him until dawn he is offered freedom. To date, none has escaped. Zaroff is surprised that Rainsford does not support his theories. Disappointed, Zaroff consoles himself with the thought that he will have the best hunt of his life. Leading Rainsford outside, Zaroff hands him a dagger —"Your fangs and claws, Mr. Rainsford." When Eve demands to know what is about to happen, Zaroff tells her that he and Rainsford are going to play "outdoor chess. His brain against mine— his woodcraft against mine. And the prize . . . Only after the kill does man know the true ecstacy of love." Eve elects to accompany Rainsford rather than remain. Zaroff consents, for "One does not kill the female animal."

At dawn, Rainsford and Eve explore the island and map out their strategy. He finds a heavy tree overhanging a path and sets about constructing a Malay deadfall, the trip-line of which is made from Rainsford's necktie and Eve's bracelet. At midnight they hide in a shallow cave nearby and watch for Zaroff's approach. As his foot descends toward the camouflaged bracelet, Zaroff steps back suddenly and fires an arrow into the trigger. The tree crashes harmlessly in front of him. Zaroff perceives Rainsford's hiding place, but cannot venture near without risking an ambush. "If you choose to play the leopard, I shall hunt you like a leopard," Zaroff shouts. Rainsford knows the hunter will return with a high-powered rifle.

With only two hours remaining before dawn, Rainsford prepares another trap by camouflaging a deep, narrow chasm. A sudden uprising of startled birds heralds Zaroff's return as Eve and Rainsford watch. Once more Zaroff triumphs, springing back from the trap at the penultimate moment. Desperately, Rainsford leads Eve into Fog Hollow, the deadly, crocodile-infested swamp where Zaroff has trapped many of his victims; the heavy fog will make the rifle useless. With only half an hour remaining before dawn, Zaroff sounds the hunting horn. Moments later his servants appear with the pack of ravening hounds. Rainsford plants a hastily-made spear in the fog-shrouded path and Ivan, pulled along by the hounds, is impaled. The freed dogs race after the fugitives as they cross a log-bridged gorge and climb into a high tree. From a limb they drop onto a rocky cliff from which a waterfall tumbles. As the dogs scramble up, Rainsford causes one of them to plunge into the fall. He kills a second with his knife and struggles with a third at the edge of the cliff. Zaroff fires; Rainsford and the dog topple into the waterfall and are swept away a moment before dawn breaks.

Later, Zaroff happily plays the piano as he recalls the pleasures of the chase. He sends the Mongol to bring Eve to him. Then the front door opens and Rainsford enters, unarmed but deadly. Zaroff offers his congratulations after Rainsford explains, "You hit the dog, not me. I took a chance and went over with him." Zaroff gives Rainsford the key to the boathouse, then draws a revolver and tries to kill him. The men fight savagely. The Russian servant enters the fray and is killed when Rainsford breaks the man's back. Zaroff seizes the war bow and an arrow, but Rainsford wrests the arrow from him and drives it into his back. Zaroff falls, mortally wounded, just as the Mongolian arrives and hurls a knife at Rainsford. Rainsford kills the Mongol with Zaroff's gun and, with Eve, finds the motor launch.

Zaroff drags himself to the window which overlooks the channel from the boathouse to the sea. Directly under the window is the yard in which the dogs are kept. When Eve and Rainsford come into sight, Zaroff fits an arrow to the war bow, intent upon killing the man who defeated him. The effort is too great; the madman falls to the ravening hounds.

Notes

In England this film was titled *The Hounds of Zaroff*. It was re-issued in the United States in 1938 as *Skull Island,* a title suggestive of its co-production. Some of the re-issue prints were printed on green stock.

A version dubbed in French, *La Chasse du Comte Zaroff,* was released two years after the first United States release, opening in Paris at the Club d'Artois on November 15, 1934. It was directed by Henri Diamant-Berger and the voices were those of Germaine Bredy, Maurice Candy, Henri Baudin, Jean Orth and Serge. In Italy the title was *La Pericolosa Partita.*

RKO re-made the subject under the original title in 1944, using more than eighty stock shots from the 1932 version. After preview the title was changed to *Game of Death.* A new script by Norman Houston changed Zaroff's name to Eric Krieger because of our wartime alliance with Russia. Noble Johnson repeated his role, this time as a Carib native. Robert Wise directed the new footage, which somehow lacked the spirit of the old.

Not only was *The Most Dangerous Game* made in tandem with early work on *King Kong,* involving the same sets and personnel, but its success undoubtedly had a great influence on the script development and editing of its more famous co-production.

Although adapted from a well-known story, *The Most Dangerous Game* contains many touches typical of the producers. Whereas Rainsford's predicament in the story results from his falling overboard, he is in the film the victim of a shipwreck brought on by circumstances not unlike those surrounding the wreck of the "Wisdom II" at Mocha. Schoedsack enjoyed some bits of dialogue that poked fun at his former enemies, the Russians.

Appendix 9

King Kong

Year	1933
Producing company	RKO-Radio Pictures, Inc.
Producers, directors	Merian C. Cooper Ernest B. Schoedsack
Executive producer	David O. Selznick
Screenplay by	James A. Creelman Ruth Rose
Idea conceived by	Merian C. Cooper Edgar Wallace
Chief technician	Willis H. O'Brien
Technical staff	E. B. Gibson Marcel Delgado Fred Reefe Orville Goldner Carroll Shepphird
Art technicians	Mario Larrinaga Byron L. Crabbe
Photographers	Eddie Linden Vernon Walker J. O. Taylor
Music	Max Steiner
Sound effects	Murray Spivack
Settings	Carroll Clark Al Herman
Recorded by	E. A. Wolcott
Film editor	Ted Cheesman
Production assistants	Archie S. Marshek Walter Daniels
Scenario associate	Horace McCoy
Operative cameramen	Eddie Henderson Felix Schoedsack Lee Davis

The controlling drawing by Larrinaga for the bottom of the canyon

Assistant cameramen	Bert Willis William Reinhold William Clothier Clifford Stine
Optical photography	Linwood G. Dunn William Ulm
Projection process	Sidney Saunders
Dunning process supervision	Carroll H. Dunning C. Dodge Dunning
Williams Matte supervision	Frank Williams
Special effects	Harry Redmond Jr.
Sculptor	John Cerisoli
Construction technician	W. G. White
Technical artists	Juan Larrinaga Zachary Hoag Victor Delgado
Associate, sound effects	Walter G. Elliott
Make-up supervision	Mel Berns
Set decorations	Thomas Little
Supervising art director	Van Nest Polglase
Costumes	Walter Plunkett
Assistant to Merian Cooper	Zoe Porter
Painting technician	Peter Stich
Camera aircraft pilots	Duke Krantz George Weiss
Technical advisors	Dr. J. W. Lytle Dr. O. A. Paterson Dr. Harry C. Raven
Art titles	Pacific Title Co.
Sound system	RCA Photophone
Running time	100 minutes

The Cast

Ann Darrow	Fay Wray
Carl Denham	Robert Armstrong
John Driscoll	Bruce Cabot
Captain Englehorn	Frank Reicher
Charles Weston	Sam Hardy
Native Chief	Noble Johnson
Witch King	Steve Clemento (e)
Second Mate Briggs	James Flavin
Charley	Victor Wong
Socrates	Paul Porcasi
Dock Watchman	Russ Powell

The "real" stuntmen sitting on the miniature log. Matted in

Six-inch models on the log

Kong shakes the log. Miniature figure in foreground

Sailor	Ethan Laidlaw
Sailor	Blackie Whiteford
Sailor	Dick Curtis
Sailor	Charles Sullivan
Sailor	Harry Tenbrook
Sailor	Gil Perkins
Theatre Patron	Vera Lewis
Theatre Patron	Leroy Mason
Reporter	Frank Mills
Reporter	Lynton Brent
Native Dancer	Jim Thorpe
Police Captain	George MacQuarrie
Handmaiden	Madame Sul-te-wan
Native Woman	Etta MacDaniel
Native	Ray Turner
Girl	Dorothy Gulliver
Girl	Carlotta Monti
Navy Pilots	Barney Capehart
	Bob Galloway
	Eric Wood
	Dusty Mitchell
	Russ Rogers
Engineer	Reginald Barlow
Flight Commander	Merian C. Cooper
Chief Observer	Ernest B. Schoedsack

Musical Score

"King Kong"; "Jungle Dance"; "The Forgotten Island"; "A Boat in the Fog"; "The Railing"; "Aboriginal Sacrifice Dance"; "Meeting with the Black Men"; "Sea at Night"; "Stolen Love"; "The Sailors"; "The Bronte"; "Cryptic Shadows"; "The Cave"; "The Snake"; "Humorous Ape"; "The Peri"; "Furioso"; "The Swimmers"; "The Escape"; "Return of Kong"; "King Kong March"; "Fanfare No. 1"; "Fanfare No. 2"; "Fanfare No. 3"; "Agitato"; "Elevated Sequence"; "The Train"; "The Aeroplane"; "Dance of Kong".

Sound Effects List and Cost Estimate July 19, 1932 (From the notebook of Murray Spivack)

MATERIAL:	Gorilla	$50.
	Chest Pounding	50.
	Stegosaurus	30.

Mostly glass, with Bob Armstrong matted in

Incomplete composite of a canyon scene. Live action shot on set at Pathe

Unfinished canyon composite

Arsinoitherium	30.
Triceratops	10.
Egothomus	30.
Sea Monster	30.
Pterodactyl	10.
Bird Wings	15.
Gun Powder	75.
Experimental	100.
TOTAL	$430.

Effects List

Wind - fix and match stock shot
Sound of Parrot
Distant traffic rumble
Background to suit stock shot of dock
Parrot - wants to fight
Ship moving slowly through oily water - Foghorn
Whirring shadow flies past
Surf noise
Drums and chanting
Ship's clock striking eight bells
Ship bell - striking eight
Parrot - talks
Air sucking back into accordion - Parrot flies away squawking
Drums from shore
Officer's whistle - distant bell
Bosun's whistle
Drums
Surf noise
Twenty-ft. drum - small drums - curious drumming (off)
Kong roars and drums his chest
Sailors firing
Fight noise
Birds
Parrot - wants to fight - squawks - spike-tailed beast advancing - beast charging and being fired at - gas bombs - beast collapses - shot
Water splashing
Kong splashing through stream
Dinosaur upsetting raft - screams and splashes
Dinosaur and shrieks of sailor
Dinosaur crunch into man
Triceratops trying to follow Kong - Fight between them - Kong hurling boulders - one of the Triceratops charging men
Sailor hearing noise - strikes head on branch
Tree crash and beast goring man as before
Arsinoitherium starting after men
Kong putting girl in tree - Kong snarls
Two-horned beast approaches - Kong roars four times - beats chest - Kong rocking log - men screaming and falling - Log falling into ravine - Kong yammering
Men landing in mud
Log and men landing in mud
Insects - lizards - spiders
Girl's screams - fight as done in test seq.
Stegosaurus disappears - Parrot squawks
Vultures feeding on meat-eater
Distant crashing sound
Man runs through pool - waterfall
Sea monster lunging at Kong - fight between them
Hisses - grunts
Sea monster dying
Kong beats chest
Screams from girl - parrot talking
Bird pterodactyl wheeling dives for girl
Kong catches bird and kills it
Driscoll and girl dive into water
Water noise - sub outlet - water sucking
Water roar
Kong roars
Water noise
Kong returning
Kong beating his breasts - roars and breast

The waterfall as shot in the High Sierra

drumming heard from behind wall
Second mate blows whistle
Arm of Kong crushing or beating sailor
Kong throwing himself at Gate
Gate wrenching loose - rips from hinges
Gate falls in
Kong stands in the Gate - snarling and beating his chest
Kong charging after men - knocking huts over - tears up tree - tears roof off hut - bites Witch Doctor in two and throws him aside - terrific snarl as Kong sees girl - bomb bursts - knocks man with sweep of paw who catapults thirty or forty ft. landing against wall of hut
Breathing of Kong after being gassed
Telegraph message being sent
City office - with wireless noise over same
Wireless ceases - Press noise supersedes it
Street noise, etc.
Crowd and street noise
Ship ploughing through rough sea - possibly Kong's howls heard from ship
Whistles blow - sound to suit stock shot
Sounds to suit stock shots
Voice over radio
Dialogue and possible street noise
Crowd roar off
Kong snarls - frightened whine
Flashlight working
Kong making whimpering noises - then roars
Kong snaps chains - beats his chest - rushes at scenery door
Kong picks up Roadster and throws it thru window - woman screaming - general noise to suit action - woman falling and landing at entrance to lobby - Kong roars as he gets Ann - Pandemonium from street below - horns, police whistles, etc. - general confusion - fire department - motorcycles and cars rush out - sirens blowing - Mounted police leaving - fire engines, etc. speeding through some well known streets in N.Y.
Kong leaps across street - confusion from below
Airplanes taking off
Noises to suit action
Kong beating his chest
Planes flying and diving
Kong grasps plane out of air - crumples it - hurls it away - plane lands in street below and bursts into flames - Kong roars - plane whizzes past and fires into Kong - Kong roars and pounds chest - planes attack together - Kong falls and lands beside burning plane.

Synopsis

Scene: the Hoboken Docks in the winter of 1932. A nattily attired man approaches the night watchman and, indicating a moored steamer, asks, "Is this the moving picture ship?" He is told the ship is indeed the "Venture" and that it is soon to embark on a "crazy" voyage. The ship, it is explained, carries three times as many crew members as it needs and is chartered by a "crazy feller" named Carl Denham, of whom it is said that "He ain't scared of nothing. They say if he wants a picture of a lion he just walks up and tells it to look pleasant." The "Venture's" first mate, Jack Driscoll, halts the conversation. The visitor identifies himself as Weston, a theatrical agent, and is told to "Come on aboard. Denham's gettin' wild."

In the captain's cabin, Denham confers with Captain Englehorn, who is concerned about a large quantity of ammunition and several cases of large gas grenades Denham has brought aboard. Denham insists the ship must get under way before the fire marshal can inspect the ship and they must reach their destination before the monsoon season starts.

Weston and Driscoll enter and Denham demands to know if the agent has found him an actress. The agent says he has not because his conscience won't let him ask a young girl to go on a voyage "for nobody knows how long, to a place you won't even hint at, the only woman on a ship with the toughest mugs I ever looked at." Englehorn reveals that even he doesn't know their destination. Denham insists he must have a girl because "The public, bless 'em, must have a pretty face to look

A beautiful composite—waterfalls from the High Sierra, painted glass and backing, miniature tree and foliage foreground, and matted live action lower right

at . . . I go out and sweat blood to make a swell picture and the critics and exhibitors all say, 'If this picture only had love interest it would gross twice as much.' " Denham rushes out, saying, "I'm going and find a woman for my picture even if I have to marry one!"

Denham is seen walking the streets, looking over the women in breadlines. He stops at a sidewalk grocery and sees a shabbily dressed girl reaching for an apple. The proprietor catches the girl and threatens to call the police until Denham pays him off. As the girl swoons into his arms Denham sees that she has the kind of beauty he's looking for. Taking the girl to a Bowery lunchroom, Denham asks her about herself. She is Ann Darrow, an orphan who worked as a film extra at the Paramount Astoria Studio before it closed. Denham's burst of enthusiasm frightens her before he explains who he is and that he has picked her as the leading lady of his new picture. "It means money and adventure and fame and a long sea voyage that starts at six o'clock tomorrow morning," he tells her.

As the "Venture" is getting under way, Ann has an unpleasant encounter with Driscoll, who is angry at the prospect of having a woman aboard. After several weeks at sea, Driscoll's interest in the girl overcomes his prejudice. He approaches Denham, saying he is worried about what lies ahead. When Denham suggests he is "going soft," Driscoll admits that his concern is for Ann.

"Oh, you *have* gone soft on her. I've got enough on my hands without having a love affair to complicate things. Better cut it out, Jack. I've never known it to fail: some big, hard-boiled egg gets a look at a pretty face and bingo, he cracks up and goes sappy. You're a pretty tough guy, but if Beauty gets you . . . why, I'm going right into a theme song. It's the idea for my picture. The Beast was a tough guy, too, but when he saw Beauty she got him. He went soft. He forgot his wisdom and the little fellows got him. Think it over, Jack."

When the "Venture" reaches a point in the Indian Ocean " 'way west of Sumatra," Denham shows Englehorn and Driscoll a map revealing their destination.

"But there's nothing . . . nothing for thousands of miles!" Englehorn protests, reaching for a chart.

"You won't find that island on any chart," Denham says. "This map was made by the skipper of a Norwegian barque. A canoe full of natives from this island was blown out to sea. When the barque picked them up, there was only one alive. He died before they reached port, but not before the skipper had pieced together a description of the island and got a fairly good idea of where it lies." He shows them a drawing of the island. "Here is a long, sandy peninsula. The only place to land is through this reef. The rest of the shoreline is sheer precipice, hundreds of feet high. And across the base of that peninsula, cutting it off from the rest of the island, is a wall . . . built so long ago that the people who live there now have slipped back, forgotten the higher civilisation that built it. But it's as strong today as it was centuries ago. The natives keep that wall in repair. They need it. There's something on the other side. Something they fear."

"A hostile tribe," Englehorn asserts.

"Did you ever hear of . . . Kong?"

"Why . . . yes," Englehorn replies uneasily. "Some Malay superstition. A god or spirit or something."

"Anyway, neither beast nor man. Something monstrous, all-powerful . . . still living, still holding that island in the grip of deadly fear. Well? Every legend has a basis in truth. I tell you, there's something on that island that no white man has ever seen."

"And you expect to photograph it?" Englehorn asks.

"If it's there *you bet* I'll photograph it!"

"Suppose it doesn't like having its picture taken?" Driscoll asks.

"Well, now you know why I brought along those cases of gas bombs."

Later, Denham directs Ann's screen test:

"Look higher . . . still higher . . . Now you see it! It's horrible but you can't look away . . . You're helpless . . . If you could only scream—but your throat's paralysed . . . Cover your eyes and scream, Ann, scream for your life!"

"What's he think she's *really* gonna see?" Driscoll asks.

The "Venture" reaches the vicinity of Denham's island during a dense fog. As the sea shallows a lookout reports breakers ahead. Anchor is dropped.

Again the waterfall, painted glass and backing, miniature Kong and rocks, and matted full-scale lower right

"That's not breakers," Driscoll says grimly. "It's drums!"

Daybreak reveals the island to be exactly as described in Denham's map. The stone wall is, in the captain's words, "Colossal! It might almost be Egyptian." Towering above all is a mountain shaped like a skull.

Denham goes ashore with a party consisting of Ann, Driscoll, Englehorn and a dozen sailors. The village seems deserted, but drumming and a weird chant of "Kong, Kong" are heard from the direction of the wall, the lower part of which is concealed from view by grass buildings. Denham, in the lead, steps out into the open and sees a spectacular ceremony in progress. Hundreds of blacks are assembled among the ruins of an ancient temple. Dancers costumed to resemble apes cavort around an altar on which crouches a native girl, naked except for garlands of flowers being draped over her body under the supervision of grotesquely-painted witch doctors. At the top of stone stairs leading to a huge double gate stands the tribal Chief.

When Denham attempts to photograph the scene, he is seen by the Chief, who halts the ceremony and, with a retinue of witch doctors, approaches the interlopers. Englehorn, who has recognised the native language as that spoken by the Nias Islanders, tries to convince the savages that the expedition has come in peace. The Witch King demands destruction of the whites for spoiling a ceremony for "the bride of Kong."

"Look at the golden woman!" the Chief cries when he sees Ann. "The bride of Kong!" He offers to trade six of his women for Ann. "Yeah, blondes *are* scarce around here," Denham observes. As the situation becomes more tense Englehorn calls for an orderly retreat before the natives think to cut them off from the beach.

Aboard ship that night Ann and Driscoll realise that they are in love. When Driscoll is called to the bridge, the Witch King and his men steal aboard ship and seize Ann, carrying her away in an outrigger. Just before midnight, Charley, the ship's cook, finds a native bracelet on deck and sets up an alarm. The sounds of a great ceremony are heard coming from the torchlit village. An armed rescue party is hurriedly organised.

Amid a frenzy of excitement Ann is prepared for the sacrifice. At last the gates open and she is taken to the top of a high stone altar at the edge of the jungle. After binding her wrists to two graven columns, each of which is surmounted by a human skull, the witch doctors hurry back to the village. The gates are closed and a huge wooden bolt is pushed into place. The horde of natives gathers along the top of the wall, their torches lighting the sky. The Chief, standing before a huge tocsin gong above the gates, intones an invocation to Kong and the gong is sounded.

Ann, sobbing helplessly on the altar, hears crashing sounds in the forest as the natives wait in hushed expectancy. Nearby trees are bent aside by a gigantic, indistinct black shape. As the shape comes into view, Ann stares up into the face of Kong, an ape many times larger than a gorilla. The cruel features of the island god take on an expression of delight as he beholds Ann. Gently, Kong releases the girl from her bonds and, sweeping her up in one giant paw, carries his "bride" into the jungle.

The rescue party from the "Venture" arrives at this moment, Driscoll barely catching a glimpse of the monster and Ann as they vanish into the darkness. The captain and half of the sailors remain in the village while Denham and Driscoll lead a dozen men into the woods.

As dawn breaks the men are deep in the jungle, following the footprints of Kong. In a clearing they encounter a Stegosaurus, a gigantic dinosaur. The monster charges toward the men, whose rifle bullets are ineffectual against the bone-armoured hide of the Mesozoic reptile. Denham brings down the beast with a gas bomb. As the men approach the Stegosaurus rises to its feet and lashes at them with its spiked tail. Again the beast falls and Denham puts a fatal bullet into its brain.

The party later reaches the shore of a fog-shrouded swamp. Kong is heard splashing across ahead of them. Hastily constructing a log raft, the men begin the perilous crossing. A Brontosaurus rises suddenly from the water, its ugly face glaring down at the men from atop a long, prehensile neck. Under a withering volley of rifle fire the dinosaur submerges, only to rise again directly under the raft. The men are flung into the water. One of them is snatched up in the jaws of the sauropod and hurled away. A sailor is dragged to his doom by the dying man. Another man is

Huts and foliage in miniature with glass and painted backing

Native huts and the Kong-trampled mannequin

Miniature scaffolding "supporting" projected natives. The rest is mostly glass

bitten and flung aside, and yet another. The survivors struggle ashore and race pell-mell into the jungle. One sailor falls behind and, seeing the Brontosaurus emerging from the water, climbs a tree in a desperate effort to escape. The dinosaur drags him from the branches.

Kong, carrying Ann, crosses a log bridging a deep chasm. He halts in a clearing beyond when he hears the men approaching. Placing Ann high in the fork of a dead tree, Kong returns to confront Driscoll and the surviving six sailors as they are crossing the ravine. Denham, having fallen back to help stragglers, stops short of the bridge. Driscoll climbs down a liana and takes refuge in a shallow cave under the edge of the cliff. The others are trapped as Kong lifts the end of the log. Two sailors fall to their deaths. As Kong shakes the log more men fall until only one remains clinging to the log. Kong lifts the log and lets it fall into the gorge. He then turns his attention to Driscoll, reaching for him. Driscoll slashes the groping fingers with his knife and Kong withdraws, angry and puzzled. Driscoll is nearly seized by a lizard-like reptile that has crawled up from the chasm, but he cuts the vine on which the creature is crawling and sends it crashing down. At this instant Kong almost has Driscoll in his grasp, but the knife again drives him back.

Ann screams in terror as a Tyrannosaurus rex, a monstrous flesh-eating dinosaur fifty feet in length, enters the glade. Kong rushes back to Ann just as the horrid jaws of the reptile are about to seize her. Kong and the Tyrannosaurus fight savagely as Ann watches in horrified fascination from the treetop. The semi-human intelligence of the ape makes Kong a fit adversary for the larger reptile. Kong is flung against the tree, which crashes down with Ann. The girl, miraculously uninjured, is pinned to the ground.

After a furious battle, Kong defeats the meat-eater by tearing its ugly jaws apart. Tenderly freeing Ann from the tree, Kong carries her deeper into the jungle.

Driscoll climbs to the top of the gorge and is hailed from the other side by Denham, the only other survivor. It is decided that Denham will go back to the village to get help and another supply of gas bombs while Driscoll follows the trail with the expectation of signalling his friends when he finds Kong's lair. Driscoll steals past the dying Tyrannosaurus, which is being fed upon by giant vultures.

Kong reaches the base of Skull Mountain and enters a cave. Inside, he deposits Ann on a ledge and leaves her for a moment. Driscoll, hiding among some boulders, sneaks toward Ann, hoping to effect a rescue. The snake-like form of an Elasmosaurus, a large aquatic reptile, slithers up from a steaming pool and lunges toward Ann. The girl's screams bring Kong, who halts the creature in the nick of time. The reptile coils around Kong's neck and for a time it appears the great ape will be strangled to death, but Kong manages to extricate himself and dashes the Elasmosaurus against the rocks, breaking its neck.

Retrieving Ann, Kong goes up to an opening near the roof of the cave, emerging on a ledge overlooking the island. Seating himself, Kong proceeds to a minute examination of his "bride," tearing away much of her clothing and intently scrutinising and sniffing the flimsy material. When Ann awakens from her swoon and begins screaming, he strokes her affectionately and then sniffs at his fingertips.

Driscoll, climbing up from the cave, dislodges a boulder. When Kong rushes inside, Ann crawls toward the edge of the "balcony," searching for a way of escape. A great flying reptile (Pteranodon) swoops down suddenly, grasping Ann in its claws. Kong rushes back and seizes the winged dragon just as it lifts Ann into the air. Ann falls to the ledge and Driscoll, while Kong is occupied with the struggling reptile, rushes to her. He finds a long liana hanging from the ledge and, with Ann clinging to him, begins a perilous descent down the sheer face of the mountain.

Kong kills the Pteranodon and throws it over the side. When he discovers that Ann and Driscoll are escaping, Kong seizes the liana and begins pulling them back to the top. Ann loses her grip and falls as they near the ledge. Driscoll dives after her. They fall into the lake at the base of the mountain and are swept down the river.

Night falls and the men at the wall have had no signal from Driscoll. Denham is assembling a rescue party when the exhausted Ann and Driscoll arrive. As everybody starts back toward the beach, Denham says:

"But what about Kong? We came here to make

Kong arrives at the beach

a moving picture, but we've got something worth more than all the movies in the world!" Driscoll angrily tells him that Kong is on a mountaintop where he can't be reached. "*If* he stays there," Denham says. "But we've got something he wants."

"Kong is coming!" a lookout cries. The gates are closed and bolted. Natives swarm from their huts to mass their numbers with the sailors against the gates. Kong attacks repeatedly, throwing his weight against the gates. At last the wooden bolt splinters and the doors swing open. An enraged Kong storms the village, crushing everything in his path. A party of native spearmen gathers on a scaffolding and hurl their weapons at the rampaging giant. Kong uproots a tree and uses it as a club to swat the leader from his perch. Grabbing up the fallen warrior, Kong bites him to death, then smashes the scaffolding to the ground with his fists. Houses are torn apart and their occupants trampled. A screaming baby is rescued from under Kong's descending foot.

At last Kong approaches the whaleboat on the beach. Denham is waiting for him. As Kong charges, Denham throws one of the trichlorine bombs, which explodes at Kong's feet. The bewildered beast falls unconscious to the beach. Denham immediately orders men to go to the ship for anchor chains and tools "to build a raft and float him to the ship."

"No chains will hold that!" Englehorn exclaims.

"We'll give him more than chains. He's always been king of his world, but we'll teach him fear. Why, the whole world will pay to see this! We're millionaires, boys—I'll share it with all of you! In a few months it'll be up in lights: 'Kong, the Eighth Wonder of the World!' "

A glittering first-night audience crowds the theatre in New York where Denham will unveil his eighth wonder. Backstage, Denham tells a group of awed newspaper reporters that he wants them to take the first photos of Kong on stage after the curtain goes up. Denham steps before the curtain to address the crowd:

"Ladies and gentlemen, I'm here tonight to tell you a very strange story, a story so strange that no one will believe it. But, ladies and gentlemen, seeing is believing, and we—my partners and I—have brought back the living proof of our adventure, an adventure in which twelve of our party met horrible deaths. But first I want you to see the greatest thing your eyes have ever beheld. He was a king and a god in the world he knew, but now he comes to civilisation merely a captive, a show to gratify your curiosity. Look at Kong, the eighth wonder of the world!"

The curtain rises, revealing to an amazed audience the captive Kong standing in chains atop a dais of structural steel. As the audience begins to panic Denham cries, "Don't be alarmed . . . those chains are made of chrome steel." He brings Ann and Driscoll on stage and tells the audience they will have the privilege of seeing the first photographs taken of Kong and his captors.

The seemingly subdued Kong becomes enraged when the flashbulbs begin to pop. He struggles against his chains, roaring in fury. Denham tries to stop the photographers—"He thinks you're attacking the girl!"—but the damage has been done.

With a mighty effort, Kong frees his right arm. It takes him only a moment to rid himself of the manacles binding his other arm, waist and ankles. Ann, Denham and Driscoll flee into the alley and dash for the hotel nearby. Kong, smashing through the stage door, sees Ann enter the building. Frustrated, he kills a man whose car has crashed near the entrance and tears the marquee from the hotel, hurling it into the terrified crowd on the street. Hearing a scream from above, Kong sees a girl looking down from a high window. He climbs up, peering into the rooms. He sees a sleeping woman in a darkened room and he plucks her from her bed. When he realises that the woman isn't Ann, he drops her to the street far below.

A further search reveals Ann and Driscoll in another room. Kong's arm crashes through a window and Driscoll is sent tumbling as Ann faints across a bed. Kong pulls the bed to the window, carefully lifts Ann and carries her to the roof. By the time Denham and Driscoll reach the roof, Kong has climbed down again.

As he nears his destination, the world's highest building, Kong is startled at the sight of an elevated train rushing past. When he perceives another train approaching, he tears up a section of the track, causing the train to crash. Many of the passengers are killed or injured as Kong attacks the cars, smashing them with his fists.

After being shelled with the gas bombs. The composite elements blocked-in for testing

By sunrise Kong is partway up the Empire State Building. The police are balked until Driscoll makes a suggestion:

"There's one thing we haven't thought of: airplanes! If he puts Ann down and they can pick him off without hitting her—"

Four Navy pursuit craft are dispatched, each bearing fore and aft machine guns. They approach the building just as Kong reaches the top, the dirigible mooring mast. While the aircraft circle, Kong places Ann on a ledge and roars defiance. This is what the airmen want and they dive toward him, guns blazing. As the biplanes swoop past, Kong makes futile attempts to reach them. A series of passes brings one of the aircraft a little too near. Kong grabs the craft with both hands and sends it crashing down the face of the building.

At last, weakened by the innumerable bullets in his body, Kong knows that he is dying. Ignoring his enemies he picks Ann up and looks at her with affection. He returns her to the ledge and strokes her gently with his fingertips. Again the airplanes dive and a last volley of bullets rips into Kong's throat. Kong topples silently from the tower. A moment later Driscoll arrives and takes Ann in his arms.

A police cordon holds back the curious throng gathered about the crushed body of Kong. Denham pushes through and gazes sadly at the dead god.

"Well, Mr. Denham, the airplanes got 'im," a police captain says. Denham shakes his head ruefully.

"Oh, no. It wasn't the airplanes. It was *Beauty* killed the Beast."

A roof-top interval. Fay Wray in miniature rear projection

Kong defies the airmen

The wounded Kong in his last moments

Appendix 10

The Son of Kong

Year	1933
Producing company	RKO-Radio Pictures, Inc.
Executive producer	Merian C. Cooper
Director	Ernest B. Schoedsack
Associate producer	Archie S. Marshek
Story by	Ruth Rose
Photographed by	Eddie Linden Vernon L. Walker J. O. Taylor
Music by	Max Steiner
Settings by	Van Nest Polglase Al Herman
Sound effects by	Murray Spivack
Recorded by	Earl A. Wolcott
Edited by	Ted Cheesman
Chief technician	Willis O'Brien
Technical staff	E. B. Gibson Marcel Delgado Carroll Shepphird Fred Reefe W. G. White
Art technicians	Mario Larrinaga Byron L. Crabbe
Special effects	Harry Redmond, Jr.
Associate sound effects	Walter G. Elliott
Cameramen	Bert Willis Linwood Dunn Clifford Stine Felix Schoedsack
Set decorations	Thomas Little
Costumes	Walter Plunkett
Makeup supervision	Mel Burns

Williams process supervision	Frank Williams
Dunning process supervision	Carroll Dunning C. Dodge Dunning
Recording process	RCA Photophone System
Running time	71 minutes.

The Cast

Carl Denham	Robert Armstrong
Hilda Peterson	Helen Mack
Captain Englehorn	Frank Reicher
Helstrom	John Marston
Chinese Cook	Victor Wong
Red	Ed Brady
Mickey	Lee Kohlmar
Peterson	Clarence Wilson
Mrs. Hudson	Katherine Ward
Girl Reporter	Gertrude Short
Servant Girl	Gertrude Sutton
Chinese Trader	James B. Leong
Native Chief	Noble Johnson
Witch King	Steve Clemento (e)
Process Server	Frank O'Connor
Bill	Constantine Romanoff
Tommy	Harry Tenbrook
Dutch	Leo "Dutch" Hendrian

Musical Score

"Runaway Blues" (paraphrase); "King's Theme"; "Ship at Sea"; "In Dakang"; "Hootchie-Kootchie"; "Fire Music"; "The Warning"; "An Offer of Help"; "Chinese Chatter"; "Love's Awakening"; "The Forgotten Island"; "Monotony"; "The Quicksands"; "The Old Temple"; "The Stegosaurus"; "The Black Bear"; "First Aid"; "The Coconuts"; "Evening Quietude"; "The Discovery"; "Johnny Get Your Gun"; "The Comedian"; "The Lizard Fight"; "Mazeltof"; "The Earthquake"; "Calm Sea". The foregoing composed and/or arranged by Max Steiner. Song, "Runaway Blues," lyrics by Edward Eliscu, music by Max Steiner. Piano music: "Maple Leaf Rag" by Scott Joplin; "Glow Worm" by Paul Lincke; "Dill Pickles" by Charles Johnson and Alfred Bryan. Banjo music: "Fit as a Fiddle" by Hoffman and Goodhart; "Billboard March" by John N. Klohr.

Synopsis

The film opens with a close shot of a lurid theatrical poster: KING KONG, THE EIGHTH WONDER OF THE WORLD. It hangs on the wall of Denham's room in a boarding house now besieged by a small army of process servers and reporters. Charley, the Chinese cook, brings a message from Captain Englehorn asking Denham to come to the "Venture." With the aid of Mickey, a friendly process server, Denham escapes in the guise of a junk dealer and reaches the ship. Englehorn suggests they flee to escape a welter of lawsuits and an impending indictment by the grand jury. Denham readily agrees and for several months they operate the "Venture" as a cargo ship in the China Sea, earning barely enough to survive.

At the Malayan port of Dakang they visit Peterson's Circus, a bedraggled tent show operated by an elderly alcoholic and his pretty daughter, Hilda ("La Belle Hélène, sweet songstress who has performed before all the crowned heads of Europe"). Denham is touched by the girl's plight.

That night, Peterson is visited by Nils Helstrom, a down-and-out Norwegian sea captain. Later, the two men argue drunkenly and it is revealed that Helstrom purposely wrecked his ship in order to collect insurance. Helstrom angrily strikes down the older man with a gin bottle and accidentally sets fire to the tent before he flees. Hilda awakens and, after freeing the trained seals and monkeys, drags her father outside just as the flaming tent collapses.

Next day Hilda confronts Helstrom and accuses him of the murder. The Dutch magistrate is supposed to arrive shortly and Helstrom expects the worst. Denham finds Hilda trying to recapture the monkeys and tries to cheer her up.

That night, Denham and Englehorn meet Helstrom in a saloon and Denham reveals that it was Helstrom who sold him the map of Skull Island. Perceiving a possible way of escape, Helstrom invents a story about a fabulous treasure left by the civilisation that built the Great Wall. Already wishing for an excuse to return to the island, Denhem and Englehorn jump to the bait and decide to set sail in the morning, taking Helstrom as an equal partner. Denham gives Hilda what money he has so that she can buy passage away from Dakang.

Once at sea, Englehorn becomes suspicious of Helstrom when he sees him whispering with Red, the surly boatswain. Helstrom is plotting to foment a mutiny and has created unrest among the crew with gruesome stories about the men killed on Denham's previous expedition to Skull Island. Tensions increase when Charlie finds a stowaway; it is Hilda, who has fallen in love with Denham. Helstrom bullies the girl into remaining silent about the murder.

The mutiny erupts on the morning the ship reaches the island. Denham, Hilda, Englehorn and Charley are set adrift in a lifeboat, in which the Chinaman has managed to conceal two shotguns. When Helstrom begins barking orders to the crew, Red orders him thrown over the side. Reluctantly, Denham rescues him.

The castaways land near the Great Wall and are given a hostile reception by the natives, who blame them for the destruction of their village. Keeping the blacks at gunpoint, they retreat to the sea and follow the precipitous coastline until they find a narrow inlet that leads to a place where it is possible to climb ashore. They are at the foot of Skull Mountain.

Denham and Hilda climb some huge steps that have been carved into the mountain. At the edge of the jungle they find the son of Kong struggling to escape from a bed of quicksand. Denham pushes a dead tree across the quagmire, enabling the giant ape to climb to safety. As Kong leaves, Denham and Hilda are convinced the ape is grateful to them. Little Kong is a youngster of the species, standing about twelve feet high.

Englehorn, Charley and Helstrom go into the jungle in search of food. They hear a terrible roar and turn to see a monstrous Styracosaurus charging toward them. Englehorn slows the dinosaur's charge with a shotgun blast and with no time to spare, the men reach the shelter of a shallow cleft. They are barely out of reach of the enraged monster, which seizes the shotgun in its parrot-like beak and destroys it.

Denham and Hilda, meantime, venture into the jungle and shoot a bird for supper. As they are returning to camp a giant cave bear lunges after them. Denham stuns the beast with the gun, enabling Hilda and himself to climb to a ledge. Little Kong hears the shot and comes running to the rescue just as the bear is reaching for its prey. A spectacular fight ensues, in which the ape finally uses an uprooted tree to drive the bear away. Kong then sits down to nurse a wounded finger. Denham binds the injury with a strip from Hilda's petticoat. When night falls the exhausted couple tend a fire to keep the animals away while Kong secretly watches over them.

At dawn Denham, convinced that Englehorn's party will not return, investigates what appears to be the sealed entrance to a pagan temple inside the mountain. Kong breaks down the stone barrier, revealing a vast cave containing a great idol decorated with precious jewels. Kong picks up Denham's shotgun and, examining it, tears the weapon apart. A moment later a dragon-like reptile enters the cave and starts toward Denham and Hilda. Kong leaps on the reptile and kills it after a savage fight.

Denham and Hilda emerge from the temple just as Englehorn's party arrives. When Kong comes into view, Helstrom shrieks in terror and runs toward the lifeboat. Englehorn, Hilda and Charley follow, fearful that the crazed man will abscond in the boat. Denham, accompanied by Kong, returns to the treasure cave. As Helstrom leaps into the lifeboat, a great sea monster arises from the depths and glowers down at him. Helstrom falls overboard and is seized and devoured by the creature.

Boulders begin tumbling down from the mountain as a devastating earthquake rocks the island. Hilda tries to return to Denham but Englehorn drags her to the boat. Denham and Kong are trapped inside as the temple entrance is buried. A violent storm accompanies the cataclysm and it quickly becomes evident that Skull Island is sinking into the sea. Fissures open in the earth, in one instance swallowing a native war party.

Denham and Kong are able to climb out of the temple when part of the roof collapses. Staying ahead of the rapidly rising waters, man and ape climb to the summit of the mountain, which crumbles around them until they are marooned on a narrow promontory. A crevice opens beneath them, then closes on Kong's leg. Denham struggles to free his protector, but Kong is hopelesslyy trapped as the waters rise about them. Denham's friends row toward them as Kong, in a last heroic gesture, holds Denham aloft even as the sea closes over his own head. Denham is hauled into the boat an instant before Kong's hand vanishes into the depths.

Days pass and the castaways give up all hope of rescue. Denham gazes ruefully at a jewel-encrusted pendant taken from the idol and wishes he could exchange it for a cask of water. Then Englehorn spies a ship on the horizon.

Safe aboard ship, Hilda suggests they split the treasure three ways instead of four: "One-third for the Skipper, one-third for Charley and one-third for . . . us?" Denham decides it's a good idea.

The big head at its frightening best

Index

Abdullah, Achmed 33
Africa Speaks 99
All That Money can Buy 11
Along the Moonbeam Trail 43
Anna Christie 99
Arlen, Richard 35, 64
Armstrong, Robert 65–6, 71, 82–3, 109–110, 161, 173, 179, 197, 199, 201, 211
Ataturk, Mustafa Kemal 27

Babes in Toyland 55
Banks, Leslie 65–6
Bat Whispers, The 50
Beast, The 57
Beast from Twenty Thousand Fathoms, The 148
Beebe, Dr. William 31–2, 78, 80
Beery, Noah 35
Beery, Wallace 48–9
Bickford, Charles 99
Bird of Paradise 23, 103
Birth of a Flivver 43
Black Scorpion 148
Boyd, William 101
Brackett, Charles 209
Brady, Ed 199
Brook, Clive 35, 64
Brown, Dr. Barnum 43, 141
Budenny, General 25
Burden, W. Douglas 37–8

Cabot, Bruce 68, 72, 82, 93–4, 101, 109, 110, 133, 136, 161, 165, 167, 173, 179, 182, 188, 190
Casablanca 201
Cavalcade 209
Celeste, Olga 66
Cerisoli, John 121
Chang 7, 32–5, 37–9, 73–4, 77, 78, 80, Appendix 2
Cheeseman, Ted 179, 181
Cimarron 50
Citizen Kane 11, 208
Clark, Carroll 64, 123
Clemente, Steve 9, 72, 84, 199
Cooper, Merian C. 7, 11, 23–8, 32–5, 37–40, 56, 58–9, 64, 68, 71–5, 77–80, 84, 93–4, 98, 100, 107, 115, 120, 127, 131, 133, 136, 146, 159, 161, 171, 173, 181, 185, 192, 197, 204, 207, 209, 211
Crabbe, Byron 59, 64, 74, 120, 136, 169, 201
Creation 11, 55–6, 58, 66, 79, 91, 99, 120, 136, 139, 182, 192. Appendix 7
Creelman, James Ashmore 59, 65, 71–2, 77, 80
Cromwell, John 64
Curious Pets of Our Ancestors 43
Curtis, Dick 85

Daniels, Walter 120
Dawley, Major Herbert M. 43, 45, 47
Delgado, Marcel 45–6, 48–9, 54, 56, 88, 94, 98, 131, 136, 141, 165, 182, 201
DeMille, Cecil B. 101, 103
Dinosaur and the Missing Link, The 41
Doctor X 101
Doyle, Sir Arthur Conan 46–7
Dowling, William 48
Dr. Cyclops 199

Dream of a Rarebit Fiend, The 41
Dunn, Linwood 99, 100, 133, 211
Dunning, C. Dodge 49, 99
Dunning, Carroll 97, 99

Edeson, Arthur 48
Eighth Wonder, The 58, 64, 209
Eliscu, Edward 204

Fairbanks, Douglas 99
Fauntleroy, Major Cedric E. 24
Fisher, Dr. G. Clyde 45
Flaherty, Robert 217
Flavin, James 85
Four Feathers, The 35, 38, 40, 73, Appendix 3
Freund, Karl 88
Frissell, Varick 40
Fulton, John P. 99

Garbo, Greta 99
Gerard, Henry 73
Ghost Breakers, The 84
Ghost of Slumber Mountain, The 43, 169, Appendix 5
Giant Behemoth, The 148
Gibson, E. B. 'Buzz' 120, 167
Gillette, William 31
Goldner, Orville 'Goldy' 120, 130, 209
Gone with the Wind 11, 207
Grant, Cary 64
Grass 9, 28, 31, 35, 39, 77, Appendix 1
Gunga Din 11

Haile Selassie 26
Hardy, Oliver 101
Harrison, Marguerite 27–8, 33
Harryhausen, Ray 148
Hathaway, Henry 64
Haver, Phyllis 83
Hell's Angels 50
Herman, Al 103, 123
Holmes, Phillips 64
Hoyt, Harry L. 47–9
Hudson, Earl 47, 49
Hughes, Howard 50
Hughes, Lloyd 48

In Prehistoric Days 48
In the Villain's Power 43
Ince, Thomas H. 107
Informer, The 11
Invisible Man, The 99
Iron Man, The 83
Its a Mad, Mad, Mad, Mad World 211

Jamboree 197
Johnson, Noble 35, 89, 199, 207

Kahane, B. B. 23, 190
Kilenyi, Doctor Edward 31
King Kong 9, 11, 23, 37–8, 66, 68, 72, 77, 80, 84–5, 87–8, 90, 99, 100, 115, 121, 123, 126, 136, 139, 146, 148, 185, 187, 190–2, 197, 201, 204, 207–9, 211, Appendix 9
King Kong Escapes 209
King Kong vs. Godzilla 209
King Klunk 209
King of Kings 11, 101, 103

La Cucuracha 211
Larrinaga, Mario 59, 64, 74, 120, 130, 136, 169, 192, 201
Lasky, Jesse L. 28, 31, 33, 34, 35, 40, 209
Last Days of Pompeii 11, 120, 121, 123, 191
Last of the Mohicans, The 82
Laurel, Stanley 101
LeBaron, William 84–5, 190
Leigh, Vivien 207
Let 'em Have It 82
Levant, Oscar 191
Lewton, Val 11, 209
Lindon, Edwin G. 123, 159, 167
Little Women 11
Lives of a Bengal Lancer, The 40, 64, 182
Lloyd, Harold 66, 101
Lost Island 209
Lost Patrol 11
Lost World, The 47–9, 54, 88, 93, 99, 139, Appendix 6
Love, Bessie 48–9
Love, Cecil 99
Lugosi, Bela 207
Luke, Keye 192

Mack, Helen 199, 201, 204
Main Event, The 82
March, Fredric 64
Marshek, Archie 72, 115, 120, 179
Marston, John 199
Mason, A. E. W. 34
McCrea, Joel 65–6
McCoy, Horace 72
Mickey and His Goats 43
Mighty Joe Young 80, 139, 148
Miller, Walter 101
Mitchell, General Billy 24
Moby Dick 81
Monkey's Paw, The 101
Montana, Bull 48

Morpheus Mike 43
Most Dangerous Game, The 11, 64–5, 68, 71–4, 78, 84, 103, 115, 133, 139, Appendix 8
Mummy, The 84
Murnau, F. W. 34
Muybridge, Eadweard 62
Mysterious Dr. Fu Manchu, The 84
Mystery of the Wax Museum, The 101

Nanook of the North 26
Nippy's Nightmare 43

O'Brien, Willis H. 7, 9, 11, 41, 43, 45–7, 49, 50, 54, 56–7, 62, 66, 75, 95, 97, 99, 111, 115, 120–1, 123, 127, 136–7, 139, 140–1, 146, 148–9, 161, 167, 179, 182, 201, 204, 208, 211
Omoolu, Mutia 99
On Moonshine Mountain 48

Parsons, Louella 192
Peters, William Frederick 35
Phantom of Crestwood 115
Phantom of the Air, The 85
Pichel, Irving 65
Pilsudski, President 25–6
Plunkett, Walter 123
Polglase, Van Nest 121
Pomeroy, Roy 35
Porter, Edwin S. 7, 41
Porter, Zoe 94, 133
Powell, William 35
Prehistoric Poultry 43
Prince, Leroy 209

R.F.D. 10,000 B.C. 43
Rango 9, 35, 39, 50, 73, 78, 185, Appendix 4
Raven, Harry C. 57
Ray, Allene 101
Redmond, Harry, Jr. 123
Reed, Luther 55
Reefe, Fred 120
Riesenfeld, Dr. Hugo 31, 33, 187
Riskin, Robert 84
Rittau, Günther 88
Roach, Hal 101
Roadhouse Murder 101
Roady, Ken 87
Rogers, Will 101, 120
Rose, Edward 31
Rose, Ruth (later Ruth Schoedsack) 7, 9, 31–5, 39, 40, 78, 80, 82, 197, 199
Rothacker, Watterson 45, 47
Rothafel, S.L. "Roxy" 192
Ruben, J. Walter 115
Ruggles, Wesley 50, 101

Salisbury, Captain Edward A. 26
Sam Loyd's Famous Puzzles–the Puzzling Billboard 43
Saunders, John Monk 84
Saunders, Sidney 88–9, 91, 93
Savo, Jimmy 191
Schoedsack, Ernest B. 7, 9, 11, 23–28, 32–5, 37–9, 40, 50, 64–8, 73, 75, 77, 79, 80, 84, 87, 101, 107, 109, 120, 131, 136
Schoedsack, Felix 40, 126–7
Selznick, David O. 23, 30, 35, 40, 55–6, 78, 82, 148, 185, 197, 207
She 80, 207
Shepphird, Carroll 121, 211
Skinner, Otis 31
Sokolowski, Lieutenant 25–6
Son of Kong, The 11, 120, 123, 133, 139, 197, 204, 208, 209, Appendix 10
Spivack, Murray 133, 187–9, 190
Steiner, Max 73, 107, 189, 190–1, 201, 204
Stine, Clifford 148
Stolen Life, A 191
Stone, Lewis 48
Sunrise 34

Tarantula 148
Tarzan, the Ape Man 99
Taylor, J.O. 123, 181
Thief of Bagdad 84, 99
Trade Winds 78
Trader Horn 50, 99

Valley of Gwangi 148
Van Dyke, W.S. 50
Vidor, King 23, 103
Von Elitz, Theodore 35

Walker, Vern L. 99, 126
Wallace, Edgar 57–9
Wedding March, The 84
Welles, Orson 208
West, Roland 50
White, W.G. "Gus" 121
Whiteford, John P. "Blackie" 85
Williams, Frank 49, 99
Wilson, Arnold 25
Wimpy, Rex 40
Wizard of Oz, The 209
Wong, Victor 85, 199
Wray, Fay 9, 35, 65–6, 68, 83–4, 89, 90, 95, 97, 101, 109, 123, 133, 136–7, 149, 161, 167, 173, 187–8, 208

Zalewski, Lieutenant 25
Zukor, Adolph 35